LEADERSHIP

VOLUME 1

TORKOM SARAYDARIAN

LEADERSHIP SERIES

Leadership Volume 1

©1995 The Creative Trust

All Rights Reserved: No part of this publication may be reproduced, stored in a retrieval system, or transmitted in any form, by any means, electronic, mechanical, photocopying, recording or otherwise, without permission in writing from the copyright owner or his representatives.

ISBN: 0-929874-25-0 (Softcover)
ISBN: 0-929874-24-2 (Hardcover)

Library of Congress Catalog Card Number: 92-82864

Printed in the United States of America

Cover Design:	*Tim Fisher* Phoenix, Arizona
Printed by:	*Data Reproductions* Rochester Hills, MI
Published by:	**T.S.G. Publishing Foundation, Inc.** P.O. Box 7068 Cave Creek, AZ 85331-7068 United States of America

Note: The visualizations and meditations contained in this book are given as guidelines. They should be used with discretion and after receiving professional advice.

Table of Contents

    Foreword v
    Preface 9
1. Vision of the Future 27
2. Leadership Essentials 47
3. Practicality in Leadership 59
4. Leadership and Vanity 67
5. Leadership and Motive 73
6. Leadership and Labor 81
7. Labor and Thought in Leadership 93
8. Group Consciousness and Group Work 101
9. The Discriminative Attitude of the Leader ... 139
10. Co-workers 153
11. Leadership and Co-workers 171
12. Cooperation 197
13. Leadership and Assistants 215
14. Leadership and Inspiration 225
15. Choosing Students 229
16. Leadership and Decisiveness 237
17. Impersonality 245
18. Leadership and Obedience 255
19. Leadership and Impulse 275
20. Leadership and Religion 279
21. Promises 285
22. Leadership and Self-Confidence 293
23. Self-Defeat and Self-Victory 301
24. Leadership and Failure 309
25. Leadership and Faith 317
26. Inspiration and Impression 323
27. The Art of Lecturing 333
28. Book Review 359
29. Effective Lecturing 363

30.	Lecturing with Feeling	379
31.	Lecturing as an Art	387
32.	Leadership and Speech	395
33.	How to Organize the Work	407
34.	Leadership and the Ability to Organize	413
35.	Festivals, Parties, and Entertainment	429
36.	Psychic Energy and Willpower	443
	Glossary	449
	Index	453

Foreword

The Leadership Series is a series of books on the subject of leadership defined for the New Era, the Future. These books are written to evoke the leadership qualities in every human being in all fields of life. Whether you are the leader of a mega corporation or the leader of a small group of people, the principles and guidelines given in this series will be of tremendous help in your daily professional and personal activities. The principles outlined in these books are timeless and relate to the core values of the human experience. All great leaders in all fields of life have demonstrated these core principles.

In all departments of human labor, there is a need for leaders who have vision, initiative, determination, vitality, and enthusiasm. There is a need for leaders who are able to stand against limitation of movement, ignorance, disorderliness, and ugliness. There is a need for leaders who are equipped with knowledge in their field of labor and who are equipped with the wisdom to protect their field of labor and their co-workers. There is a need for leaders who understand core values and principles and stand on them regardless of the common practices to the contrary.

The ideas given on leadership in these series of books are taken from a lifetime of experience in leadership. They cover every area of leadership. These ideas can be applied in any field. The principles are the same; a true leader can learn from one field and apply his learning to any other field.

Leadership is

- example
- sacrifice
- wisdom
- daring
- fearlessness
- nobility
- humility
- gratitude
- courage

Any leader in any field needs these principles.

Leadership is the answer of a need and it is the future. On one hand, the leader responds to the need; on the other hand, he is the leader of the future.

In any field a leader must respond to the need as well as carry out his labor in order to meet the needs of the future.

If the reader thinks that I am referring to a leader of a particular field in these series of books, he must know that he is hindering his vision.

Leadership is not gender specific, nor is it specific to any field. It is not specific to a particular form of dress, physical characteristics, or ways of behavior. Leadership in its essence is based on deep inner values and a commitment to the advancement and continuous growth of others. A true leader is a spiritual teacher and is found in every field of life such as science, religion, politics, arts, and business. The spiritual teacher does not mean a religious teacher, but a person who *ever seeks new ways of approach, new fields of discovery, new levels of consciousness both for himself and others.* In a sense, any leader equipped with such tendencies is a spiritual teacher and a leader.

These series of books can be used by a corporate executive as well as a church priest, a parent, the individual who wants to lead himself out of limitations, as well as the teacher in a classroom.

One of the greatest abilities of a true leader is inclusiveness or synthesis. For him, each field of human endeavor is not a separate world but a department of the one field of life. A true leader can fit into any department in a very short time.

After you study these series of books, you will be able to see how true leadership is inspired and directed by great principles and values in all fields of life, and how leadership is the common denominator of all fields. We hope that the leader existing in you may be evoked and you too will take the responsibility of leadership.

These pages carry my experiences of forty years. I give them to those who can use them in their self-sacrificial service for the entire humanity. Most of these chapters were used as study papers for a selected number of students.

Here then is ***Leadership,*** Volume One.

Torkom Saraydarian

1995

Preface

Life is built on the principle of leadership. The principle of leadership is the source of evolution, of the Law of Karma, of striving, and of sensitivity to the Cosmic Magnet. The whole Cosmos reflects this principle.

In each atom you have the nucleus. In each plant you have the controlling system. In each animal you have the guiding core. In each man you have the brain and the soul. In each planet you have the planetary life. All are based on the Law of the Hierarchy, the law of successive experience, and on the principle of leadership.

Evolution is not carried forward all on the same level. Each becomes according to what he does. Each is drawn forward according to his sensitivity to the Purpose of all creation.

There is a false idea which confuses people; it emphasizes group work without leadership. This idea is based on an inner failure on the path of leadership. Those who even deny leadership are led by their own ideas, by the examples of others, and they themselves try to impress and lead others to follow their path. Concealed hypocrisy flows through such activities.

Leadership is not imposition. Leadership is achievement. Leadership is the ability to conduct an orchestra, to guide a nation, to contact the highest light possible, and to reveal it to the multitudes. Leadership is the ability to sacrifice, to be the cement for a cathedral.

Only those who do not have contact with their Real Self wander, barking against the principle of leadership.

Without the principle of leadership, we will end in anarchy.

Leadership is vision. Leadership paves the way for freedom. Leadership is not dictatorship. Leadership is the ability to go ahead with one's own evolution and share his achievements with others.

Those who achieve more than others naturally impress and inspire others. Those who are impressed and inspired by those who achieve great heights follow their steps, not to imitate them but to learn the ways and means of achievement.

Those who know more are naturally leaders to those who do not know. Those who have greater strength are naturally leaders to those who are weak. Those who function on higher levels of awareness are the leaders for those who can only function on lower levels and need guidance.

It is not only illogical to ignore the principle of leadership, but it is also insanity and vanity. Look at your body. There is harmony in it. Every part is precious, but you have the leader of the body which is *you*. If you are absent, there is no leader. . . and you are dead.

It is true that many so-called leaders have exploited human beings, countries, or nations. But what about those Great Ones in all fields of human endeavor who inspire people and lead them one or two steps higher on their evolutionary path?

Bees are more intelligent in recognizing their leaders than those who advertise group psychology but try secretly to be their leaders.

When the leadership acts against the interests of others, it turns into a source of exploitation. When the leadership imposes its will, it turns into dictatorship. Such a leadership destroys itself through these two means, only to open the way for new leaders who live for the interests of others and protect people from their own weaknesses; who release the power of striving in others, challenge them to new achievements, and inspire them every time they fail.

Often when people think about leaders, they think about impostors, dictators, and totalitarians, and they develop in their hearts some kind of refusal or denial of the idea of leadership

A leader who imposes himself on others is not a real leader. A real leader is one who realistically realizes that he should lead people because all of them need the guidance that only he can give them. He leads people not by using them for his advantage but by working for their advantage, serving their interests. This is a very different concept of leadership. A leader is not a boss; a leader is not an object of worship. He is truly a servant, but a servant far more advanced in virtues, in knowledge, and in skill so that without vanity he can invite people around him that they may follow his steps — not to reach him, but to reach their own Inner Self and the treasury of their inner potentials.

There was a big fire in the mountains. Fifteen people were trapped on a highway surrounded by the burning forest. When everyone was desperate, a little girl jumped out of her car and said, "Follow me. I know a path which may save us." She led them to the seashore by a shortcut and saved their lives.

This is a very clear example of leadership. She made people follow her and save their own lives *only* because she knew the path.

Those who have no outstanding spiritual gifts and are tired of not reaching a higher level, refuse leadership. Because they can no longer become leaders, they do not want anyone else to become a leader. This is a very sad phenomenon especially in so-called new age groups which, loaded with vanity, selfishness, and self-interests, do not tolerate anyone to be a leader.

People who are polluted within their own heart with negative emotions and vanity prevent others from making a breakthrough and standing outside of their locked chains or circles. They excuse themselves with the deceitful logic that they advance together and they do not need any leader to tell them what to do. But the pitiful point is that they do not see that already they are *followers* of some idea given by somebody else, whose name they would never mention. And the most pitiful point is that they want, by all means, for people to *follow their steps*.

The principle of leadership is found in every walk of life. One must have spiritual humility to see where he is on the chain of the evolution. There is the one who is above him and the one who is below him. With one hand he holds the hand above him to raise himself up; with the other hand he pulls up the one below him. And this chain is the chain of leadership. Everyone is a leader; everyone is a follower; and only vanity and self-deceit will curtain the eyes and blind them from seeing this fact.

On the path of leadership, one needs education and training. When a man advances from one position to another position, it is like graduating from one class and entering a higher class.

In each higher class the *student* needs to learn more in order to expand his consciousness, to observe objects and events from more viewpoints, to use the law of synthesis more, and to see the greater need. With this learning he will notice that his expanding consciousness and increasing viewpoints put a tremendous pressure on his physical body and its various systems. Here his training starts: to adapt his physical, emotional, and mental nature to the incoming, increasing flow of light and to the revealing needs of the field in which he is situated at the time.

The progress of the leader is like a walking cross. His feet are on the ground of human need. His head is immersed in the will and purpose of life. His hands are ready to lift and guide.

On each level of his leadership path the leader deepens his wisdom, expands his consciousness, and appropriates his physical, emotional, and mental instruments to the incoming light and to the demands of the need.

Leadership is a training ground and an opportunity to develop, unfold, and expand the activity of the sense of synthesis. The greater a leader is, the more unfolded is his sense of synthesis.

It is very important that a leader is open to new viewpoints and is ready to learn and to change the narrower viewpoints he had before. He will, however, be very careful that he is not carried away by separative but "intelligently" prepared viewpoints, which are intended to limit his expansion and use him for separative ends.

The leader has a great opportunity to come in contact with many hidden motives, with self-seeking interests and plans. The psychology of individuals and groups can be an open book for his studies.

The leader's intention is to serve the highest good for the greatest number of people and find ways and means to expand the consciousness of those who are inclined only to care for their own separative interests.

Thus the office of the leader is a classroom where he reads the pages of the Book of Life and prepares himself to serve in larger fields and for the higher interests of the people. He learns every minute, and he has the opportunity to train himself with each drop of learning.

We are told that the Hierarchy[1] is formed by those individuals who worked and served as great executives in many fields of human endeavor and, in the meantime, served the Plan with their whole heart. But they started the path of service in their homes and carried it out into their groups, nations, and humanity with a sensitivity to the Plan of the Hierarchy. The Plan of the Hierarchy was the source of their inspiration and orientation.[2]

Thus you are a leader wherever you are. You lead yourself to the field of service, to the field of greater light, to the field of greater synthesis, to the field of greater sacrifice.

You do not force people to follow you. You shine your light; you increase the intensity of your light through your experience and wisdom. You increase the resources of your psychic energy by coming in contact with your Inner Divinity. Thus you become a challenge to others and a beauty for their hearts and souls.

It is only challenge and beauty that create the most irresistible magnetic currents and put the centers in human beings into motion. One must strive toward higher and higher summits.

Leadership belongs to all human endeavors. The real leaders are those who, in their particular field, cultivate the principle of sensitivity and direction toward the Common Good and who, in cooperation with all other fields, respond to the principle of synthesis.

Every single person in each field of human endeavor will eventually learn to cooperate with those who are working in different fields for the Common Good. The common denominator of all fields is the one human life.

---

1. See also *Challenge for Discipleship*, Ch. 57, "Hierarchy."
2. Note: The Plan is the formulation of the Purpose or Will of God into a workable program for this planet.

The common denominator of the leadership of all fields is the good of all humanity, in all dimensions of life. When we are referring to leaders, then, we have in mind the whole field of life with its specialized sections in the One field.

We must remember that a leader is *not an authority*.

An authority is one who is considered infallible in his knowledge, decisions, plans, and directions.

We have never seen nor do we expect such an authority. Such an authority will be a prison for the human soul and will hinder his progress for ages if imposed.

We know, however, that every entity in this Universe is progressively going forward on the path of evolution. This statement does not deny that there are people who are far more advanced than we are on the Path. This does not deny that there are people who have greater insight, deeper foresight, and a more powerful ability to synthesize. We call these people our leaders, and they lead us by the power that their own evolution has given to them.

We call them our teachers who teach us, not because they need to teach us but because our response to them creates the link for transference of wisdom. Those who are further progressed and wealthier by their deeds of sacrificial service are those to whom we look for guidance and for courage.

In its positive and relative meaning, we respect authorities. Such authorities are great specialists in any field of human endeavor. They are not absolute sources of knowledge, information, or direction but they are great treasure houses of experience, information, and wisdom. We love and respect such authorities without abandoning our right to question them, to reject them, even to disbelieve them.

No power in the world must use its position to enslave the human soul. The greater the power, the greater the freedom it inspires in you because by freedom one proves his level of achievement and affirms the true nature of his beingness.

There is an increasing need for leadership in the field of esoteric knowledge. More and more people are becoming disillusioned with the teachings given to them by opportunists, by people who have good intentions but are full of glamors and vanities, or by people who want to use the Teaching as a business to raise money.

Great damage is done to people who approach the Teaching with sincerity in their heart and are caught in groups, institutions, or organizations that are only for social activities or that function as traps for exploitation. Some of these searchers gradually forget about their quest and adapt themselves to their environment. Some of them totally suppress their aspiration and spiritual striving because of their disillusionment. Only a small percentage, through discrimination, continue their search to find the proper field where they can grow and serve.

The number of true searchers is increasing. We must prepare ourselves to meet their need and at the same time safeguard ourselves from the dangers of falling into vanities, glamors, or of using the searchers for our own interests.

A leader must always stand on guard. There are so many temptations in his environment, in his work, in his relationships with people. Those who come to him may bring new temptations. That is why the leader must stand on guard and not let his personality vehicles negotiate with temptations. Some of these temptations are money, sex, praise, flattery, need for friendship, and need for security.

The leader is not an angel. He needs money, he needs love, he needs friendship and security; but he never uses the Teaching as a fishing net to catch people and use them for his own ends.

The leader must be so careful that he does not despise anyone who comes with the sincere desire in his heart for spiritual development and service.

The leader also must know that all who come to him are not really coming for the Teaching. They may come for the leader's beauty, manliness, womanliness, or money; they may come to secure positions for themselves through side doors. Such people appear very sincere, intelligent, and full of the zeal to serve. But the leader must recognize them.

Some people do not like spiritual discipline. They can be tested easily. Some of them do not commit themselves to heavy labor. Some of them are not punctual or they are jealous or they do not like to sacrifice. They appear very obedient. They like to praise the leader in public. They like to show off. They criticize when the opportunity is given. They like high positions. All these signs in the newcomer indicate the need for extreme caution by the leader.

It is difficult to uproot a tree which has been kept in the wrong place for a long time.

Some people just like to stay in a group by any means and gather information that can be used against the leader if he does not satisfy their secret motives. The leader must be alert to the first signs of dishonesty or treachery, but also give such people a chance to contact their Soul and choose the noble path of sincerity and renouncement.

The best students are those in whom you see sincerity and the spirit of renouncement and silence.

There are also people who appear sacrificial in order to hold offices, but once you depend on them they express their true colors and present their various demands.

You can see how delicate is the task of the leader.

A leader is a leader not to satisfy and enjoy his leadership or to enjoy the friendship of thousands of people, but he is a leader under the command of his Soul or his Master. He may personally love you, need you, or enjoy your friendship, money, or position; but if this relationship does not fit the plan of his Master or Soul, he instantaneously cuts it and renounces all his ties. This is why an experienced leader creates as few ties as possible to be able to sever them in due time without doing any harm to the work or to the person.

Let us repeat here that a leader has no favorites. He can negotiate with someone with whom he had no former interest and cut off someone with whom he was very close if the work requires such actions. He also takes such actions sometimes to test his co-workers or to remove hindrances on the path of service.

The demand for New Era disciples is increasing daily, and leadership must prepare itself to meet the need — not only the need of true disciples, but also the problems of false disciples.

We must repeat here that you cannot prepare leaders and you cannot create leaders. They are the result of their own labors of many lives. But you can instruct those who already are leaders by birth, or by the labor of many lives. You can recognize them. They have all the weaknesses of average people, but they have a few signs by which you can recognize them, no matter how deeply they are covered with superficial activities.

They love labor; they love striving. They do not give up. They never hide and never like to show-off. They stand as they are. They see their mistakes and admit them when you point them out. They never talk ill about a co-worker, even if they are hurt. They do not act in pity; they have a tendency to make people stand on their own feet.

also a clear intuitive perception, a faith by which they accept the Teaching as it is given by the Christ, Buddha, or Krishna. It is only an accepting disciple who can be led on the path until he becomes an accepted disciple.

An accepted disciple is one who is accepted by his Soul, by his Master, or by his Ashram. He knows that he belongs now to an Ashram. He has contacts which verify his faith. Leadership must try to create those conditions in which such disciples grow and mature without wasting the time and energy of the Masters.

It is very important to emphasize that the leader must create the right conditions for growth, for unfoldment, for testing — even through crisis — but always after examining his own motives.

5. The leader must prepare his lectures and classes carefully, even if he knows what he is going to talk about. Remember that lectures serve two purposes:

   a. To lead, inspire, and encourage people, unfolding the true beauty of the Teaching in them.

   b. To prove to the watching Master or senior disciple that the Leader is unfolding through continuous striving and preparations. The Leader should not be content to give the things that he knows, but must find new things. He must present the things that he did not know but learned as he prepared the instructions and lectures.

The Guide watches you to find out how much new light you are bringing in while you are serving other people. A true lecture is the extension of your Divine Self.

When the leader does not have new inspirations, people feel it and leave him alone. Our magnetism increases only when we transmit new inspiration, new facets or hues of the Teaching on the same foundation.

6. The leader not only must prepare his lectures, but he must also rehearse them. Rehearsal is very important. It is rehearsal that sustains the flow of renewal and improvement. Rehearsal gives confidence and freedom of expression and enlarges the channel of inspiration.

Rehearsal builds those vibrations around you which, as the need arises, come and flow through your speech.

Rehearsal breaks those thoughtwaves which are antagonistic to your topic or destructive to your goals. When you rehearse, you clean many obstacles which could make it hard for you to speak creatively.

Rehearsal attracts help from invisible beings. Some of them like people who strive. They feel joy in the presence of striving leaders.

Rehearsed lectures are those which are less clichéd and freer. Non-rehearsed lectures imprison the leader.

7. The leader must make a one year plan for the daily classes and activities of the group. The plan must be made in such a way that it can be adjusted, added to, and improved upon without losing the principal purpose. Those who are dealing with plans must be very careful that every change they make brings the plan closer to the original purpose.

The leader must prepare the future courses, which can grow in a gradient scale and in conformity with the need and purpose. It is very easy for young leaders to be trapped in nice activities to such a degree that eventually they can lose almost a whole life cycle before they free themselves from unnecessary engagements. Honest leaders are mostly tempted by sidetracking activities, especially through their glamors.

A leader is an engineer. He provides the blueprint and the various materials to build the Inner Sanctuary. To do this, he plans his lectures and activities in such a way that people grow harmoniously.

Sometimes we like to emphasize only one part of the Teaching and forget other parts. Thus we create unbalanced growth in our students. When only one part of the Teaching is taken as the whole Teaching, we create fanatics or blind people.

So the leader will be like a wise cook who gives his people a well-balanced diet by which they are well nourished.

One of the areas in which the leader must work is meditation. Meditation does not necessarily start from below; it may start from above. The leader works for radiation and service or creativity. He starts with contemplation and goes toward meditation, concentration, and formulation.

Formulation is the stage of expression in any form according to our Ray.

In contemplation we contact energy and change it into concepts, then into ideas in meditation, and thoughtforms in formulation. Thus the form through which the idea will be presented to the world is progressively formulated.

In the basic meditation process, we eliminate obstacles and hindrances and let the light coming from the higher mind or Intuition pour down, nourish, and energize our threefold nature with ideas, with aspiration, and with vitality.

In basic meditation there is no imposition. You are not imposing anything on yourself, but you are increasing your light to see more, to realize more, to be more. Through meditation you expand your space in which your influence and creativity grow.

A leader is one who leads himself to higher levels of consciousness, to new dimensions of sincerity, solemnity, dedication, honesty, and renunciation. When you lead yourself, people will know that you are a leader and they will join you with their efforts to form a group leadership.

A leader conquers the subjective fields first and proves himself to be a leader in his consciousness and in the subjective side of his life. Any victory achieved on subjective levels reflects itself on objective fields, and a subjective leader becomes a reality on the objective field. You do not need to make yourself be elected. You will be accepted as the leader because a true leader opens the sense of recognition in others.

When you decide within your heart to serve people without expectation and without reservation, no matter how the life tempts you to escape, to exploit, you turn into a leader because whatever a man thinks in his heart, so he is.

Leaders are magnets because they are led by the fire of their Soul, by the fire of their Ashram, by the fire of the Hierarchy. Once you are in tune with these Centers you turn into a magnet. People, subjectively first and then objectively, are attracted to you, not to worship you or to obey you but to take part in your great labor of helping the Hierarchy to restore the Plan on Earth.

No one can be magnetic if he has no contact with his Soul; this is the first charge of magnetism.

When the guilt feeling or feeling of failure starts to descend upon you, reminding you of the chain of your failures, withdraw yourself into the Self and say:

> *More radiant than the sun,*
> *Purer than the snow,*
> *Subtler than the ether,*

> *Is the Self,*
> *The Spirit within my heart.*
> *I am that Self.*
> *That Self am I.*

Try to work from the level of Self because the most effective technique of the dark forces is to discourage leaders with their own failures and blow them out of proportion so that the leader misjudges himself and quits the battlefield of service.

Those leaders who are protected by the shield of their Teacher always try to act and serve as souls and not as personalities.

The following pages will strive to unfold the spirit of leadership in its many petals.

1
Vision of the Future

Vision is an image of yourself projected into the future. It is an active, dynamic image which inspires you and pulls you up and forward on the path of your evolution.

Vision is what you want to be and what you want to do for the service of humanity.

Vision is a two-sided magnetic field. One side represents your aspiration, dedication, and striving. The other side represents the projected plan of your Soul into your personality. Actually there is no vision if these two magnetic fields do not fuse within each other.

The Soul projects into the sphere of your mind a part of the plan which you must accomplish in your life. This is given by your Soul as a magnetic field. When the developing human soul comes in contact with this field and tries to understand it, a vision is the result, which he tries to translate and actualize or materialize with his aspiration, dedication, and striving.

Vision is the part of the Hierarchical Plan which you can materialize. That part of the Plan is your duty which you can fulfill at your level, in your cycle, and with your capacity. But no matter what that vision is, it pulls you up and forward toward perfection, toward greater service for humanity, and toward greater cooperation with the Plan.

Visions can be given to us from various sources. We have personality visions which are mostly our dreams and aspirations. We have visions projected from our Inner Guide, visions projected from the Spiritual Triad or the Hierarchy, and visions projected from the Monad or Shamballa, or still higher visions coming from higher centers in the solar system or galaxy.

- Vision projected from the Inner Guide is related mostly to our evolution on the Path.

- Vision projected from the Hierarchy or from the Spiritual Triad is related to the Plan and to the service of all humanity.

- Vision projected from Shamballa is related to the Purpose of the Planetary Logos.

- Visions projected from even higher sources are related to solar and galactic fields of service. Thus, as you have contact with higher visions, the field of your service expands. The rule is that there is no vision if it is not related to a field of service.

A vision always evokes from your Real Self an aspiration to sacrifice, to give, to serve, to radiate, and to uplift people. There is no vision if it is not associated with the idea of service.

Suppose a man makes a vision for himself and says, "I want to make one million dollars and enjoy my life." That is not a vision but an exploitation of the laws and principles of the Universe for his personal ends.

Let us say that you have a vision. When that vision breaks the limitations of your selfishness or separatism, the walls and bars of your consciousness, and expands your awareness to such a degree that you clearly realize that you are a part of Nature instead of thinking that you are a separate being in the Universe, this is a great breakthrough.

Vision takes you into inclusiveness, wholeness, no matter what part you have to play in the Plan.

The vision given in the Spiritual Triad — in the plane of the abstract mind, Intuition, and Atmic levels — is very dynamic, and it wipes away almost all obstacles on its path of fulfillment. Vision given by the Spiritual Triad is charged with the electricity of the highest level of intellect, with the fire of Intuition, and with the flame of Willpower. Such vision demands from you Enlightenment, Intuition, and Willpower to be able to materialize on Earth.

You can try to express such a vision with your elevated intellect, but it does not work. You need Intuition and you need Willpower, which wipe away all obstacles.

Visions are given to you according to your past service and present potentials and demands.

It is always emphasized that you must be ready to accept and understand a vision. To be ready means to have a healthy body, positive emotions, and a well cultivated mind. Your physical life, your emotional and mental life are the interpreters of the vision. Vision is translated on the level that you are. If your personality is not ready to absorb that high-voltage energy, the vision cannot find a healthy expression through you, and it reflects in your personality vehicles as a distortion. Your life turns into a life of confusion and a life of distortion.

The most dangerous human beings are those who contact a vision and the vision penetrates into their distorted system with a high voltage and creates great confusion, purposelessness, and diffusion.

When the vision is contacted by a purified and ready personality, the vision brings about a great change in your life. If you do not change and progress steadily, and if you are not stepping on what you were yesterday and raising yourself upward, you do not have vision or you are unable to assimilate the vision. If you cannot assimilate the vision presented to you from your Soul, you live through a distorted vision.

The Plan is a great dynamic thoughtform created by the Hierarchy as a blueprint for the construction of a new humanity.

Your Soul holds a small part of the Plan for you. The construction is like a huge jigsaw puzzle. Your part is a small piece of it. Your duty is to find your right place and to fill it to make everything else more complete. You see how your vision is related to the whole. You try very hard to be the embodiment of the vision that your Soul holds for you and to fill that space which, when filled, makes everything else more complete and more beautiful. Your destiny is not to live for yourself but to live for the whole.

In the overall picture of the Plan, you are nothing as a separate piece but are everything when completing that picture. Your value lies in completing the picture because you will never be able to complete yourself until you sacrifice your ego to complete the picture.

This is not understood by contemporary humanity which emphasizes separatism and self, national, and party interests. Such groups and nations are working against the laws and principles, forces, and energies of the Universe. That is why we do not have a harmonious world but a world which is full of pain, suffering, fear, disease, wars, and crime.

When you create a vision, you create a magnetic pull in the higher dimension, in the future. Your thought goes and builds an image for your future Self. In the process of understanding, translating, and formulating your future, you must ask yourself, "What do I want to be in the future?"

Whatever you want to be in the future, that is your vision. But if that vision is not related to the service of humanity, you do not have real vision, and you are creating a short circuit in the energy patterns of the Universe. You distort the electrical networks of the laws and principles of the Universe because you are exploiting them and using them for your selfish interests instead of using them to fulfill the demands of the laws and principles.

When you are thinking and meditating about what you want to be in the future, always try to relate it to the big jigsaw puzzle, to the overall image of the Plan. You are important because you are a part, and you must find your right place to complete the global, solar, galactic, and Cosmic pictures. If you really find your place with the right level, the right voltage, you become a conscious part of that whole. The energy of that great existence makes you go forward and forward on the path of your perfection because now you are a part of the energy network, and the Presence flows through you in its Cosmic Beauty, Goodness, and Truth.

People can also become blockages in that system if they work for their ego.

Let us remember that all is energy; all forms are condensed energy floating in an ocean of energy with their individual fields of energy. When you are fused with a great vision, the energy of the vision comes and passes through the network of your creative electric system and then passes through your fingers and pencils or brushes onto paper. It becomes a writing, a painting, a piece of music, etc. and radiates out in a pattern you created through your art. This pattern of energy continuously radiates through your creation, and when people come in contact with your creativity, they find a path through which they can contact the source of your vision.

If you do not have a vision you are becoming a failure. Failure means not to have a vision or not to follow your vision.

Vision is a dynamic power that leads you forward. When a little girl is playing with her doll and caring for it, she is building a vision or responding to a vision, which is the vision of motherhood. Thus, the Soul on every stage of your life projects a vision, if you are sensitive enough to grasp it. It is through vision that the Soul moves you forward.

There are individual visions, group visions, and global visions. Individual vision can be achieved when every day for a few minutes you think about your future service for humanity. Every day read a fairy tale or legend in which the spirit of heroism, nobility, and sacrifice is demonstrated. Every day think about a great hero who brought more beauty into the world. Every day read such things to your children or friends.

I was reading a fairy tale to some teenagers. It was written that a beautiful young knight, when riding on his horse, found a girl who was wounded and almost exhausted from bleeding. He bandaged her wounds, took her to his castle, took care of her, saw to her training in the womanly arts, and married her.

Look how beautiful this is. The fairy tale is creating a vision in you that is beyond you and which challenges you and inspires you to be a knight instead of a cowboy who kills his neighbor for an acre of land.

You have lots of literature on the market which takes you down and down toward your toes. The legends that present to you the beauty of service, inclusiveness, purity, simplicity, fearlessness are good means to achieve visions. This kind of literature must be read to your children before "their house is on fire." They will reject any instruction from you at the time of the fire. You must prepare them from their childhood, even from pregnancy.

I was talking with fifteen teenagers. I asked what they wanted for the future. Some said, "A good car, a good home, a good friend, wife or husband, and money to enjoy life." Some said, "We want to be leaders in the world, to make people follow our instructions and orders!" One of them said, "I want to educate myself and build myself in a way that I serve humanity." "Thank you," I said, "You have a vision, and do not let that vision fade away."

In our education the only thing lacking is vision. There is the spirit of competition, separatism, and self-interest but not vision. Our children are not taught the science of service for humanity. There needs to be a curriculum which inspires the students to work for humanity, to create one humanity, to eliminate all discrimination, and to develop sacrificial will to dedicate themselves for the upliftment of one humanity. This is the failure of education. This means that contemporary education has no foundation. It can give knowledge and information and let it be used against the survival of nations and humanity.

I want to see a course for those who want to be world citizens, for those who want to eliminate all barriers between nations, for those who want to protect their freedom from any separative interests. Such a teaching will be stronger than communism, stronger than democracy.

This does not mean that there are no great humanitarians and people of vision, but at the present they do not have enough power to change the curriculum of the schools in all nations.

The goal is not to be a doctor but to be a doctor to serve humanity with utmost selflessness and without exploitation. The goal is not to be a lawyer but to be a lawyer who is dedicated to the service of those who are mistreated and exploited. The goal should not be personal interest but the interest of others. If your vision is not beyond your own interests, you do not have vision.

Is it necessary to have vision?

I would say that without vision man will slowly descend into apathy, inertia, depression and become suicidal or criminal. If you want to cure such people, give them vision. Give them hope and future. Show them what they can do for others.

One day a girl came to me who was very depressed. Fortunately, one hour before another girl had come also with serious depression. After talking with the first girl, I told her to wait in the garden until I saw the new girl. While I was conversing with the new girl, I said to her, "You know, I want you to help that girl in the garden. She is so depressed."

I introduced both girls. "You help her," I said, "until I finish a letter and come back." Half an hour later they were laughing. I said, "What is the matter?" They were almost unable to talk to me because of their laughter. Eventually one of them said, "It is so silly. . .you played a nice trick to make us expose ourselves to each other and find out how ridiculous were the reasons for our depression."

The secret was that each of them saw a need in the other and tried to help her, giving a new hope and a new vision. And when they saw the vision, both were relieved.

To prevent crime you do not need more laws and more police. You need teachers to give vision to the youth. Give vision to children, and you will see the disappearance of crimes. But then a few million people will lose their business without crime. But our taxes will be less!

Whenever one has no vision, he is destructive. Without vision you go toward separatism, selfishness, and matter. It is only vision that carries you up into beauty, inclusiveness, and righteousness. Inclusiveness and righteousness mean cooperation, harmony, service, and adjustment.

When you build your vision through meditation and thinking, you will proceed on the way of your evolution. It is impossible to have a vision and not see its blooming. It is impossible to plant any healthy seed without expecting its germination. Whatever you sow, you reap. Building a vision means to put a seed in fertile ground.

When you create a contact, a vision, you create focus. Whenever you have focus, you have energy circulation around the focus.

Space is static. There is no movement in space. Motion starts in space when you have focus. That is what the whole creation is. The manifestation or the creation as a whole is a focus and has billions of smaller focuses in space. It is because of these focuses that we have energy and energy circulation.

Creation is projected by the Cosmic Mind to create motion in the static space, to create circulation of energy and polarity. You create polarity through having a vision. The polarity is between you and the vision, and the energies of the Universe start to circulate through you and your vision according to the level and intensity of your focus. If the vision is as negative as you are, there is no polarity. Your vision must be so beautiful, so universal, so progressive, and so magnetic that it creates a positive polarity in relation to your negative polarity and puts into action the creative energies in Nature. That is why if you have vision, you are creative.

When you have energy circulation, you have a continuous and ever-expanding source of inspiration and impressions from higher sources. Thus, you elevate and sublimate yourself through contacting energies coming continuously from higher sources.

One must have a vision. If you do not know what you are going to be, then you are going to be nothing. You became a human being because you strove for the vision of a human being. You became an artist because you had the vision to be an artist. Whatever you are now, that was the accomplishment of your past vision; and whatever you will be in the future is based on the vision that you build in the present.

Try to have a vision of being something that is for the service of humanity.

Immediately when you create a vision, you are caught in the whirlpool of the vision. The vision will pick you up like an eagle. If you have a vision from which you cannot escape even if you try, you have a real vision. Vision is the vehicle of your Higher Self, and once the Higher Self has a means to contact you, you will never be the same.

If you go and ask Christ, "Why are you talking that way? People will kill you?" He will answer you, "Go behind me, Satan, and leave me alone to bring my vision to humanity."

Your vision eventually will burn all that is not worthy of the vision and will wipe out all that stands on the path of the manifestation of that vision.

The power of a vision is that it is a part of the Divine Plan, a part of the Divine Purpose, and you are letting loose the energy of the Plan and Purpose to carry your vision into fulfillment.

Once a man told me that Christ does not exist. "I do not care," I said, "as long as I can create Him as my vision and hold Him as my vision."

When you establish polarity between you and a vision, you are drawn to your vision. It will take time for you to identify yourself with your vision if it is too high, but the time period is the period during which all obstacles on the path of your vision are gradually eliminated, leaving you free to be your vision.

Vision is like a seed which we put under the earth. Now the seed is thinking, "I am a fragrant flower." The sand or the earth around it will hear its words and say, "You are crazy. What are you talking about?"

And the seed will say, "Never mind what you think about me. I am a beautiful, fragrant flower which will be carried to the tables of knights and kings."

Because the vision is inside of the seed, it is impossible for it not to be the vision, the fragrant flower.

The seed is you. You are the seed of the Cosmic Almighty Flower. Because God is in the seed, it is impossible not to be like the Father.

It is impossible not to be the likeness of the Father if we are created as His likeness. Then why do we have all these failures, crimes, and insanity?

The answer is that a man not following a vision creates a miserable life for himself, and for a long time his life is a process of building without a plan and destroying without a purpose.

Such insanity descends on us when we try to have and not give, to raise ourselves and not uplift others, to have light and keep others in darkness, to be powerful but try to perpetuate weakness, to expand and make others contract, to be happy but keep others miserable; in a word, when we do not try to bloom toward our own innate vision.

In one of the monasteries that I visited I saw a very interesting structure. There were two long walls forming a path. One could enter this path hoping that it would lead somewhere. After you walked fifty yards, you found yourself before a wall eight feet high. I was very curious, and one day I climbed the wall. Walking on a side wall, I saw that after another fifty yards there was another wall, another wall. . .five walls interrupting the path I had been following.

I was curious about why these walls were here. In front of the last wall there was a huge marble coffin. I thought, maybe this is not a usual building with four rooms! It has no doors and no windows!

One day I went to a very old gardener in the monastery and asked, "What is this building?"

"Did you see how it is built?"

"Yes."

"How?"

"Five walls and four rooms. . .and a coffin."

"How did you see them?"

"I climbed on the wall and discovered its structure."

"Ah," he said, "that is the way not to be trapped in those rooms. Did you see lots of people trapped in the rooms?"

"No, I did not see anybody."

"Well, imagine millions of people trapped in those rooms."

"Okay," I said, "but how did they go in?"

"They fell in."

"Why the walls?"

"Imagine. . .the walls are five traps which trap people and do not free them to bloom."

"And what are they?"

"I will not tell you for six months. You think it over and find out."

For six months I went through agony, every day going there for a few minutes and trying to solve the riddle. I could not.

Six months later I went to him and said, "Well, here I am. I could not find the meaning of the walls."

"Really? Are you *angry*?"

"No."

"Are you *afraid*?"

"No."

"Are you *greedy*?"

"I don't think so."

"Do you *hate*?"

"No."

"But maybe you are *jealous*?"

"I am not. Why to be jealous?"

"I don't know. But you see, you know the answer."

"How?"

When I said "how," he shouted in a loud voice, telling me to go to hell and find the answer. I ran away, thinking that the gardener was crazy.

At night when I was resting and thinking about the walls and reviewing my conversation with the gardener, suddenly I sat up in my bed and exclaimed, "My goodness!"

"What did you say," asked a half-sleeping friend.

"My goodness!"

"What?"

"I know the meaning of the walls in which people are trapped."

"You are stupid."

"I am not."

I walked to the bed of my friend and whispered in his ear, "The first wall is fear. The second wall is anger. The third wall is greed. The fourth wall is hate. The fifth wall is jealousy. I've got it!"

He sat up in bed. Opening his eyes, he said, "You are crazy. Go away."

This is how the seed is imprisoned within five walls and cannot bloom.

Our vision must not have these five traps which sometimes are called the five monsters.

Those who can *surpass* these five walls, because of their vision, will surpass the human level and become the members of the kingdom of God, or members of the community of flowers. The majority of humanity has been too long on the human level, just like a child who does not want to leave his kindergarten because there are lots of toys there. Similarly, man says, "Leave me alone. Give me my television, my car, a girl, and some money, and I will be happy."

Man stays perpetually at the level he has reached instead of going to the next stage of his evolution. The reason is that his vision in the seed has not fallen on fertile ground and been activated there.

Man must step onto his path of superhuman evolution. This is done only through a great vision.

Man has had enough pleasure throughout ages. He has eaten lots and possessed lots and left all his possessions millions of times. It is the time now for him to come to his sanity and proceed with his superhuman evolution toward "the kingdom of heaven." We have had enough of kingdoms of sex, food, and property. They do not satisfy us any more. We need to proceed toward the kingdom of Beauty, Goodness, Truth, simplicity, and wisdom.

We must also work for group vision.[1] To achieve group vision, we must subordinate our individual visions to the group vision. Real groups only come into

---

1. See also *The Psychology of Cooperation and Group Consciousness*.

existence when the members have vision and are able to subordinate their vision to the group vision.

Group vision is the service which the group can render for humanity. Group vision comes to the group especially at the time of full moons when the planet, the sun, and one of the zodiacal constellations are aligned with each other, thus providing a channel through which zodiacal energies penetrate into the sphere of the planet and reach the group.

At the time of the full moon, the Hierarchy uses the opportunity of the alignment to impress the Plan on the stream of energy and contact humanity as a whole. Times for greater visions are at the full moons of Aries and Gemini. The highest moment of contact is the Taurus full moon. It is at this full moon that Shamballa sends the impressions of the Purpose along the streams of energy penetrating the planet.

It is through individual and group meditation at the full moon times that the vision comes, and insight and the future are revealed to the group.

How can our vision manifest?

1. By visualization, as if an accomplished fact is in operation

2. By every day feeding the thoughtform with the fire of enthusiasm

3. By keeping ourselves healthy, clean, and as pure as possible

4. By maintaining strict purity of speech, non-criticism, and eliminating gossip

5. By being noble and honest in our lives

6. By offering our lives and money to the vision

7. By always being patient about the vision

In these three full moons we receive three kinds of vision. One is related to human intellect or to abstract thinking and the art of programming of human affairs. The second is related to love-wisdom, to the Plan, a part of which is impressed on the minds of the disciples. The third is related to the Will, to the Purpose of the Almighty Life.

Through these three full moons we shape our vision, bringing it into completion, and we start manifesting it throughout our lives.

It is very important to see the difference between the Plan and the Purpose.

The Plan is the blueprint for the future of humanity, for the future of the world. Labor on all levels is the action to bring the Plan into manifestation. The Purpose is the "why" of the Plan.

You want to build a castle. The laborers are working on a given blueprint. Then you ask, why does this castle have to be built? How does it reveal the purpose and the will behind the purpose?

The Plan can change. The techniques of the labor can change when you have closer contact with and more understanding of the Purpose. For example, my purpose is to serve in various places. Engineers planned a carriage. After using the carriage for a while, I saw that the carriage does not meet my purpose. So the engineers built a steam engine. After using the steam engine for a while, I noticed that it does not completely serve my purpose. So eventually they built a car, then better and better cars, and then the airplane. My purpose remained the same — to go and serve in various cities, various states and countries, various planets.

In all these developments the plan cyclically changed; the laborers used more sophisticated techniques, but the purpose remained the same.

When you come closer to the essence of the Purpose of the Captain of the World, you adjust your plans continuously. Also, as humanity progresses, the Plan changes.

An engineer can have great plans, but seeing that humanity is not ready, he gives to humanity only a simplified portion of the plan. Thus, the plan is in continuous change due to the closer contact of the engineers with the purpose, and due to the advance of humanity and its technology.

The first contact with the Purpose reveals itself as a vision which in time grows and builds in details. At the first contact with the vision, we go through psychological changes.

For example, every vision, if it is true vision, increases the sense of responsibility within you. You do not have a vision if you do not feel a sense of responsibility, a new discipline to face your responsibility. The sense of responsibility is a sign that you have a vision. When you lose your vision, you lose your sense of responsibility and begin to hurt people with your attitudes, deeds, gossip, nosiness, and criticism; you fall into the five traps, or into the stagnated lake of your selfish interests.

Group vision is the sum total of the vision of the members of the group. When the members raise their spiritual frequency and eventually hit the layers of the Plan, the Plan evokes in them a vision toward which they strive.

Groups can actualize their vision on one or many of the seven fields of human endeavor. A group can try to materialize its vision in politics, in education, in the field of communication or philosophy, or in arts, sciences, religion, or economics. Wherever the majority of the group members fit, there is the field of service.

A group must ask itself, "Where do we fit in these seven fields?" Once the field is found, then the cycle of heavy discipline begins to fit the group to the requirements of the field in order to carry on a great service and make part of the Plan materialize through the group.

The Hierarchy has seven main Ashrams of specialization to translate the Purpose into the Plan. Groups have seven fields of human endeavor to make the Plan manifest through their vision. This can be explained as follows:

The Plan is a great symphony. It is a universal vision for those who contact the Plan. Humanity is divided into seven fields of human endeavor. Each field is a group of musicians playing the same instruments. The cellos come together and say, "Let us make our part perfect." The violins come together and say, "Let us do our part as well as possible." The other instruments do the same. When all the groups do their best, the whole orchestra does its best, and the symphony manifests in its total beauty.

Joy, health, and success are only possible if you have a great vision.

Vision is the summit of a beautiful mountain, and your heart urges you to climb that mountain and reach the summit.

What are the signs that a nation is losing its vision? There are many:

— increasing crime

— pornography

— injustice

— totalitarianism

— lack of the sense of righteousness

— materialism

— greed

— loss of respect for each other

— pleasure seeking

— anarchy

— drugs

— sexual license

— hate

— criticism

— discrimination

— separatism

and all their relatives and children.
There are also signs that a man or a group has vision:

- discipline
- cooperation
- respect
- silence
- creativity
- joy
- health

- mastery
- solemnity

If individuals strive to reach a vision and manifest it in their life, they uplift a nation and enable it to receive a global or universal vision.

We say to each other, "Happy New Year." Actually we must say, "Happy Year." When you do not have a vision, the year is not a new year but the continuation of the old year. If we have the same life, the same "dress," the same pains, sufferings and worries, the same likes, dislikes, and pleasures, where is the newness in it?

We can have a new year, a new life, a new beginning, only when we renew our vision, contact a vision, or penetrate deeper into our vision — a vision that is not handicapped by our personal, group, racial, national, traditional, religious, political, or social limitations. Visions must stand beyond all this if we are going to serve humanity.

When we are receiving any impression from any limiting field of consciousness, we are losing a part of that vision.

In the fire of vision, true leadership comes into being. The more you actualize your vision, the better leader you become. Your vision charges your aura with magnetism and radioactivity. You become a walking vision for others. Every true leader is a walking vision. People touch your vision through your presence, and your vision builds striving in them to reach their inner vision.

2
Leadership Essentials

True leaders are those who are able to lead themselves — their physical, emotional, and mental nature — toward new standards of living and operation.

The leader must realize that he cannot lead others until he knows how to lead himself.

He who is a sincere and devoted student of the Ageless Wisdom and who is very anxious to take his evolution into his own hands must know that leadership is the result of such realizations. Without these realizations, there is no leadership. Once a man is led to himself, he then becomes a man who awakens other people, not by trying to do so, but spontaneously. His existence creates conflicts, striving, and self-exertion in others, and they become their own leaders, not his followers.

A true leader not only awakens in others self-exertion, striving, and conflict but also the presence of his realizations urges them to be creative. Creativity, in this sense, means to express the level of achievement which one has reached. The beauty one has touched within comes out as a creative expression in his life. Once a person starts to be creative, he will lead himself into sacrificial service.

No one can lead other people to such realizations if he causes those around him to become "monkeys," artificially oriented and imitative.

Leadership does not mean to lead other people in your steps. Leadership means to cause others to be led by their own high spirit, high sincerity, and highest values. They must be led by values which they have within themselves. Once three or four people are really led to themselves by themselves, then a leadership group may be formed. A leadership group is formed by those disciples who have contact with their own Souls.

The leader is the "troublemaker" in that he presents opportunities for people to strive toward their True Self. A "troublemaker" is the custodian of the Plan. He presents the Plan and gives people chances to work, as much as they are able, without pressure of any kind. In this way the modern leader keeps his own freedom and does not violate the free will of others.

A real leader is an achievement and a path of achievement for others. Because of such an achievement, a possibility now exists for us; a path is now open.

Every leader must be able to say, "I am a point of light within a greater Light." He is not saying that he wishes that there were a light and that light would come and enter his head. When he says, "I am a strand of loving energy," he is affirming his own achievement within the stream of divine Love. He says, "I am a point of sacrificial fire, focused within the fiery Will of God. And thus I stand. I am a way by which men may achieve...." He does not say, "I am a way by which men may come to me."[1]

This is the mantram of the real disciple.

Because of his Light, because of his Love, and because of his Power, others are challenged to go more deeply within and to achieve within themselves.

The term "leadership" does not necessarily refer to the head of a group; rather it refers to a person who is trying to lead himself into light.

When a person is leading himself into greater light, into greater sacrifice and service, and into greater cooperation with the Hierarchy, he is a leader. When he is leading himself, he is leading other lives around him and around his bodies. He is leading others who are karmically affiliated with him. His leadership is not by force but because of his achievements.

On this path the greatest trap for leadership is vanity. Vanity is a state of mental illusion when a man thinks that he is something which he is not. When a man is after transient objects or values, he is a man of vanity.

This is a very important point. When you see a man who is emphasizing things which are really useless and without value from the standpoint of the Eternal Presence or the Eternal Now, then he is a man of vanity because he is running after shadows.

Every time we overemphasize secondary things, things which are not really eternal, spiritual, or do not present a value that gives greater freedom to humanity, then we are running after shadows. These shadows may be in the form of objects, states of consciousness, or illusions and glamors.

---

1. "Affirmation of a Disciple," *Five Great Mantrams*, p. 31.

Even if people want to possess things for the sake of possessions, it really means they are running after vanity because they are after transient objects, whether subjective or objective.

The greatest obstacles for humanity are those people who are running after vanity. They do not present real values, and thus they use their positions and opportunities only for their own little selves. Such people burn cities for their own vanities.

Some people like to shine by the light of others. This is also vanity. They may read something beautiful somewhere, repeat it, and cause people to think that they are great. And if they really enjoy doing this, then they are deeply involved in glamor.

Leadership requires continuous freedom from any kind of object, whether it is outside or inside. Leadership means decentralization of yourself.

There are four important qualities which a leader must cultivate, sometimes very cautiously or painfully. These qualities must be practiced in his daily speech, thoughts, and activities.

The first one is *objectivity*. A leader is a "down-to-earth" man. He is practical and realistic and does not run after glamors or illusions. This does not mean that he denies abstract values and realities but for him they are objective because of his intuitional faculty. He has the ability to see things as they are, with their true value and connections.

The second quality is *sincerity*. A leader must be sincere with himself and with others. Sincerity evokes spiritual recognition and a cooperative spirit in others. Sincerity inspires faith and trust. It is the ability to face oneself in the light of reality and relate oneself to others as you are in essence.

The third quality is *directness*. This is the ability to dissipate those factors which can distort your image as you really are. Directness is the shortcut. The leader never loses time and never looks for detours, but he deals with the right person in the right way at the right moment. He puts his finger on the exact problem and emphasizes the most important key to the problem.

Directness means that you contact the people to whom you direct yourself. Directness means center-to-center communication, complete communication of everything that you want to say.

If a disciple does not learn directness, he becomes a victim of his own glamors, illusions, and maya. He must destroy these and face himself.

Directness saves time and energy. Directness creates shocks and makes people face reality. When you are not direct, you create many complications within yourself and others.

When a leader is indirect, he loses his prestige; people eventually mistrust him.

The fourth quality is *gratitude*. A grateful man is a man of magnetism and cooperation. He attracts higher qualities. Gratitude is the recognition and appreciation of the help given to a person. Through gratitude we help people to be better, to be more beautiful. Gratitude increases the soul quality in others.

When these four virtues are developed, they dissipate vanity and the leader stands within the light of his Essence.

Vanity can be defined as self-deception. A man who is caught in vanity tries to make people believe that he is not as they see him but is one who knows more, is more, and has more.

Vanity is adherence to transient values.

We can learn the true esoteric value of virtues when we really try to demonstrate them or be them. The leader must use these four virtues in his daily practical life.

There is a great law that a leader cannot proceed on his way to greater service until he prepares people to take his place in the field of service. One cannot advance in the field of service when he is attached to his level. The work of the Hierarchy demands a chain of workers to replace each other on higher and higher spirals.

Leadership is so subtle, and it cannot be learned. We may only learn the techniques of how to lead by leading ourselves. Then do we become leaders.

People will come to you and ask for answers to their questions. Here again vanity enters in if you are not careful and if you think that you are omniscient, that you can do anything, or that you will be respected and loved because of your demonstration of your abilities. This will cause intrigues in you, and it presents a great danger because it will prevent your self-exertion. You will think to yourself, "Now everyone is coming to me because I know. If I know, why should I know more?"

Self-exertion is the primary weapon for leaders. Do not be satisfied with what you are. On the contrary, where you are is total darkness compared to your Real Self. Understand this. You can respect your former self, but you do not want to be stuck to that level because of the praise of others. Any time people praise you, there is the danger that you can become cemented or trapped on the level where you are. If a leader believes the praise that he is great, he wants to perpetuate his present level and he is dead. The leader must see his level as the past, with so much still before him, and say, "Who am I yet?"

Have your self-respect. Self-respect is very important, but self-respect and selfishness or showing off are totally different things.

Solemnity means to respect the Divinity within yourself. A solemn person does not gamble with his Inner Divinity.

There are two ways of praising. One way causes you to stick to your former level. The other creates in you a tremendous self-exertion. For example, someone says to you, "You know, you took the first initiation; how beautiful it is! But there are eight more waiting for you yet. Now, no matter how heavy or fast or deep, you must struggle and strive to reach those." This is creative praise; but excessive praise without vision acts as an obstacle.

A man of leadership does not learn these things. He knows them without learning them, or he has some intuitive sense about them because he has already passed through these experiences and does not need to deliberate upon them in order to know how to act. The leader has that psychometric mechanism or sense in him which measures people and life.

The most important thing is not to learn the techniques of leadership but rather to learn how to reach greater awareness and deeper experience within your inner world. The rest will be given to you. As Christ said, "Seek first the Kingdom of Heaven, and all else will be given to you."

The leader has higher frequencies in his sphere, greater expansions of awareness, and greater radiations and vibrations which he generates. When someone else's mental aura meets his and a question comes to the person, that person will know the answer or the reality more clearly because there is a dynamic center of energy near him.

A leader is a source, a battery, which is filling the weak batteries of others.

Leadership is your achievement. Because of your achievement and by your achievement, you are creating a tremendous vacuum in a field. For example, when you are in a boat and you push the paddle into the water, you create a hole into which more water races. Because you move a quantity of water, its place is filled by other water. Allegorically, such a movement is formed by your movement into yourself. Your expansion creates a space, an opportunity for others, via the vacuum you created, to move into themselves, into the next level of awareness out of which you are pushing.

Nicholas Roerich did a very beautiful painting of someone sitting and throwing arrows. It is of a blue mountain and arrows being thrown into space. The man in the painting is throwing his thoughts. Who knows where they came from, but they impress people, influence people, and expand their consciousness.

This is similar to climbing Mt. Everest. Because there is an Everest, a great mountain, an achievement in front of us, we cannot help but climb it. We do so because we want to *be,* because it is reminding us of our future possibilities.

Leadership is not a wish or a desire. Leadership is *willpower.* The difference between a leader and a non-leader is that the leader uses his willpower. A non-leader uses his aspirations, emotions, and imagination, but the leader acts. When the time comes, he acts, he demonstrates, and he proves. The leader does not imagine and lose time; wishful thinking is inappropriate for leadership.

Leadership must also be very flexible. At certain times a leader must retreat to win. He must let people win if their success will make them better servers, or if their success makes them give him more freedom to work.

Sometimes co-workers are built by allowing them to take on positions and responsibilities. There are occasions when your personal success or victory over others is your failure. The leader is not interested in any personality success or failure. . .if the Soul is in victory or if the Plan is in manifestation.

Leadership is watchfulness. A leader in action is one who knows dangers and from where they come.

Once I was preparing to visit a Brotherhood as a young man. I did not know where I was going to stay at night and under what conditions. My father told me, "There are two important things to know when you go to a house. First, you must know where the bathroom is." I laughed then, but I saw later he was right. "The second thing you must know," he said, "is a way to escape." Later this saved me from many dangers.

When I entered a house where I was going to stay for two or three nights, I looked around and found a place from which I could escape if anything happened. And indeed it happened that I made use of it many times! There was the danger there that while you were sleeping, people would rob or kill you. Therefore I would sleep near a window, and, when I sensed danger, I would jump out and run or sneak away.

The leader must be aware of the conditions, and when it is best to keep silent, must keep silent.

The primary danger for humanity at this time is obsession and possession. Obsession and possession are gradual. When men or women are going to be obsessed, their walk changes; their eyes change; their looks change; they speak differently; and they undergo other changes. They may love you one moment and hate you the next; different personalities and different faces appear in them. From these signs you may immediately know their condition.

There is another danger which those who are striving to be leaders must be made aware. This danger may be referred to as "evoking the emanations of the past."

It is necessary to study attentively the cases of so-called dual existence. At its worst, it is a type of obsession. At its best, a survival of former incarnations. Sometimes

> *the spirit approaches his former incarnations to such an extent that he relives them. It is necessary to observe solicitously this condition, which does not enter into the consciousness of the present incarnation. One should not trouble him with questions...You notice that we touch upon past incarnations only in cases of necessity, in order not to evoke the emanations of the past from* Akasha.[2]

Being stuck to the past occurs when through some ways or means a person is in rapport with the memories of his past, either consciously or unconsciously. For example, though a simple woman now, she was a queen in a past incarnation, so she tries to act like a queen now even though she is not. This creates a tremendous conflict.

"The emanations of the past" are your emotional, mental, and karmic radiations or waves of energy and force. If you go too deeply and really start reliving your past incarnations, you will eventually attract all your former emanations and make a mess of your present life.

Leadership is used as either power or domination. Power is the result of knowledge, expansion of consciousness, creativity, purity of observation, and contact with the Higher Worlds. Power is impossible without an elevated and expanded consciousness.

Domination is the result of a narrow consciousness full of fear and self-interest. A leader who wants to dominate and dictate is not a true leader. Leadership is not domination but the ability to awaken in others the sense of direction, discrimination, and the sense of the most essential.

---

2. Agni Yoga Society, Agni Yoga, para. 230, 1980 edition.

With the beauty of his ideas and the inclusiveness of his consciousness, a true leader gains respect. People listen to him, not because they want to be dominated but because they want to learn and be protected from their own mistakes. A real leader protects the freedom of people, but he neither praises their weaknesses nor encourages them. He even does not criticize them, but vigilantly follows their steps to stop them at the brink of the abyss.

Domination is the characteristic of weak people who are afraid of losing their position and self-interests. Domination paralyzes the consciousness of other people and does not let them find themselves. The goal of the true leader is to make you meet your True Self. Domination makes this almost impossible. To dominate means to prevent others from meeting their True Self.

The leader stands for success because he tries to take his steps very carefully, with full circumspection in regard to his possibilities, the environment, and the people involved.

In spite of many careful considerations and preparations, a leader may fail. But a leader is one who cannot be defeated by his failure; on the contrary, the failure awakens in him a greater striving to achieve a greater success.

What does a leader do after a failure? He sits down and considers the factors that led him to failure. Were these factors in him or in his co-workers? Was it a question of time, conditions, calculations, etc.? Through factual confrontation he finds the errors which led him to failure.

During such a procedure he does not criticize, scold, or belittle any one of his co-workers, but he tries to analyze the situation from as many viewpoints as possible and take constructive, instructive, and disciplinary action to eliminate the failure-causing factors. Such analysis or research enriches him and his co-workers and strengthens their ties and mutual respect.

After the factors of failure are found, he can organize the next adventure in a better way. This organizational process must be done by all those who were involved in the failure and by all those who had the positions as well as those newly appointed.

The greatest aim of the leader is not *success* but the preparation of men and women who can be future leaders. Leadership is often learned not through success but through labor, conflict, and failure.

In olden days, those leaders who did not have disappointments, failures, and conflicts were not counted as promising leaders. Many old kings sent their sons away from home to make them learn the battle of life and reach maturity through successes and failures. Many kings organized games for their children and conditioned their defeat so that they created in them a greater striving for victory.

You can see this game in the play of wild animals and also with cats and dogs. They play with their little ones and give them a hard time, again and again, until they awaken in them the spirit of fighting and the will to overcome. In this way they prepare future victors.

Life does the same thing if we understand its technique. After each failure and defeat we see the awakening of a new spirit which we did not have before.

Leadership stands for success, and by all possible means the leader must strive for victory and success even in his worst defeats.

3
Practicality in Leadership

Leaders are not daydreamers. They are very practical and, at the same time, very idealistic people. They have an innate sense of measurement which senses the need, the time, and the dosage of the help to be given.

As a leader you must give to people what they need at that time, plus a little vision for the future. You may want to give very precious ideas, but if your audience cannot use them for their needs, it will be a waste of energy on your side and a matter of confusion on the audience's side.

There is a funny story in which a rooster was lost in the desert and was looking for some grain, but instead he found some pearls and a diamond. Angry with what he found, he exclaimed, "My God, I do not need diamonds or pearls. They cannot kill my hunger. I want a few grains. . . ."

This teaches us that we must try to feed the need and not present fantastic ideas or visions, when the need is for a few grains.

Showing off is a miserable sickness, originating from vanity. Do not let people starve, presenting to them your philosophical speculations when they need a few concrete suggestions.

Showing off, when accepted by your audience, builds in their minds a false picture of the real you. This picture or image eventually can be imposed upon you to such a degree that you begin to accept it as your own true image. Once you accept it, the conflict will start within you in a very subtle and hidden way. Eventually you will find yourself in a confused state of mind. You will hate "yourself," identifying either with the false image or with your Real Self and hating your false self when you see the real you as you are. This divides you into two.

Your show-off image is not so dangerous when it is not projected to the audience. Once it is projected to the audience, the audience feels it, charges it, and crystallizes it into a more concrete form.

Once I wrote a comedy about a man who has around him ten to fifteen pictures, and he does not know which one he is. He decides to be one each day, but eventually he finds out that he does not really exist.

Alternating from picture to picture totally wipes out of your mind the true image of your self.

I was reading an open letter from a leader of a group. Addressing his followers he said, "I am in the Himalayas. All the Masters are sending their greetings to you."

This is a false image building process and a technique which runs directly opposite to the interest of the Hierarchy. He is building a false image in the minds of others that he is a messenger of the Masters, that he can come in contact with Them, that They spoke with him and sent Their greetings, etc. So, he is a very important man, and because he is important you should listen to him...and prepare for slavery.

It is so important to keep your image clear in the minds of others because their love and energy will reach you in a clear and pure way. But if your image is false, distorted energies will be projected on you.

People often think that leadership is some kind of dictatorship. The leader — they think — must forbid certain things, allow certain things, and dictate certain actions.

Leadership is exactly the opposite. A true leader never dictates or forces any course of action. He analyzes, he explains, but leaves people free to follow their own path.

Leadership stands for principles and emphasizes principles but leaves people free to choose and discriminate.

The leader develops dignity and leaves people free to do whatever they want, shielded with dignity.

You do not say to your follower: do this, do that, do not do this, do not do that. Instead you explain to him that everything he does affects his immediate circle of co-workers and friends; either he complicates their lives and increases their obstacles, or he makes them freer to carry on their service with the fewest hindrances. Once he knows this, it is up to him what to do, how to live, and whom to love, or with whom to relate.

The leader stands on principles, and principles do not force anyone. They are there as guidelines for correction, for adjustment, and for re-polarization. To be in harmony with principles is a source of joy and energy.

In group life the leadership has the right to isolate people who bring confusion, misrepresenting the group through their behavior and wrongdoings. People who are irresponsible and retard the unfoldment and expansion of group service can be eliminated from the group. Of course the group members are free to choose their own life outside of the group — their religious activities, their political and social activities, and their personal affairs — as long as they are not involving the group in any way.

There is a very fine line between what a group member can do privately and what effect it can have on the group life. This is why it is so important to choose group members very carefully so that they do not use the group for their own advantage or defame it through their insane activities and behaviors.

With all the above, the leadership must find the ways and means to transform a man rather than to throw him out. Every transformation of character is a great service. It is easy to separate drug users, smokers, and criminals from a group and leave them to their own fate. But it is better to transform their life, even at the cost of certain labor, etc.

Hierarchical groups are not only service centers but also refineries where people go and pass through a transformation process until they are able to serve others with firsthand experience. This transformation process depends on the efforts and the exercise of free will of the aspirants and the choices they make.

Hierarchical groups provide the conditions, the atmosphere in which you bloom by your own choice, at your own speed and beauty. Any forceful imposition upon another fellow being creates disturbances in the etheric body.

Aspirants lose their path when they are forced in any direction for these reasons:

1. They develop an imitation mechanism, a hypocrisy.

2. They depend on you and others.

3. They become subject to hypnosis.

4. They fail to develop striving efforts and stand on their own path.

5. Their brain and mind become mechanical. They do not think but want others to think for them.

Leaders of the Future must emphasize the subjective values, the subjective virtues, causes, and motives, and explain how the form is the shadow of what goes inside our emotional and mental bodies.

Once a man told me that we must cultivate, develop, and unfold our brain. "How do you do that?" I asked.

"By right food, by accumulating knowledge, data, and by living a busy life," he said.

I told him that the brain can only unfold and develop if we expand our consciousness through right thinking, right living, and developing virtues.

Subjective values, the consciousness, and thoughts charge the brain and make it a better mechanism to be used. Matter does not charge the consciousness, but thought and consciousness charge the matter. This is to say that a car cannot drive the gasoline, but it is the gasoline that drives the car.

This is why the disciples of the world must emphasize the causal values, the motives, the consciousness, the thoughts, the beingness, the principles. When the subjective side is taken care of, the objective side will follow. Behaviors, events, phenomena, and forms will be changed because of the change of cause, principles, thoughts, consciousness, and motives.

Those who work on the form to change the Spirit will eventually be disappointed.

Through education we can change the life and the consciousness. We can apply this method throughout our whole life. People with wrong motives know this technique and apply it every day far more than those who want to serve humanity.

New causes must be introduced in our life to make the life change, and the quality of life will depend on the introduced cause.

I believe in slow change. I believe in the transformation process through education and experience.

Accumulation of knowledge and its technological uses will not help us to mature and grow if our hearts are still full of glamors, if our minds are full of illusions, if our bodies crave various non goal-fitting pleasures, and if we have an ego and are full of vanity.

The educational process is a process of release and freedom. In true education you do not impose, but you evoke understanding and cooperation.

People want to bring fast changes in life — in their own life, in the life of society. Until the real causes of dissatisfaction are gradually annihilated, the imposition of new changes will create more problems because human nature has the tendency to react if there is any imposition of a new rhythm.

That is why the leader is not flattered or bribed with immediate and fast success. He has a long-range vision, and sometimes to reach that long-range vision and success, temporary withdrawals and apparent failures are necessary.

If one reads the history of humanity esoterically, he will not have difficulty in seeing the victory of basic principles flowering age after age, despite the bonfires of temporary successes of all those forces working against those principles. Take, for example, the principle of freedom. History shows great victories against freedom in which freedom, in its many expressions, was defeated — but only for a short while. You see in history the undercurrent of freedom flowing faster and stronger than before and cyclically demonstrating its power through great events, activities, and achievements.

In the history of humanity, the adversaries of the human spirit and freedom are like boats on the ocean of freedom boasting of their power to use the ocean and control it. But once the tide swells, the boat perishes cycle after cycle and, unfortunately, the adversaries learn their lessons very slowly.

Any violation of human freedom in any form and through any technique gives momentary satisfaction and success, but it does not serve even the violators. Real success can be achieved only in a free society. When success is achieved in violation of freedom, the field of an enslaved society gradually turns into a great failure for the violators.

Future leaders will work for long-range goals with the basic principles of the human soul such as:

1. Freedom
2. Love
3. Unity
4. Harmony
5. Cooperation
6. Forgiveness
7. Beauty
8. Goodness
9. Truth
10. Self-forgetfulness

11. Harmlessness

12. Right speech

Leaders of the Future will work in the spirit of these principles. Success achieved through these principles will last forever.

4
Leadership and Vanity

A leader never makes claims. If any person on the path starts making claims, it is a sign that he is cracking under the pressure of the Teaching. This cracking takes place when the seeds of vanity exist in the secret chambers of his being. To satisfy his vanity and to attract attention, he slowly begins to declare that he is an important person. He follows the well-known path of *descent*, going down step by step every few years. These are the claims he makes:

1. He is an important person.

2. He has psychic powers.

3. He is a disciple.

4. He is an initiate.

5. He has contact with Masters.

6. He channels Masters.

7. He is a Master.

Unfortunately, average people do not see the disintegration of his soul through vanity, and they come closer to him and fall into the path of illusion. It is so painful to awaken such followers of pseudo masters. Sometimes it is better to let them learn in their sleep than to awaken them by a shock because it leads to confusion, hopelessness, irresponsibility, and insanity. Great care must be taken to introduce light into their minds, slowly replacing their illusion.

Pseudo disciples and masters are everywhere at this time because the average person is not trained to discriminate and he encourages such leaders with his money and service.

A real disciple never takes advantage of the naïveté or ignorance of people. He never takes advantage when people are desperate and psychologically ready to surrender. He never takes advantage with his knowledge, position, or wisdom. On the contrary, an honest disciple speaks about his failures, struggles, and problems and proves that he is a human being. He shows people how to strive and how to overcome their problems by his own example. He does not make people depend on him but on their own Selves.

The greatest damage that a disciple can do is to form a false image of himself in the minds of others. Once a so-called great master came and was giving a talk. Suddenly he stopped his talk and said, "You must hear the sign of higher forces." Everyone was spellbound. There were irregular knocks on the roof. I went out to see the "higher forces." They were there; four squirrels were fighting with each other.

Another teacher claimed that he was having conferences with Great Ones every day, but he was caught smuggling drugs. Claim-making is a sign that a person has no values and standards upon which he can stand. Once my Teacher said that if you meet someone who makes claims, run ten miles away from him and never look back.

A real disciple stands upon the virtue of his sacrificial life, on his striving, beauty, joy, humanness, study, meditation, and most of all on his humility. He tries to teach the path of discipleship only through his life-example. Not only does he not make claims, but he also feels indignant when someone for any reason makes claims on his behalf. His vision and understanding of greatness is so clear that he does not dare to minimize the higher values by making any claims about his personal achievements.

One day my father, another boy, and I were picnicking in a beautiful field full of flowers. My friend was holding up his thumb and looking at a mountain next to it. "What are you doing?" asked my father.

"I am measuring the mountain with my thumb."

"How big is it?" asked my father.

"It is just the size of my thumb. I can even cover it."

I remember this conversation every time people declare themselves to be initiates, masters. Their greatness is equal to their thumb.

The greatest damage to the Teaching and to the great Teachers is done not by its enemies but by those who measure greatness by the thumb of their claims. A wise man once said, "Do not measure greatness with your petty achievements."

Once my Teacher was going to give a lecture in a big city. In order to draw more attention, attendance, and money, the organizer printed a very inflated advertisement. One hour before the lecture, my Teacher saw the advertisement, and he felt very grieved. When it was time for him to speak, he came to the podium and said, "I am not the person advertised in the flyer. I will give him a chance, whoever he is, to speak to you." And he walked away.

I was very upset, but in my heart there was also a deep joy. On the way back he did not talk. My father was with us. When we left my Teacher at the monastery and were going home, I said to my father, "People were surprised and the organizer was very upset."

"But your Teacher gave the greatest lesson in solemnity and dignity," said my father.

People use fancy names to impress their followers or the public. Or they hide in the shadow of great leaders in order to feel glorified in their shadow. They tell stories of how they visited famous scientists, artists, and politicians and had long conversations with them; how they were visited by invisible ones and initiated into mysteries and became their messengers; or how they changed their name and now they are a new being. All this indicates vanity and hidden motives to show off and impress people.

The real light does not need such advertising agents. A disciple must stand on his own value, labor, and dedication. He must radiate his pure essence, and people will come to him for guidance and labor.

On the spiritual path one must always appear as he is. Any effort to build an exaggerated image of oneself in the mind of the public creates a heavy blow to his spiritual quest.

One of our Teachers in a monastery said at the time of graduation, "Do not try to appear to be more than what you are. Do not make claims because life will demand of you whatever you claim. Do not manipulate the names of Great Ones in your work. But try to shine with your real light and increase its radiation through dedication and sacrificial service."

5
Leadership and Motive

Leadership is of two kinds: leadership of the personality and leadership of the Soul.

The leadership of the personality is a leadership for the benefit of the personalty of the leader.

The leadership of the Soul is a leadership for the benefit of the spiritual progress of those for whom the leader stands as an inspirational source for the Plan.

The personality-oriented leader is interested in the physical, emotional, and mental separative interests of himself or his followers. Such a leader makes people serve his personality.

The Soul-oriented leader is interested in the development of the Soul quality of his co-workers so that they eventually become their own leaders and then the leaders of those who respond to the keynote of their Soul and the Divine Plan.

If the leader is not beyond his personality, he is caught in the turmoil of his own maya, glamors, and illusions.

Leadership, whether it is on personality or Soul levels, evokes energy from the reservoirs of willpower within the man. If the personality is not purified, the energy that pours down from the reservoirs of the will increases the force of maya, glamors, and illusions of the leader, and the leader becomes the victim of his own power. Maya, glamors, and illusions combined form our ego, and when this ego is open like a sail to the winds of our vanity and to the winds of flattery, it eventually turns into its own enemy and prevents the leader from walking on the path of perfection. It becomes the traditional Dweller on the Threshold.

The destruction of a leader begins with the weakening and eventually the deterioration of the structure of the principles, moral values, and spiritual virtues for which he stands. After a while he works diametrically opposite to his own values and principles.

It is after this period that the deterioration of the form of his organization takes its course. This is true for a family, group, business, or nation. The leader holds in his hands the possibility of development, unfoldment, and success or the possibility of the decay and destruction of the people.

Soul leadership is unpleasant for those who still live in their own personality interests. Soul leadership tries to make such people renounce personality direction and re-orient themselves to spiritual values.

Soul leadership is the highest joy of those who are travelers on the path of spiritual values. Such joy is the joy of striving and labor.

Personality leadership stands for accumulation and possession. Soul leadership stands for sharing, right distribution, and renunciation.

Personality leadership is divided into two branches. One branch is the total exploitation of the followers. The followers must forget their own lives and serve the leader as if they were his own property. In the second branch the leader helps his followers prosper and then uses their prosperity to increase his own prosperity. Such a leader is totally prosperity-oriented and does not care about moral and spiritual values.

The leader keeps his position as long as he satisfies the greed of his followers.

In spiritual leadership the people are invited to strive to get rid of their attachments and personality habits. A leader in such a field is not a pleasant person but, rather, a troublemaker. This is why spiritual leadership is established not by the choice or vote of the people but by the self-choice of the leader.

No one can truly be a spiritual leader unless he has continuity of consciousness. This gives him power and right direction. His direction does not come from the desires and wishes of the people. It comes from inner Ashrams, from his own Master, or from his Soul.

You cannot elect a spiritual leader. You cannot replace him. The only way to increase his effectiveness is to develop your own continuity of consciousness and become aware of the Plan and offer your service to him.

In spiritual leadership there is no competition, ego, supremacy, and jealousy. In spiritual leadership you must have total understanding of the Plan and try to fit yourself to the Plan.

The leader is a very important part of the group because of his ability, knowledge, and willpower.

Many personality-oriented leaders raise their level and eventually become spiritually-oriented leaders because of their followers. When the fellowship of a group is on the path of striving, sincerity, and simplicity, eventually the whole aura of the group helps the leader of good intention to step up and work on a higher dimension.

It is very true that groups or nations cannot have leaders for which they are not worthy. Advancing fellowship urges the leader to make greater breakthroughs. An intelligent leader receives inspiration from the progressive achievements of his followers.

A selfish leadership, or a leader who exploits his followers, is to be blamed less than his followers. The followers are responsible for having a selfish leader, a leader oriented to material values. If the followers are really oriented to spiritual values, no materialistically oriented leader can continue his job among them.

Leadership is attacked mostly because of jealousy, self-interest, or politics.

A man of *spiritual values* will never attack his leader, if he wants to be a leader in the future.

In very serious cases of doubt, he must go and talk with the leader, analyze him, understand him, and see his viewpoints, and on special occasions try to help him see a better direction, without demonstrating vanity or the spirit of criticism.

A truly spiritual leader will give his people opportunities to cooperate with him in leadership. He will prepare co-workers and even those who will succeed him at the time of his promotion.

Leadership, apart from the really spiritual field, is subject to various kinds of interests, but even ego-oriented leadership has its benefits for those who karmically are attracted to such a leader. These leaders are the response to such followers.

Spiritual leaders work on different levels. They appear differently to the lower levels of the fellowship than they appear to the highly developed members.

People condition the level on which a leader acts. It is not the imposition of the leader that is the hindrance on the path of your progress, but it is the crystallization of your consciousness, jealousy, hatred, greed, and ignorance that is your own hindrance. Any kind of leadership cannot stop your creativity if you are really creative, and often *because* of suppression your creativity increases a thousandfold.

Leadership is the moment when you impress on the brains of the people that there is a great need, and meeting that need is your greatest interest. This is true leadership.

There should be no choice when the command comes, not because the leader wants it but because the need demands it.

You must prove to your people that you really know their needs and at the right psychological moment meet their need. Only an obedient fellowship can pass onto the path of leadership. Leadership is the response of your level.

A Hierarchical leader must always aggravate your personality. He is not going to be pleasant or please you; he is always going to put his finger on your wounds and challenge you to discipline yourself.

The spiritual leader has a compass in his hand; he has knowledge of the pole star. He has vision. He has purpose and motive power to go forward in spite of all hindrances.

Motivation is the compass of life. Without a compass, you have no direction.

The pole star must be the guiding star in our direction, and the pole star in man is the radioactive center of Beauty, Goodness, and Truth.

The motive power behind all our actions, words, feelings, and thoughts must be

1. How to create Beauty in others and be myself beautiful

2. How to create Goodness and be myself a distributor of goodness

3. How to create Truth and be myself righteous and truthful

Right motivation is the ability to choose the right direction in relation to the pole star within us.

Our actions, emotions, thoughts, ideas, and plans will have value and bring permanent assistance to ourselves and others if they are efforts to radiate Beauty, Goodness, and Truth.

The greatest need of human beings and of humanity as a whole is to have a compass and to set its direction right.

People act like children. They try to accumulate possessions and educate themselves in many branches of knowledge in order to have more power and higher positions; but all that they have and all that they know eventually work against their own peace, joy, and survival if they do not have a compass and are not aware of the "pole star." The pole star is the purpose of the human soul. The purpose of the human soul is to bloom into his divine Beauty, Goodness, and Truth.

Motivation is the focused will of the human soul to direct himself toward the purpose. Motivation is the response of the human soul to that purpose.

The right motive is the realization of the purpose. When the purpose impresses the human soul, we say that the human soul has a *vision*.

Motive is dynamic willpower to actualize the vision on the path toward its source, the purpose.

From early childhood vision must be given to human beings. They must be aware of the pole star within themselves, and in all their life the awareness of the "pole star" must create direction in them.

Without the pole star, without vision and direction, we will create with all our thoughts, feelings, and actions our own prisons and our own weapons to destroy ourselves and our planet.

6
Leadership and Labor

One of the greatest means to develop real psychic powers and higher senses is labor.

The Great Ones create opportunities for us to serve. It is through labor that the sources of beauty, creativity, and willpower are opened and the Divine Self begins to manifest.

Those who escape from labor weaken their moral powers, lose the vision of their soul, and fall into the trap of pleasures, pain, and suffering.

The greatest sign of a disciple or an initiate is his joy and gratitude when he finds an opportunity to labor. He performs his labor without expectation because his greatest reward is the opportunity to serve. It is at the moment of a dedicated labor that the transformation of the personality takes place and the resources of the spiritual *gifts* begin to open their gates.

Such a transformation and unfoldment cannot be bought with money, flattery, or any kind of compensation.

There are many levels of graduation on the path of life. Real graduation is not the certificate and power that you receive at the end of your schooling, or at a certain level of your academic learning. Real graduation is the gradual change of the focus of your consciousness from lower and narrower fields to higher and expanding fields of consciousness. Real graduation is step-by-step transformation of your beingness.

Such a graduation is offered to you every time you totally forget yourself in labor, with firm dedication, having in mind that you are not serving any person, but through the technique of labor you are trying to manifest your love, your wisdom in helping a vision to actualize and turn into a path of liberation.

Every moment of dedicated labor is an opportunity to meet yourself and see yourself as you are. Self-discovery is not achieved in learning but in labor.

It is through labor that the tendency to spiritual beggary is overcome. Most so-called spiritual people are beggars. They read spiritual books; they attend lectures and seminars; they even offer money to spiritual causes just to feel secure and protected. There is selfishness in their hearts. Their only motive is to gain for their pitiful selves. Offer an opportunity to such people to labor and work and they slowly fade away and hide in the caves of their pitiful selves.

If you do not feel joy in labor, if you dwell on thoughts of praise or expectation, if you think that you are doing a special favor for someone, if you feel that someone is using you or exploiting you, if you feel that your labor is not recognized and acknowledged, if you feel that you must labor in "this" field to express your hatred or revenge for "that" field, if you feel that you are wasting your time, it is better for you to go to the bazaar and learn the contemporary ways and means to make money by selling your soul.

"What do you gain if you lose your soul, but gain the world?"

The soul is gained, actualized, and brought into manifestation only through self-denial and through renunciation in labor.

It is also true that a misfortune is the effect of a past moment in which you denied *labor*. A moment of refusal of the opportunity to labor is a moment in which you cut the power lines which will light your electric bulbs in future lives. Every time you escape from an opportunity to render a labor, you deprive yourself of a future success, abundance, and joy.

All success, joy, health, and prosperity that you have in your life is because you labored in the past to serve people and cooperate with the forces of light, love, and beauty. It takes many years for life to bring us to the witness stand. All the efforts of life are wasted when one escapes from the witness stand.

Denial of Self is the moment when you escape from the field of battle, the field of actual witness. The greatest act of witness is the labor carried on in the name of the Omnipresent Self in every living form.

The spiritual Path prepares us for a supreme honor. This supreme honor is the developed ability to stand as a *witness* for all those *values* and *treasures* of wisdom which are inherited by us.

Realization, actualization, and transformation of our nature take place the moment when we stand as a witness for the Source which gave us wisdom, love, and the power of striving.

Window-shoppers seldom enter higher levels of consciousness. They imagine that they have all those things that they see. One cannot expand without paying the cost of expansion. The cost is the ability to stand as a witness and prove yourself with your unselfish and sacrificial labor.

Those who escape from labor turn into gophers in the group. They act in a very subtle way to disturb or distort the focus of the group by imitating certain activities which slowly take the attention of the workers away from the principal direction. Time and money are wasted on things which are emotional and worldly but which are covered by sentimentalism to hide personal vanities and interests.

The success of a group is in its focus. All time, energy, and money must be directed toward its responsibilities. The group must create one-pointed focus to:

— Remove maya

— Dispel glamor

— Annihilate illusions

— Reveal the Divine Self

If the focus is kept, success will reveal itself.

Faint-hearted ones, window-shoppers, and fearful ones can cure themselves from such diseases only by standing as witnesses and manifesting their attitude through sacrificial labor.

Life has a technique to teach very painful lessons to those who neglect or deny their responsibilities. Life takes away the opportunity that was given to you to labor. It takes away the tools that were not used in labor. This is considered a great disaster by the Great Ones, and They warn us not to lose any opportunity to labor.

Service is the fragrance of labor. Service is the radiation of psychic energy. Service is the distribution of love, wisdom, gratitude, and the power of the will through labor.

It is in true labor that you become a distributor of divine treasures.

There is no small or big labor. There is only a small or big heart. If you have a big heart, a living, radiant heart, every opportunity for any kind of labor is an opportunity to serve the Infinite Source of life.

Contact with the Divine Presence is achieved only through labor.

Leadership is labor, increasing labor. The reward of the leader, which he receives from the life as a response to his labor, is more work, more *labor*, expanding on various fields and on various planes.

The leader is a source of labor; he is not only engaged in a sacred labor, but he also draws from the whirlpool of labor all those who are related to him. No one can sit and wait or remain lazy once he comes in contact with a true leader. A leader initiates labor incessantly, in many forms and in many colors. This is one of the signs of the leader: that he evokes labor, not for his personality but for the Plan of the Hierarchy, for the Teaching.

A leader is one who has annihilated egotism, and the pure energy of action pours through him and kindles the fire in others. In the presence of a true leader the first thing you ask is, "What can I do? I must do something."

Thus, leadership is organized labor with a plan and with a purpose.

No one can achieve true leadership unless he is an embodiment of labor.

When you increase the numbers of those who love labor, you change groups, communities, nations.

Labor is the effort to manifest Beauty, Goodness, Righteousness, Joy, and Freedom, in harmony with the Divine Plan. All oppositions to our labor evoke energy from within us, strengthen our willpower and make us ready to labor on greater heights where there is more danger, greater joy, and the possibility to serve more.

Labor starts within ourselves. Labor means to change, to transform our personality, to make it an expression of Beauty, Goodness, Righteousness, Joy, and Freedom. Our labor outside of our personal field can be successful only when we first labor within ourselves. Those who try to liberate people before they liberate themselves can eventually be trapped in their vanities or be rejected by those who have common sense.

It is interesting to note that if we are serious with our own selves and in our labor, the spiritual forces will be serious in helping us and in cooperating with us. We cannot evoke help unless we prove that we did our best. The door must be knocked upon with all our might, and it will open if the forces know that we have really decided to enter.

Labor can be performed in a better way if you do not try to increase your karmic debts. No one can labor comfortably with a heavy load on his shoulders.

Those who labor eventually turn into transmitters. Labor channels higher energies according to the motive behind it.

There is a subtle point here. People who serve in any field of human endeavor are continuously subject to failures and successes. Some failures originate from their personality weaknesses; some because of their lack of sufficient discipline; but they should never give up and never stay depressed. They put on their new tires and enter the race. They do not condemn and criticize themselves, but after true observation they shape themselves up and start again. If their failure was very serious, they go back and try to see the cause of it, and sometimes for years they work upon themselves until they feel once more that they are ready for another round of labor.

Self-condemnation and self-criticism are not for leaders. Leaders must use heavy, selfless, detached observation of their motives and actions. Unless this is done one will repeat his failures.

Some of the failures of the leader do not directly originate from his weaknesses but from surrounding conditions, even from his overemphasized virtues. In any case, the leader never runs away from the field of service because of his faults. This does not mean that he repeats his faults. Every failure must make him more alert because as a leader advances in his service he becomes responsible for more people. He can damage or save more people. This realization deepens his sense of responsibility.

Self-condemnation is a method to freeze yourself, impressing the image of failure upon your mind.

Observation gives you enough freedom not to identify with the failure but be able to insulate the failure and handle it in the best way possible.

Many leaders abandon the field of service, becoming shocked by their insignificant failures. In such cases, the fellow leaders must encourage the person to prepare himself for another term of labor.

If one is not a leader and has no proof of his being a leader through the fruits of his life, if he is full of the vanity of leadership and is indifferent to the well-being of other people, he must be closely observed and not encouraged when he fails. It is better to leave such people alone to measure their own weaknesses and find out for themselves.

False leaders have the following characteristics:

1. They want you to work, and they enjoy the fruits of your labor.

2. They impose their ideas and their will upon you.

3. They limit your freedom.

4. They are interested in your lower nature more than your soul.

5. They do not meditate.

6. They do not pray.

7. They bribe you in various ways.

8. They are jealous underneath the appearance of carelessness and indifference.

9. They do not live what they teach.

10. They manipulate people through their weaknesses.

11. They do not care about humanity as a whole but only for certain parties.

12. They do not confer and share their plans with their people.

13. They like to shine at the expense of others.

14. They lack justice and honesty.

15. They try to change others without changing themselves.

A real leader never runs after people for fellowship. People come to a leader because of the labor he is presenting. They stay within his leadership because they want to labor with him.

Any leader who tries to own his followers and enslave them by these many tactics is a false leader. Remember, the greatest task of the leader is to make you own yourself, to make you the leader of yourself, to make you free and independent. Any effort from his side to make you follow him will be a negative sign.

You never follow a leader, but you cooperate with him in a plan presented by him and approved by you in your freedom.

True leadership is a process of initiation as a group. The leader is the catalyst for those who work with him. The greatest intention of the leader is to help you make your Divinity manifest.

Initiation is often considered to be progress from outside to inside. For me it is the reverse. Initiation is the externalization of your True Self. It is your Divinity gradually revealing itself in creative Beauty, Goodness, Righteousness, Joy, and Freedom.

When Christ was emphasizing that you must be born again, He was referring to initiation. That deeply hidden, inactive, concealed Divinity within your frame must reveal itself. Your Divinity must be active in your life and manifest itself stage by stage until it reveals itself in the clear light of day. This is how the sons of God come into being.

People think that we must be initiated into a higher plane, into a greater sphere of consciousness. Of course, this is a way to talk to those who do not know the mystery of the Self. But the Self is already in the highest plane; it is a Ray originating from the Sun. It is more radiant than the Sun, purer than the snow, subtler than the ether. . . . Why, then, will He be initiated, and into what?

The process of initiation is to make that Self manifest. Each stage of manifestation is an initiation until the whole Divinity manifests itself here on earth in a physical body.

That is what Christ demonstrated. He, as a Self — as *the Self* — let His light shine out; He lived as a god. He demonstrated perfection in his physical body. He spoke with the Father. He healed; He controlled Nature; He raised the dead. He walked on the waves of the sea.

All these stories or symbols tell us that we must strive for perfection here on earth and reach perfection here on earth.

The periods between lives are periods of digestion, decision, and planning; but the battle must be won while you are in the body until you reach the Fifth Initiation — the perfection. Until you reach such a perfection and conquer death, you cannot manifest your Divinity on subtler planes and you must always come back to prove your Divinity.

Initiation is a purification process in which the Inner Light shines more and more.

There are four signs in which you can see the proof of progress. In each stage of initiation, which means in each step of manifestation of Divinity in you:

1. You awaken in a greater degree to new values of life.

2. You register impressions from higher and higher centers more accurately.

3. You demonstrate deeper responsibility in your entire field of relationships.

4. Your creativity increases until it embraces many fields of human endeavor.

1. As the Divinity within you manifests itself in a greater light and splendor, you gradually detach from the values related to your separative interests and the interests of the involutionary lives within your threefold bodies. For example, you appreciate truth and honesty more than money. You appreciate beingness more than havingness. You give priority to the interests of others

over your own interests. And people often cannot understand this, but you go on with your labor.

2. You receive impressions from greater centers, from your Master, from Ashrams, from the Hierarchy, Shamballa, or even from galaxies. As your Divinity releases itself, you come in contact with greater fields because the Self is one; the Self is the Communion or Communication itself. Greater Self-expression, greater unity and oneness are sensed. Unity and oneness are the essence of communication. Thus, you are guided by greater centers. And because of your communication with higher powers, you know better how to navigate your ship in space.

3. Deeper sense of responsibility is the sign of a true disciple and full proof that he is on the path of initiation or Self-actualization.

The sense of responsibility manifests within a man when the Self manifests Itself more and more and floods the brain consciousness with the ideas of unity and oneness. From that moment on you live in such a way that you respond to the needs of people and become a true server. You evoke beauty, courage, daring, and solemnity in people, and you protect the progress of humanity with your life.

The sense of responsibility is the awareness that your thoughts, your emotions, your decisions, or your actions can influence people and affect their lives, either in the right or the wrong direction. You become aware that creating hindrances upon the path of people hinders your own path, and the assistance you give to others opens your path.

The sense of responsibility gives you the power to stand for the rights of the people and resign from your own rights, if it is necessary to gain their rights.

The sense of responsibility gives you the power not to interfere with the karma of others but to inspire them to overcome their karma the way they want or they can.

The sense of responsibility is an awareness that you and other human beings are immortal souls.

4. Divinity is creativity. When your Inner Self manifests, every step of coming into manifestation is an act of creativity.

Initiation makes you a conscious part of the creative Power in the Universe. You become an extension of this creativity. You create beauty, vitality, radioactivity, visions, plans, and those art forms which bring the Self closer to the multitudes and build a bridge between man — the reflection — and the true man — the Self.

Thus leadership means to bring out the Sleeping Beauty, the sleeping Divine Spark in every man, and release It to master Its vehicles.

The Self abides in His individualized condition on the Divine and Monadic Planes, but these planes are not organized or are not in use. He must come into physical manifestation and start His great labor to organize His physical body and gradually higher and higher bodies in order to make His personality reflect all that is achieved on deeper or higher planes.

The work starts here, in our physical body and in our brain, and goes deeper and deeper until each vehicle is organized in such a way that the Divinity or the Self can shine out through all of them and use them as vehicles of contact and creativity. Such a labor challenges our resources and leads us to the path of new achievements.

7
Labor and Thought in Leadership

...To love the endlessness of labor is already an initiation of considerable order; it prepares one for the conquest of time. The state of conquest of time guarantees a step in the Subtle World, where labor is an absolute condition, just as it is in the body. A complaint against labor can only come from slaves of the body.[1]

Labor is a work carried out on yourself to shape yourself, to transform yourself, and to transcend yourself

---

1. Agni Yoga Society, *Heart*, para. 79.

— closely watching your thoughts, emotions, words, and actions.

Never get tired of labor. If you worked on one side of yourself, work on another side of yourself. When you learn the secret of labor, you are an Initiate of high degree. But do not forget that labor is related to your spiritual development.

Those who labor on themselves have three signs:

1. They love labor.

2. They are always unsatisfied with what they are.

3. They are always joyful in their labor.

You can do any kind of labor and make it a means through which you expand your consciousness and build higher vehicles for your spirit.

Any time you begin to be proud of yourself, you fail in your spiritual progress. Spiritual development is achieved when you do not have expectations from your labor. When you work on yourself, your thought is to improve yourself in order to help others.

When you are satisfied with yourself and feel happy, you create a false unity within yourself. There is no improvement except when there is duality within you. Duality means *dissatisfaction.*

Discipleship is a continuous process of striving toward your vision. Labor means to make every kind of effort to bring out the latent Beauty, Goodness, Righteousness, Joy, and Freedom.

Labor is contact with your True Self.

Labor leads you to the level where you conquer time. This means that you can do in one hour what you used to do in one day. Labor gradually makes your speed faster.

If you repair cars for ten years, your speed of repairing cars improves and you repair more and more quickly. This is how you conquer time.

Through labor you eliminate obstacles existing in you, for example ignorance, lack of experience, laziness, inertia, lack of concentration, and patience. As you conquer these things your speed increases.

Speed increases as your skill-in-action improves, as your knowledge and experience increase, and as you see the vision in purer light.

The greatest obstacle is falling in love with yourself, and most of us fall in love with ourselves. Once you fall in love with yourself you lose polarity, and you fail in your evolution. There are many who sleep on the road of evolution under the heavy blankets of their vanities and self-love.

Unless one conquers time, he cannot enter into the Subtle Worlds consciously. The conquest of time is increasing speed, the ability to do things, creativity, freedom from limitations, and self-forgetfulness. Once you demonstrate these qualities, you find yourself in the Subtle Worlds consciously.

In the Subtle Worlds you do not have your physical body; you are not limited by the time concept; you do not need to sleep and rest and take a vacation: you are in continuous labor.

If you demonstrate in your life that you can labor as if you did not have the limitation of time, as if you did not have any expectation for compensation, and as if you love labor for the sake of labor, you are ready to enter into the Subtle World consciously.

Imagine a car which is running one hundred miles per hour and which you somehow manage to hang on to. What happens? The speed destroys you. This is the Subtle World. You must be used to the speed through agelong labor.

Increase your speed through labor; increase the speed of your thinking, actions, decisions.

If you are decisive, you conquer a certain portion of time. You do not lose time saying this or that; you act on your fast but correct decision. And your decision will not be the result of mental calculation but the result of your Intuition.

Often people wander between many crossroads and lose time. We have many expressions which are the symbols of lack of decisiveness, for example "maybe," "perhaps," "on the other hand," "I have to think about it," "it seems." The light of the Intuition does not need such expressions. It is decisive.

We must always think about how we can conquer time — through continuity of consciousness, through unceasing labor, through enlightenment, through self-forgetfulness, harmlessness, and right speech.

Those who are not in harmony with their Self are always lost on the path. Those who are harmful always face obstacles on their path. Those who do not exercise right speech are always stuck in the mud of their karma. These people are the "foolish virgins."

Everything on the path of perfection is related not to pleasing the masses but to speed. The purpose of speed is to annihilate itself and thus prove that there is no time when the speeding one enters into the sphere of omniscience.

On the thread of speed you see forms, colors, sound, heat, and rays. As speed increases it turns into light, and eventually speed becomes Space.

Materialization of Space produces time. Spiritualization of matter annihilates time. Speed is the enemy of time and the enemy of matter. Victory in the Future depends upon speed.

The Great Ones send a call. One responds after two hundred years; one responds in three years; one responds in twenty-four hours; one responds immediately.

These are the speeds of responses. One can have a higher sensitivity if he is disciplined in conquering time and matter through labor.

In the Subtle Worlds "labor is an absolute condition." You are closer to the Central Magnet; you are in continuous motion. "Accustom yourself to labor."

"A complaint against labor can only come from slaves of the body." Each complaint is a weakening step. Each complaint indicates the spirit of failure, withdrawal from the path of striving and labor. Each complaint indicates the disappearance of vision and future.

In the Teaching we are told about petty thoughts which enter into the structure of great plans and decisions and destroy them. One must refuse to listen to petty thoughts about his plans and decisions, and he must isolate himself from people and from their old ways of thinking until the plan is put into action.

Together with such actions, one must be careful that petty thoughts hidden in the layers of his mind are not evoked. Many great decisions were destroyed by a word or a gesture carrying a petty thought.

Petty thoughts are those thoughts which carry with them a disturbing force. They are rejecting by nature. They suggest that the plan is worthless and useless. They indicate failure. They ridicule your capacity and efficiency. They evoke memories of failures from your mind. They project an image of hopelessness and retard and destroy your creative energy.

Ancient kings use to keep people with petty thoughts away, especially at the time of great decisions and plans, and surround themselves with those who had an intuitive grasp of the plan and were positively ready to actualize it, in spite of all difficulties. They used to emphasize the importance of the moments of failure during a construction, as if these moments were charges of a new catalytic action. Through such fortification of the minds of co-workers, they protected them from petty thoughts.

Petty thoughts are especially powerful when a leader is in a moment of extreme tension or crossing a dangerous bridge in the labor.

The leader sees in the accumulation of antagonistic forces the sign of his victory. This is mostly a very intuitive awareness in front of accumulating danger. A petty thought released at such a moment of extreme tension destroys the opportunity of the victory, and the warrior puts his arms down at the moment when the victory was going to destroy the accumulated opposition.

We are told again and again not to give up when we feel we have failed, but to feel that what we do is *worthy*, is a *service* for the human cause, is an *act to express* our gratitude to Great Ones, is a part of the Plan.

Victory is gained at the tip of the rising wave. One of the techniques of great warriors is to evoke the accumulation of all opposing forces. Each accumulation evokes greater preparation and strength within the warrior. Each accumulation brings closer the moment of victory. Victory is achieved by the total destruction of dark forces. The warrior evokes total accumulation and prepares himself to meet it on the summit of the wave.

In such a moment of extreme watchfulness and tension, the warrior of spirit must have around him only those who are armed with the vision of victory and future.

When Great Ones speak about labor, They also emphasize that labor cannot be carried on to its destination if the spirit of a warrior is not present in it.

Spiritual labor is a continuous striving to meet the demands of the Call of the Spirit.

People justify themselves: If we have plans and great visions but do not have the ways and means to meet them, if our conditions do not allow us to engage in the labor to actualize our visions, is it not better to worry instead about our daily bread?

First of all, we must know that it is the plan and the vision that prepare the ways and means for their actualization by creating the right conditions. All conditions and facilities were created not by conditions and facilities but by the plan for the future and the vision.

Plans and visions create polarity in matter — in the physical, emotional, and mental spheres — and this polarity accumulates all the personalities and elements necessary for the manifestation of the plan and the vision. Things start moving by an inner force, by an inner organized force, to provide the vehicles for the manifestation of the plan.

Secondly, those who run after their "daily bread" and forget about "the kingdom of heaven" not only lose the "daily bread" but also "the kingdom of heaven." The depression and the catastrophic condition of the economy all over the world are clear indications that man was running after his daily bread and neglecting the call of "the kingdom of heaven."

Daily life will eventually evaporate into the air if that daily life is not reinforced by the values of the future, by the virtues of the soul, by the longing of the spirit, and especially if it is not a response to the call for improvement and perfection.

8
Group Consciousness and Group Work

Group consciousness is found in many stages.

Herd consciousness is the lowest manifestation of group consciousness. Animals, insects, and birds have a sort of group consciousness by which they act and react as a group.

On the human level, this state of consciousness has its stages. We have a kind of consciousness which is called mob consciousness or crowd consciousness in which the crowd follows a certain path inspired by the collective consciousness of the crowd. Then we have party, gang, racial, and national group consciousness. But all these are steps leading to higher group consciousness.

On the human level, group consciousness is divided into three stages. The first stage is when one joins a group dedicated to a lofty plan or goal. In this stage, group consciousness is the ability to think about group members as if they were you and relate to them as if they were more important than you. In group consciousness we subordinate our interests to the interests of group members. We highly respect them and try to create opportunities to serve them and to uplift them.

A group-conscious member is very sensitive to the needs of others, and he sincerely tries to meet those needs until they are able to stand on their own feet. During the time of sickness, tribulation, and sorrow, a group-conscious person stands as a tower of courage, love, and inspiration without personality involvement.

Group consciousness means involvement with the life of the group, with the plan and purpose of the group, through self-forgetfulness, harmlessness, and right speech.

In this stage those group members who seek their personal interests, or use the group members or the group for their personal goals, or engage themselves in criticism, hatred, gossip, malice, and slander are proving that they were not able to develop group consciousness in spite of being a member of the group.

Other signs of lack of group consciousness are the inability to serve, sacrifice, and help the group with dedication, devotion, and intelligence.

The next higher stage of group consciousness belongs to those who are able to function on the higher mental plane in subjective and objective realms.

Group consciousness is the result of a progressive response to the Law of Synthesis.

The Law of Synthesis acts on various levels of existence with various intensities and manifestations. For example, it acts through the sacral center and produces family relationships. It acts through the solar plexus and produces racial relationships. It acts through the heart center and produces international relationships. It acts through the Inner Guide and produces great servers who lay down their lives for the liberation of humanity as a unit on the planet.

The Law of Synthesis throughout the ages stimulates the center of unity within each human being and draws him toward synthesis. This is how families, races, cooperatives, nations, and the United Nations are formed, leading humanity toward world brotherhood and one humanity.

All resistance to the Law of Synthesis produces suffering, delay in growth, and eventual degeneration.

Group consciousness cannot develop in one jump. It develops gradually. The first sign of its development is a sense of responsibility which a human being feels toward other human beings. This sense of responsibility makes him feel that he must be careful of what he does, speaks, or thinks so that he does not hurt anyone in the world. He checks the motives of all his expressions as much as possible. This leads him gradually to right human relationships, inclusive thinking, and actions that are based on goodwill.

After trying to live in such a state of consciousness, he becomes an attractive unit to those who are on the same path of group discovery, and through them he expands the horizon of his inclusiveness and lays the foundation for true group consciousness.

Groups that are dedicated to Christ and to the Teaching of the Great Ones are challenged to develop group consciousness.

Group consciousness is the totality of the consciousness of the group. As the individual man has his own mental sphere and the lighted area in it which we call consciousness, so has a group. The mental bodies of the group members gradually come together in the same frequency and form a united field of electromagnetic energy. When this energy field of mental substance is built, the Souls of the group project Their intelligent light upon the sphere and create a lighted area of extreme sensitivity, which eventually records the impressions coming from each person and from higher centers. It is at the center of this lighted area that eventually an accepted disciple or an initiate locates himself and serves as the Soul of the group.

This unified field of lighted area acts as a group-conscious mechanism, and we say that the members of the group have achieved group-consciousness.

The signs of group consciousness are

1. Striving for improvement and perfection in the skill to use the mechanism in the field of their individual service.

2. Intuitive response to each other's needs to further each other's spiritual progress.

3. Seeing the greater vision and the project to be fulfilled in the light of a greater plan.

4. Intelligent cooperation in the group work.

5. Increasing joy for each other's achievements and beauty.

6. Total silence toward personal weaknesses and failures.

7. Increasing creativity of each member.

8. Similarity of motive behind all their actions.

9. Intuitive response to the call of the Hierarchy.

10. Deep honesty and sincerity toward each other.

11. Elimination of all tendencies to use each other for personal ends.

12. Increasing spirit of solemnity, gratitude, and simplicity.

13. Transformation of the aura of the group into a sphere of vibratory energy which heals or eliminates the undesirable.

14. Transformation of the aura of the group into a sphere of light which causes enlightenment in those who come within its radius of influence and leads them into serious decisions for their own spiritual path. It reveals also the dark areas in their nature, which can be honestly met by them and cleared away.

Thus the sphere of group consciousness eventually becomes so organized that the group members telepathically share each other's aspiration, insight, vision, and joy. If this continues for a long time, they even attract greater waves of wisdom from the Hierarchical sources.

When group consciousness exists, it attracts the attention of the subjective guide of the group who comes closer and begins to inspire the group to greater service and greater sacrifice for humanity.

As the subjective guide anchors itself in the electromagnetic sphere of the group consciousness, the members of the group feel closer and closer to each other until a spiritual family comes into being. The members of this spiritual family *share each other's karma*, and because of their spiritual striving each one helps to pay each other's karma. In this way, the group's mortgage of karma is eventually paid, and the whole group is set free for real Hierarchical work.

It is at this stage that the Great Ones can come in contact with such a group and initiate them through the stages of discipleship until the group becomes a Son in the heart of the Master. The greatest reward of a group is when the members are able to serve the Hierarchy in Their Cosmic vision.

Such groups are very, very rare, and we are told that the Great Ones are trying Their utmost to create such groups. This is what is called the externalization of the Ashrams. Our *Souls* are members of the Ashrams. Once we are able to live as Souls and tune with each other like the strings of a lute, we become manifested divine beauties in the world, radioactive Souls externalized on objective levels. Such an achievement is not only a victory for the group members, but it is also a victory for great Teachers because only through such groups can the salvage of humanity be carried out and the purity of spiritual life be maintained throughout the world.

There are obstacles on the path which make such an integration, fusion, unification, and service impossible for a long time.

The first obstacle is the tendency of the group members to create relations with each other based upon personality interests. This can be on the physical, emotional, mental, or even on business levels. Such relationships, if not based on spiritual vision and on striving toward sacrificial service for humanity, create a complicated and polluted atmosphere in which the germs of criticism, dislikes, partisan spirit, greed, and matter grow in such an abundance that the flame of spirit dies.

The second obstacle comes into being when some group members do not respond to their duties, obligations, and responsibilities; for example, when they do not follow the rule of "unanimous and simultaneous" meditation, study, and labor and miss various service activities. Such an attitude makes the group membership lukewarm and increases the karma of those who are striving hard to meet all that their Soul requests. The group karma increases when some of the members keep their membership but dedicate themselves to various interests which do not agree with the aspiration, vision, and sacrificial dedication of the group.

Group consciousness cannot come into existence when a member stays away from the group physically and spiritually but attaches to it with different personality interests or just for the sake of formality. It is only your spiritual frequency which you are radiating out through your meditation, studies, and group labor that creates unification.

A group that does not strive for spiritual achievement as a whole slowly degenerates.

The group is just like a big family in which a few members may continually become contaminated in their own lives and bring their germs to the group, time after time. Such a family can do two things:

- Either welcome contamination and retard their own evolution or
- Eliminate germ-bringing members from their family or group

Sometimes we think that we have to welcome the suffering brought upon us by our self-seeking brothers or sisters. Such an attitude is a positive encouragement for them. You may help your brothers and sisters when you teach them to stand on their feet and face their own problems by their own means and do not let them load the group with their own personal problems and negligence.

so that the plan or the meaning is expressed or worked out and the purpose is reached.

An esoteric group is formed around a *plan*, not around a personality. The head of the group represents the Plan. He is as successful as he understands and lives according to the Plan. This Plan is the expression of the Purpose.

The Purpose is related to Shamballa, the dynamic center of the Will of the planetary Soul. The Plan is related to the Hierarchy, the dynamic center of Love-Wisdom of the planetary Soul. The members are related to humanity. The Purpose is the Will. The Plan is the attractive power between the members.

The group is the field where the Plan is understood and worked out, and because of this relationship, the electricity of Shamballa flows through the group. The love of the Hierarchy holds them together, and the need of humanity evokes sacrificial service from the group.

Groups are formed to meet a *need*. To meet a need for an esoteric group means to apply the Plan through the seven fields of human endeavor. As the Plan is worked out, the Hierarchy enters into closer relationship with humanity.

In the formation of a group no pressure must be exercised on the members. They must come together as the magnet of the Plan attracts them. An esoteric group is formed by those who have a certain degree of Soul contact. It is this contact that will reveal to them the Plan.

What must a member expect from the group? The answer is

— Enthusiasm

— Non-criticism

- Loving understanding

- Indifference toward his personality

- Example of labor

- Striving

- Silence

Every time the group reveals in him his touchiness, pride, vanity, showing off in any way, he must consider this as a gift from the group. He must understand that the group stands there only to encourage his spiritual striving. The only way he can "criticize" the group is when he becomes an example of humility, generosity, and labor without showing off.

In all esoteric groups it is witnessed that only those who practice great discipline of silence and can retreat into the shadow of humility are promoted by the light of the need to the positions of great sacrificial service.

The Teacher says,

> Group integrity... *will come if each of the group members will simply mind his own business and permit his group brothers to mind theirs; it will come if you keep your personality affairs, your private concerns and troubles out of the group life; it will come if you refrain from discussion of each other and of each other's affairs and attitudes....*[2]

It is also very important to ask ourselves, "Is my presence in the group an example of selfless labor?"

---

2. Alice A. Bailey, *Discipleship in the New Age*, Vol. I, p. 60.

To keep the group alive, the electrical current of the Hierarchical Plan must freely circulate through the members. That is why there exists the need for "unanimous and simultaneous" meditation because it puts the group members in contact with the Plan through their Souls.

The goal of an esoteric group is to reveal the concealed Divinity within man and Nature.

It is possible to have a unified group-consciousness even if individual members do not meet with each other on personality levels. Such members are like *notes* by which the Master plays His music of service. They are tuned with each other and unified in the will of the Master. That is why they can serve as a group.

But before we reach such a state of subjective unification, we must prove that we can build a group on the physical level through which the music of our Soul can manifest. And the only proof that we can demonstrate is "unanimous and simultaneous" discipline.

It is not imperative that the members of a group be in one location and physically in contact with each other in order to serve or to unfold, but it is imperative that they are tuned with the group and are in the one labor of "simultaneous and unanimous" discipline to increase the manifestation of their souls.

There are two kinds of service — the most essential service and non-essential service. The unified group is one that is dedicated to the most essential service according to the immediate requests of the Hierarchical Plan. If the Hierarchical Plan is requesting an *ark* to save humanity and a group of people is dedicated to build that ark, others can argue and say that they too are serving by planting trees and building houses. The unified group knows that though such people are serving, they will be very unfortunate when the doors of the ark are closed and they are left outside. The ark is group consciousness. . . which individual members build by working for it.

The quality of our service depends upon the spiritual group or focus from which we derive our inspiration. As the Ashrams are inspired by the Hierarchy, so each member of the group can be inspired by the unified group focus to carry his soul light wherever it is needed. The group not only inspires him, but also it keeps his standards high and becomes for him a source of energy and courage. That is why the individual must have a source of inspiration in the unified group consciousness and in the unified group striving.

An individual who follows the drives of his personality is a "free" agent. He does things as he wants. But a disciple is one who renounces the freedom of his personality and enters the discipline of his Soul. An Initiate is not a free agent; he is the servant of the Plan. An advanced Initiate eventually renounces even his will and says, "Father, Thy will be done."

In group formation, it is the highest vision of the group that frees his will, annihilates the personality or separative walls, and lets the group vision express itself through the sphere of the unified will of the group.

A real group must have group consciousness. No group can have group consciousness if the members of that group arc not totally free of obsession and possession, or if the members have not renounced the tendency to violate the individual wills of others and impose their own will on them. A spiritual group is formed by those who make their own life beautiful only to make the life of the group beautiful. In a spiritual group the ruling agent is the vision and the service is the gradual revelation of that vision.

The question arises: How must the group deal with those delinquent members who knock again on the door of the Ashram? The answer is: Give them a plan of discipline divided into four fields:

1. Physical and emotional

2. Study

3. Service

4. Donation

1. The physical and emotional disciplines can be related to food, drink, sex, and labor.

2. Give them a course of study, a book, or a set course of lessons which they must study and answer questions.

3. Give them work; typing, copying, cleaning, watering the plants, selling books, etc.

4. Challenge them to donate part of their income to the group need or help those people who need financial help.

When these four disciplines are carried out for a period of one to two years, the true nature of the delinquent member will appear and show you the right action to take.

An attitude of pity carries with it irreparable damage to the delinquent member and to the group as a whole because in one case the member will not exercise mastery over his problems and in the other case the group will be contaminated again by the weakness of the member.

A group can create group consciousness not because its members are on the same level of achievement but because they are striving toward the *same goal*. This is how the group becomes a ladder extending from the lowest to the highest. Group consciousness is not formed by different degrees of education; it is a sphere of consciousness and a state of the *heart* or intuitive perception, resulting in right motive. Such a group evokes the highest from each member and makes each member flourish.

The Great Teacher says,

The heart centre cannot react, except under group impetus, group happiness or unhappiness, and other group relations.[3]

There are many doors and windows closed within our nature. There are great beauties waiting for manifestation if the rays of the sun touch them. It is only a group on the path of spiritual striving that opens the closed doors and windows, removes the barriers within our being, and releases unexpected beauties.

The reason for this is that as the group Lotus comes into formation and gradually enters into the stage of unfoldment, it evokes the spiritual seeds latent in other members to come into living activity under the protection of the group aura. No individual achievement can be compared with achievement in a group because of the group demand for improvement and perfection. One can render individual service in many fields without an apparent affiliation with any known group, but such people are very rare. If you study such situations, you can find in many cases that they were drawing their inspiration from those visions which were projected into

---

3. Alice A. Bailey, *Discipleship in the New Age*, Vol. II, p.114.

Space by various groups during many centuries through their aspirations discipline, and striving.

Most great servers are subjectively in contact with Ashrams, but to reach such a subjective contact one must first prove his fitness in a group through his group consciousness.

Many, many times we are told that the Soul is group conscious.

One who becomes at one with this Soul develops group consciousness. No one can advance without being a part of a group, as no building can come into being if the different materials do not come together under the inspiration of a plan.

Many thousands of years ago, some people tried to build a tower in Babylon. The tower was never completed for only one reason: they suddenly stopped understanding each other's language.

What happened was that they lost the vision and the ability to respond to that vision. Their attention was scattered into various conflicting directions. Then the intuitive center, the heart, ceased to function as a center of communication or a center of contact between group members, and the tower remained unfinished. That is why the challenge for spiritual discipline, spiritual striving, and unified group endeavor is needed to build the Tower of the Future.

There are four stages of leadership:

1. The leader is the commander and he demands total obedience.

2. The leader leads the group in cooperation with the intuitive acceptance of the fellowship.

3. The leader presents the Plan and lets the group follow.

4. All group members are in contact with the Plan and the group is guided by a Master.

All these stages are evolutionary phases through which a group and a leader pass.

Failure is registered when the leader does not recognize the level and the type of the group and uses advanced or obsolete methods.

Schools or groups that are working under the inspiration of the Hierarchy cannot be run by committees but by Initiates who, because of their stature, run the group according to the Plan and inspiration of the Hierarchy.

An advanced Initiate, by his own virtue and attainment, is always the leader both in the subjective and objective worlds. He is the one to whom is given the responsibility to guide, to educate, and to lead those aspirants and disciples who are karmically in tune with him. No advanced Initiate lets himself be conditioned by the votes of his students. He does consider the time, the conditions, the maturity, and the responses of his people and tries to unfold and develop their consciousness, giving them *duties* that require initiative and independent decisions.

The signs of an advanced leader can be found in the responses of his group members. These are his "fruits." We may enumerate them in the following way:

1. The group members cooperate with him.

2. They respect his vision, his plans, his ideas, his personality and protect him from any kind of attack.

3. They make necessary sacrifices to help him achieve his goal for the Plan.

4. They love one another to a degree that they see each other's beauty and leave each other free in the light of their Soul.

5. They work cooperatively on projects presented by the leader.

6. They take initiative and build their own field of service.

7. They work as parts of a total plan.

8. They keep maximum silence about each other's personality affairs and never interfere with the Hierarchical service each one is rendering for humanity in his separate field.

9. They continue the work in deep cooperation and selflessness in the absence of the leader.

10. They develop and build upon the plan presented by the leader, adopting, if necessary, new techniques and new ways and means of service.

11. When the leader designates any officer, they show the same respect and cooperation toward him.

12. In the case of the sudden departure of the leader, the group unanimously chooses a successor for life through meditation, silence, and prayers, if the leader had not already appointed one.

13. Every year they expand the field of their service with new projects, without falling into time-consuming social activities.

14. They put great emphasis upon self-realization, upon transformation, and Transfiguration, rather than on self-demonstration and various kinds of showing off.

15. They see in their leader a path, not an end. They see in him a man who does not want to please their personalities but wants to cooperate with their highest strivings.

16. If a leader is on the right path, the majority of group members will have self-initiative efforts in their own way, in their chosen field.

17. The group members try to live in beauty.

18. The group members develop an adaptability as a result of their deeper understanding of life.

Do not forget that these are signs of the real value of a Teacher reflected in the response from his co-workers.

When the watching Master sees these effects of the leader, He promotes him to heavier duties and greater responsibilities.

Alice A. Bailey wrote a letter to the secretaries of the Arcane School on November 9, 1941, in which she said:

"One thing, however, is necessary to make clear. No esoteric group is ever handled by a group. This is a basic statement. Always at the head of every real esoteric school or group stands a world disciple. He is the responsible agent, and no such disciple can ever relinquish his post to a group to handle the work for him. He is responsible to the Hierarchy for the group keynote, the group teaching, and the choice of the group workers. This in no way involves a dictatorship. Where a dictatorship is present, you have a disciple working under glamour or under the goal of personal ambition. There is no such thing as authority as the world understands it in an occult school. There is a voluntary standing together of all in the group, complete identity of purpose between the group members and the guiding disciple and *no trace of coercion*. Where the spiritual will of all concerned is evoked there is a unified recognition of means, of truth, of methods of work and sphere of influence. The spirit of the Hierarchy runs through the entire group — the spirit of love, of understanding, and of unity of objective."[4]

The guiding disciple is the link between the Ashram and the members of the group. He is the point of inspiration and guidance. He is the answer to the spiritual need of his group, and he stands responsible for the service the group renders for the Hierarchy.

Persons who do not respond to the presented vision slowly drop away, caught by their own illusions, glamors, maya, and resultant problems. The attitude of the group members toward the dropped ones must be one of total detachment, if possible, in order not to infect the group with the aura of a dropped person. New members must be tested at least two years, and certain group members must watch them very closely to see if they are striving to improve themselves, to sacrifice, and to serve.

Group members can progress only by striving toward perfection and preparing themselves for world service without being caught in the pleasures of the world. Each warrior eventually sees the five-pointed star leading toward the Path.

Group consciousness is a state of consciousness which is charged with harmlessness and oriented toward the welfare of one humanity. Such a group consciousness

---

4. Author's private collection.

directs all your thoughts, words, and deeds toward synthesis and unity.

People have the idea that group consciousness is the ability to work in a group through personality relationships. This is wrong. Real groups do not exist below the higher mental planes; one cannot be a member of a real group if he has no access to higher mental planes.

Groups of the Future are formed only around the Plan of the Hierarchy, or around the Purpose to uplift, unite, heal, and transform humanity. Those people who come together to serve their own interests or to create protection for their members or even to save their souls are not considered groups.

The membership of New Era groups is formed by those who are conscious of or are intuitively drawn to the Plan and have dedicated their lives to fulfill the Plan.

It is possible that the group members live in different areas of the world, in different races, in different fields of human endeavor. Members can even be on subjective or objective planes. But they form a subjective group when they have the same purpose and a similar dedication to achieve the purpose.

Personality relationships do not contribute to group consciousness if not handled in impersonal ways. It is possible to externalize a subjective group, but it is almost impossible to make a subjective group formed by and based on personality relationships.

In personality relationships we want to be, to do, to achieve, and to serve because of what people expect or demand from us. We are controlled by others and by their actions and reactions.

In subjective groups this danger is eliminated. It is the Purpose, the Plan that controls the group members, not the members, nor even the leader.

In subjective groups the leader is the spearhead or the custodian of the Plan. He stands and works as an example of achievement. He never imposes his will, but he reveals the Plan and makes the members sense the Purpose behind it.

Advanced leaders do not compromise and negotiate when the motives of certain elements reveal themselves to be degenerative or destructive. Their will, like lightning, smites the glamors, illusions, and maya of such elements and reveals what they are and toward what they were supposed to strive.

Those who most identify with the Plan with all their being become leaders of subjective groups. Such leaders are those who were able to conquer their self-will and self-interest. They represent the power of the Plan and the power which manifests through the actualization of the Plan.

Groups formed on personality levels disintegrate when the energy increases in them because it increases their glamors, illusions, and maya. Groups formed on subjective levels expand and grow as the energy increases because it increases their virtues and relates them to higher sources of energy. When such groups externalize, they bring a great voltage of beauty, culture, joy, and light. Sometimes their lifespan can extend to five thousand years or more!

Groups formed on personality levels survive through personal interests or group interests. They continue to exist as long as the energy from spiritual sources is not released. Immediately when this energy is released, conflict and disintegration set in.

The members of groups formed on personality levels have different orientations and expectations, and their centers and vehicles are differently unfolded. For a while this difference does not hurt the group integrity due to the presence of beliefs, leadership, dogmas, traditions, or interests. The group, just like a nest of insect eggs, remains quiescent, but when higher energies are invoked, every egg turns into a different insect and all fly in different directions.

People sometimes attack groups to destroy them. Such an effort often fails if personalty ties are strong and expectant interest is great. Such attacks even strengthen personality-oriented groups.

The best way to destroy a personality-based group is to increase the vision of certain members and make them strive to expand their consciousness. This will bring in a great amount of energy which will create conflict and eventually disintegration. But such disintegration is a great service for the group members, releasing them from their glamors, illusions, and maya and giving them an opportunity for a new start.

When we say groups, we refer to religious groups, churches, cooperatives, companies, corporations, brotherhoods, orders: all those groups whose members come together by the power of a vision, faith, service, research, education, personal interest, protection, or crime. Their motives range between darkness and light. All these groups and others create a life according to what they are in essence.

As in the individual, so in group formation. Our bodies, or organizations as a whole, are built according to our responses or reactions. Reaction or response is a mechanism of attraction and assimilation. When you act in certain ways you attract to your aura certain elements, and with these elements you build your aura which conditions your entire life.

When you react negatively you attract negative ions, which create many disturbances in your system. When you respond positively you attract positive elements, and they do great, constructive work in your aura.

Reactions are always negative attitudes, and they move out from the physical, emotional, and lower mental planes. They are often associated with glamors, illusions, maya, inner commands, and posthypnotic suggestions.

Responses are always positive because they emerge from the soul, Intuitional, and higher Planes, and they attract life-giving, enlightening, strengthening elements emanating from higher realms.

Thus, response to the energies released at certain times from certain luminaries attracts positive ions in Space. Response to these energies attracts the energy released from these sources to higher centers in man. Response expands our consciousness. Reaction causes contraction in it. Every event, every problem, or every condition evokes either reaction or response.

In reaction there is friction and negativity. In response there is a wise solution or a constructive attitude which attracts constructive elements to our aura.

Our life is a film produced between these two forces: reaction and response. It is possible to change our life by cultivating an attitude of response toward life in general and toward certain energies in particular.

In response we relate ourselves to constructive, enlightening, expanding energies. In reaction we relate ourselves to the forces of glamor, illusion, and maya.

The life around us mirrors what we are in essence. This essence grows and manifests through response to higher energies found either in light, color, sound, beauty, ideas, visions, revelations, love, or joy. The essence contracts and even fades away when reaction increases in man. Reaction collects those elements which bury the essence.

It is the essence that attracts success, joy, health, prosperity, beauty, harmony, light, and wisdom. When the essence is buried, the negative shell which we call the personality attracts disturbing events, elements of failure, sickness, distortion, attacks, etc.

The essence grows through response. Response is the means of communication of the liberated human soul on three levels:

1. When he is on the higher mental plane, or soul level

2. When he is in the Spiritual Triad

3. When he is in Monadic awareness

On the soul level he responds to the energies of light and draws the energies of light into his system. On the level of the Spiritual Triad, he responds to the energies of love and compassion, and through his response a flow of the elements of attraction fill his aura. In Monadic awareness he attracts through his response those energies which guide his direction to the Cosmic Magnet.

Subjective groups — those which are formed on the soul level, on the level of the Spiritual Triad, and on the Monadic awareness level — are mechanisms of response through which creative energies are circulated or forwarded for specific purposes. Such groups are totally impersonal and do not have a separative identity. They provide a mechanism which great Lives utilize to promote the Purpose of the Cosmic Magnet.

Groups formed on personality levels attract those forces which create separatism, congestions, and confusion and lead the groups to those actions which are self-destructive and retrogressive.

In every subjective group an inner core must stand watchfully to observe any movement in the group which tends toward personality reactions. Such movements must be handled wisely, evoking a response from the higher realms of those individuals who are responsible for such movements.

Group consciousness will eventually create a response from the soul of humanity. When this response is strengthened and carried on in all departments of human endeavor, the age of synthesis will begin. The unfolding synthesis will eventually reveal the oneness of life and the oneness of the purpose in humanity.

Group consciousness is achieved when people realize that people come into incarnation in group formation. When they find the group members and have right relationship with them in a definite plan of service, group consciousness grows fast. Life after life they come closer to each other, until their consciousnesses merge and form one center of light, inspiring each member of the group to engage in harmonious labor for the Plan.

Group consciousness can only exist in relation to a plan and in the labor for that plan. As the labor of each individual synchronizes to meet the requirements of the plan and its actualization, the group integrity progresses and creates a great field of magnetism to which new souls are occasionally attracted.

The group works on subjective and objective levels simultaneously. This is the reason for its effectiveness.

The subjective group works mostly with the thoughts of the objective group, releasing inspiration and imparting new visions. The objective group prepares those forms and activities which help the visions and inspirations of the subjective group to actualize.

In most cases the subjective group holds the integrity of the objective group, and often subjectively it repairs the damages done to the group mind by the negative thoughts of the objective group members.

When any disunion and ugly conflict starts in the objective group, the subjective group feels great distress and pain as if its members were caught in a tornado of destructive thoughts. This temporarily damages harmonious cooperation between the subjective and objective groups — though the subjective group, being aware of the thoughts and motives of the objective group, tries to enlighten and guide them into right lines, inspiring tolerance, forgiveness, patience, love, and understanding. Such inspirations sometimes telepathically reach the members, sometimes as dreams.

No force or attack can hurt an objective group if its subjective counterpart is integrated on higher planes and is in contact with the Hierarchy of Light.

Some members of the objective group form part of the subjective group, too, if they have contact with their Souls, or if they have developed their continuity of consciousness. Actually, the subjective group occasionally holds a conference with the objective group members during certain nights and strengthens their relationship with each other.

Those group members who hurt the group through gossip, evil thoughts, and dishonest actions cause much trouble to the subjective group. The entire group in a subjective conference has a discussion to advise such members; otherwise, they decide to expel them from the group. It is on such occasions that certain members, feeling their inadequacy, leave the group and go after their personal interests. But the tie still remains for a long time, and the group Soul always expects them back.

It is also a fact that many unrelated groups, or groups which do not know each other on the physical plane, are part of one group in subjective levels. Each carries out its own labor to build the Temple of the Lord. This is why new-age group members are advised not to attack and hurt other kinds of groups with fanatical and negative criticism, not knowing that they are working in the same field with different names, books, and techniques.

Often ten, fifteen, or more groups work objectively in separate fields, but subjectively for the same plan. When people develop continuity of consciousness, they will realize this fact, and great respect and cooperation will be established between the groups.

Interference with the tasks of other groups is forbidden. The disciple of the Future is advised to carry out his responsibilities

> "through self-forgetfulness,
>
> harmlessness,
>
> and right speech."

In the future it will be possible to put into conscious contact the leaders of closely related groups and eventually create a multidimensional group under one leadership group. We are told that the Hierarchy is the highest example of such group activity and leadership.

One of the resources of group work is its synchronization and unanimity. This is created by group members reading the same materials and doing the same meditations.

A group is not powerful unless it has a rhythm, an accumulative tension, and a planned service for humanity.

Rhythm produces force and momentum. That is why all movements of the planets, solar systems, and galaxies are based on rhythm. Rhythm relates, synchronizes, and creates accumulative force within the form.

A group must follow the law of rhythm through meditation, study, and service. These should be carried rhythmically in the right measure, synchronously, and unanimously. Lack of rhythm makes group integration impossible.

Through these three actions each member of the group creates a wave of energy with a special frequency, and all these waves eventually attract each other and form a magnetic thoughtform for Hierarchical service.

Esoteric groups have no other purpose than to create such a magnetic field by which they attract impressions from the Hierarchy. Eventually, as such groups unfold and develop, they will be a part of the externalization of the Hierarchy.

Thus, as the group receives impressions from the Hierarchy and receives greater wisdom, knowledge, and guidance, the Self within its form will gradually establish a conscious relationship with the Hierarchy and become an extension of the Hierarchy on the physical plane.

All the failures and shortcomings of the individuals in the group eventually can be wiped away as the synchronous and unanimous meditation, study, and service establish the psychic rhythm and let loose within the group the psychic energy from higher sources. That is why Christ said that if three people are united in His name, He will be among them. United refers to the synchronous and unanimous life of study and meditation as a service for Him, the Head of the Hierarchy.

The Hierarchy is not interested in our physical plane successes and failures. They are interested in our subjective life and in the contribution we are making to the integration of the group.

When a group integrates, it radiates specific Rays and symbols and attracts the attention of the Hierarchy. When the group is watched by certain members of the Hierarchy, it immediately receives a great inflow of spiritual, uplifting, purifying, and charging energy which reveals the Plan and challenges the group to take a more conscious part in the Plan.

The goal of esoteric groups is to be impressed by the Hierarchical Plan and manifest it through all group activities and services to such a degree that the group initiates itself into the field of the Plan and becomes a part of the Plan in manifestation. This is how the externalization of the Hierarchy is carried out.

The group members individually and the group as an entity will gradually be more careful to make sure that all their expressions are synchronized with the Plan and manifested unanimously.

Group members can help such a process by checking and observing their thoughts, emotions, activities, and speech and by eliminating those factors in their lives which are not in tune with the Plan and with their goal. This creates a group life and an individual life based on goal-fitness.

This happens naturally when group members create that magnetic field of dedication, the synchronization of higher values, and the rhythm of group service and meditation. Their Souls eventually feel each other's vibrations and relate to each other on higher planes. Their Souls impose upon their personalities a new rhythm which will purify the vehicles and dispel those elements which are not in accord with the goal of the group.

It even happens that the group radiation rejects those members who are burdens or who create disturbances in the energy field of the group.

When a disciple is living in such a group rhythm, he develops the sense of the "most essential." The most essential is followed in his activities, words, thoughts, and relations. The most essential sorts out all unnecessary elements from his nature and gradually makes him a fit note in the symphonic life of the group.

This leads him to the conscious use of energy. He learns that without energy he cannot reach his goal. Hence, he imposes upon himself a discipline of economy — economy in words, in thought, in emotional responses and reactions, in imagination, in activities, in money, in time, etc. All these help him accumulate energy to be used for the Hierarchical services only.

It is very difficult to reach such an elevated stage of living, but that is the goal. There are many who have reached such a degree of awareness and realization. All that they have and are belongs to the Hierarchy, and they are advanced and trained to use it wisely and goal-fittingly.

An esoteric group is like an engine, a complicated engine. If the engine has eighty percent new parts, but the rest are not really fit for the work of the engine, the whole engine suffers.

There are two things that the "invisible" engineer does: he replaces the parts or repairs them. To repair means to keep the old parts but inspire further discipline, clean them, and eventually make them work properly in the engine.

An intelligent member of the group who feels his weakness can do a great service for the group if, after consultation with its leader, he resigns from the group for a short or long period of time and works on himself. In this period of absence, the rule is "absolute silence about the group life" and a very sincere detachment from the group life. This will help him see himself clearly. Later, if he feels that there still is a great aspiration in his heart for correct group work, he imposes a special discipline upon himself and with his silence proves that he is fit again for a group test. He can be re-admitted after due observation. Such a discipline has nothing to do with secrecy, etc.

Esoteric groups do not have secrets. They do not have underground activities. All they want is to bring the Kingdom of God to earth and create a world of prosperity, joy, health, harmony, and beauty.

When such groups come into formation in various parts of the world, eventually it will be possible to relate them to each other and start a greater discipline of synchronous and unanimous meditation, study, and service. That is what the Hierarchy is expecting from all those students who are coming in contact with the Hierarchical literature. It is such a world wide group that will assist the Hierarchical consciousness and produce those heroes of spirit who will serve in the great task of human transfiguration.

A group must develop its energies of attraction and repulsion, attraction of those impressions that are coming from higher sources through the Plan and through the Purpose; repulsion of those impressions which are coming from the sources of distortion or from the sources that are consciously acting against the Hierarchical Plan. Once such a balance is established within the group, the group Soul automatically repels and rejects undesirable forces and attracts spiritual energies.

The same energies can be used to keep a balance between the personality and the Soul of the group. The same energies can be used by the leader of the group to create the right personality and Soul distance in the group members in relation to him. He keeps them at the right distance so as not to energize them beyond their capacities and not to reject them when they need him.

In the discipleship groups one is free to express his dissatisfaction with certain things that are related to him or to the group, but he presents his dissatisfaction in a different way than a complainer does. He finds the cause; he clearly sees the result; and he tries to find those ways and means through which he hopes to put things in a satisfactory condition. His motive is not destructive but constructive and is not influenced by his glamors, vanities, jealousies, or hatreds.

The first thing he does is to present the plan to the leader, and then he tries to receive feedback. If he proves that he is right and honest in his presentation, the leader takes action to correct the situation or the leader suggests that he make further studies and have further consultations at a later date.

As the study of the situation goes on, the leader watches him very closely and even passes him through certain tests to discover his real motive. Sometimes the leader finds him honest and sincere, and things become corrected and improved. Sometimes a dark viper begins to reveal itself, and the leader takes right action to awaken him, to discipline him, or to drop him from the discipleship group.

Some enemies of discipleship groups gain their positions by showing great interest and zeal for the progress of the group. Thus, they gain recognition and positions and continue their work more dangerously.

If a complainer shows the same weakness that he complains about in others, he is already revealed. If a complainer does not show the same weakness that he sees in others but has cravings for showing off or thinks he is better than others, the leader leads him into hard discipline to break his ego.

Sometimes improvements must take place gradually, cycle after cycle. A strong complaint to push things faster may reveal a dark motive or a glamored mind and ego.

Certain unsatisfactory conditions can serve to reveal many motives. Often it is better to continue an unsatisfactory condition than to improve it and create an ego. Sometimes unsatisfactory conditions can turn into causes for striving and discipline. Sometimes they can be opportunities for those who serve their egos.

In discipleship groups the most important thing is to develop loving understanding, patience, pure discrimination, and selflessness. Egos, whether they are right or wrong, must not be encouraged, and they must be watched very carefully so as not to let them grow out of control.

The major task of the leader must be to prepare leaders to cooperate with the Plan and eventually form a leadership group which works in unison and in closest cooperation. This will be possible when people advance spiritually, developing high morality and self-denial. Once such a group is formed, the leadership will not only be strong but also invincible, and the plan of the group will move forward with more surety.

Leaders in the leadership group will take responsibility in different branches of the work and make their decisions and solve the problems of their particular field with the leadership group. Every leadership group must have the most experienced one as their chief who will offer his help in difficult situations. He also must have the last word.

Ambition, love for position, touchiness, ego, self-interest, anger, impatience, lack of control upon speech, and jealousy are very negative signs which must carefully be watched in those who prepare themselves for leadership.

When the leadership group is formed, like the presidents of different factories, they must come together regularly to discuss and to improve the service of the Plan in the field of each leader.

All decisions must be based on the Teaching. Its principles and laws must be applied in each decision. Earthly arguments must not be encouraged even if they provide shortcuts.

To discipline those who fail in their responsibilities or tasks, the leadership group must not use common, earthly procedures. Punishment, taxation, and rebuke are not Hierarchical methods. The real causes of the failure must be found, and the failure must be handled as if it were a mechanical problem. The individual who failed must be subjected to a period of intensive training or recapitulation.

All decisions must be affirmed and approved by the leadership group as a whole.

In conclusion, first there must be a self-appointed leader who has a plan which, in fact, is a part of the Hierarchical Plan. The Hierarchical Plan is the Plan through which humanity may continuously progress toward perfection in Beauty, Goodness, Righteousness, Joy, and Freedom. The leader will attract those who can respond to his plan; this is the discipleship group.

The next duty of the leader is to select those who manifest leadership qualities. Such a selection will be a slow process through observation. The candidate must be watched in many situations, in many conditions — in labor, in rest, in play, in study, in creativity, in speech, in silence, in vices or virtues — and he must slowly be promoted through trying conditions.

After one person reaches a leadership position, it will be easier to find the next person.

The leadership group must not exceed seven members.

The original leader must stay in the group as a moral authority and source of wisdom and experience. He must choose his successor many years before he passes away so that he has time to train him sufficiently. Thus, a leader advances more when he prepares people to hold his position.

Leaders must have close contact with their Solar Angel, and they should have built their continuity of consciousness.

There are certain kinds of students who in the Far East are called wanderers, beggars, or tasters. They go from group to group to satisfy their changing tastes, and to each new group they say, "We did not learn from the other groups."

Beware of these people. Sometimes they are traitors; sometimes they seek easy ways for pleasures; sometimes they come to hide; sometimes to satisfy their laziness. They demonstrate an aura which can have decomposing effects on other auras and infect the whole group.

We call them "restless ones." They are sometimes covered by hypocrisy and they show off; sometimes they present you with an offer of great service. They use all sorts of tactics to make room for themselves in your group and teaching until they are saturated, confused, or satisfied.

When such people are insincere, they have a layer over their mind through which the Teaching cannot penetrate and nourish them. The best way to teach them is to reject them. Then if they persist, give them heavy labor. This will bring their colors out.

Do not give them any responsibility. That is not their intention. Keep them away from sensitive tasks, but assign individual heavy labor to them to be done privately at their homes.

When people come to you and insult their former teachers or groups, or belittle them through their judgment, you must know that they will possibly do the same to you. One of our teachers used to say that such people enter the group as a needle but they leave the group as an elephant, creating a big hole in the aura of the group.

Lack of gratitude and respectfulness toward their former teachers are clear warnings to you. Sometimes they try to hide such feelings; but if you try to dig them out, they will come to the surface.

Such people also carry with them many entities or one entity that does not let them start roots anywhere. Sometimes such entities bring contamination to the group Soul.

On the other hand, a few of such wanderers can be saved, if one deals with them in a direct and stern way. You must expose their psychology to them clearly but very cautiously because they may add your name to the list of those whom they hate.

Some of these people may have graduated from the high school and college of the Teaching and they need to find their special, straight path of preparation for Hierarchical Teaching. If this is the case, you can tell them to check their physical, emotional, and mental life and their motives to see if they see the need to change a few things and make themselves up-to-date. If they say that they found a few things to be changed but they did not change, it means they are not on the Path. If they did change, then they must want to meet a Great One. If the Great One does not appear and they get tired of waiting, this means they are deceiving themselves.

Looking for the Path in many teachings and groups signifies that this person is running after his own tail. The Path is within him, but he must open the gates to the Path by his efforts to *change* himself.

A young man came to me and said he had been with the Sufis, with Gurdjieff, with the Catholic Church, and he was still looking for the Path! I said, "Do you know how many people became Great Ones through the Sufis, how many people found their innermost center through the teaching of Gurdjieff, how many Holy Ones, striving lights, were produced by the Teaching of Christ?"

He said, "I know."

"Then where are you looking for a path?"

Whenever or wherever you contact the highest within you, that is the gate to the Path. One must find those elements within himself that are obscuring his vision from seeing the Path existing within himself.

The Path can be found only with an intense desire to change yourself and forget yourself in the service of humanity. The Path can be found through sincere confrontation with yourself and by making firm decisions to commit yourself to enter the path of perfection.

9
The Discriminative Attitude of the Leader

In choosing individuals who will study the advanced Teaching and in the future will possibly be co-workers, you must be careful of certain types of people:

1. Those who are lukewarm or are flickering lights; those who waver. You will look for those who are enthusiastic, steady, and striving. The former ones will waste your time and energy, and in due time will create problems for you and hinder the expansion of the Teaching.

2. Those who do not stand for the truth, for right, and are afraid to resist evil. These are the channels through which dark ones enter the strata of sincere disciples, disturb their focus, loosen their striving, and eventually lead them into a life which is self-oriented,

selfish, and dedicated to self-gratification rather than to self-sacrifice. There is no true Teaching without self-sacrifice. Lukewarmness is condemned by great Teachers.

Those who have courage to stand against injustice and corruption will eventually find their way to the Hierarchy.

3. Those who have advanced minds but retarded hearts. A mentally advanced man, if not balanced by the heart, serves dark forces, spreads doubts and confusion, and leads the group to material values and selfish interests. He also kills dedication, faith, and trust.

4. Those who are in continuous irritation, full of anger and hatred, or bear a hidden grudge against you. Such vermin are used by dark forces against the leadership and the Teacher. In critical times these polluted associates deliver the fortress into the hands of the enemies and join them to secure their interests.

5. Those who criticize and gossip. These people plant animosity among the members of the group and sow separatism and distrust. One of them is enough to destroy a group, if the leader is not awake to the issues.

6. Those who try to secure their personal interests from duties and responsibilities entrusted to them. Such people try to increase their own interests in the name of the group and at the expense of the group. It is observed that such people steal, lie, and play office politics. Watch small signs and you will reveal their actions and motives.

It is important that you test the applicants for a minimum of one year and see if they steal, lie, distort the truth, keep their word, and if they are solemn. The Teaching creates violent reactions and strengthens their vices and weaknesses. Thus, before they are part of the group, they must be cleared in special disciplines and studies.

We are told that dark forces love those who enter the spiritual Path and see in them an opportunity to deteriorate the work in subtle ways.

Most so-called new-age groups, cults, and religious organizations work under the subtle direction of the dark forces. The signs of wrong direction are

— Greed for money and its wrong use

— Emphasis on form

— Totalitarian attitude

— Conspiracy

— Separative, political interests

— Sectarianism, fanaticism

— Physical pleasures

— Socializing

— Intrigues, gossip, criticism

Helena Roerich once wrote:

"Many naive people think that the dark ones act only through evil, corruption, and crime. How wrong they are! Only crude and relatively insignificant forces act in this way. Much more dangerous are those who masquerade under the Light of the Teaching."

"Ignorance and lack of intuition push many into the arms of darkness, and deprive them for a long time, if not forever, of the salutary influence and attraction of the rays of the great Stronghold of Light."[1]

7. Those who have strong ambition and vanities may display the following tendencies:

— To run the show

— To control people

— To have higher and higher positions

— To manipulate people and their personal lives

Such people can do much harm and damage to the group without the slightest feeling just to satisfy their ambition and vanity.

People must be promoted very slowly. The leader and his co-workers must watch to see the signs of

- Dedicated, selfless service
- Humility
- Heart quality
- Discrimination
- Control of the mouth
- Nobility
- Sincerity
- Loyalty

---

1. Agni Yoga Society, *Letters of Helena Roerich*, Vol. II, pp. 6-7.

These are the guidelines, and no one must be promoted until these qualities are revealed in them or painfully developed.

The leader must know that the real Ashrams are formed with only a few people. Increasing the membership loosens the spiritual direction and tension of the group. Each person brings his karmic burden and his own web of glamors, illusions, and motives.

The Ashram is a field of self-transformation. People must join the Ashram to find those conditions in which they are challenged to cultivate their virtues, to develop their spiritual senses, to learn how to serve, to learn the reality of the subjective world. This means that not everyone must be taken into the Ashram. People sometimes need long ages of suffering before they are able to function in an Ashram.

It must also be mentioned that those who are trained in Ashrams must still keep their contact with life in general. Ashrams are not escapes but schools to train people to transform life. Spiritual progress must be proven in our daily labor and relationships.

8. Reject also dependent ones. These are people who are used by stronger ones to satisfy their vanity and self-interest. They are used for ugly missions and as unwise channels between group members.

Young souls who are after the satisfaction of their glamors encourage weak ones to depend on their advice, money, and security. And once self-dependency is taken away from them, they fall into the path of treason, the path of betrayal. In general, they relate to the leader in pleasant ways; they use flattery and obedience without respect. Often they bring gifts, and then they bring information about others and their activities. This is one of their secret weapons. They try to gain trust by bringing you news of the private affairs of the members or news related to the group welfare.

Unripe leaders encourage such people to gather information. In so doing, they allow them to come closer to their life and to the sensitive nerves of the group. Their whole intention is to shrink the group.

The leader must be austere and stern with them and keep them at a distance, not only from himself but from the members of the group.

9. The leader must be careful of those who promise but do not fulfill their promises. Of course, this will be watched for a period of a year or a few years. Such people are inflamed by the Teaching momentarily and they feel urged to promise to serve or to give, but their promise is often not fulfilled for various reasons. Give them another chance, and see if they promise and play the same game.

If such people by chance render a good service, do not allow yourself to trust them. Be always watchful because they may quit their duty in a moment of dire need and leave you in serious trouble.

The Sages recommend rejecting such people from Ashrams because those who promise and do not keep their promise have a very subtle disarrangement in their mental body which turns under pressure into treachery and hatred against the Teaching. Sometimes such behavior is related to a weak will or to a busy life. But the reality is that behind this behavior there is a heavy karma, instability of direction, and lack of responsibility.

10. The leader must be careful of bullheaded people. Bullheaded people are those who want everything around them to be done according to their own thoughts or will. Bullheaded people are those who force the issues without considering related problems. Bullheaded people want things to be done without considering the

viewpoints and interests of others. Bullheaded people use heavy emotion and selfish logic. Such people are used to disintegrate groups and dissipate the focus of harmony and unity.

Bullheaded people do not follow instructions and rules, and they reject advice. Sometimes they show obedience if they feel that through obedience they can succeed in their own ways.

Bullheaded people identify themselves with their property, office, and rank. Their computer belongs to them; their office belongs to them; their rank is an emblem of power for them. The leader will have a very hard time making new arrangements if he has bullheaded people working for him.

11. There is another type which may be called the "I know" type, and it must be carefully avoided. This "I know" type is a show-off type, and it creates real problems in the group. Instead of working on his own self-actualization, such a person forces himself on others to feel superior and to make other people follow him.

Such persons are often found in the list of betrayers. They measure things according to what they think they know, and if their knowledge is not affirmed they create hatred and disturb the forces of the Ashram. "I know" people cause various embarrassments to the leader and mislead other people by distorting the leader's direction. They lack Intuition and co-measurement. It is very difficult to teach them because before you open your mouth they already "know."

In one of the monasteries, when a student started to develop the "I know" attitude, the Teacher used to give him the most humiliating job and almost ignore his presence. Very often he was dismissed from the school. Humility is the first door to true knowledge and cooperation.

12. There is another dangerous type, which is called the "what is going on here" type. All he wants is information, which is taken superficially and later used with deliberation to distort the true facts. Such types bring light-mindedness into the group and sow the seeds of distrust, superficiality, and lack of a sense of responsibility. This type never makes commitments and lives by the labor of others.

In esoteric Ashrams those who do not grow spiritually hinder the progress of the rest.

Such types often are the best sources of information for the enemies of the group. They translate things as they see them from their own viewpoint. Fortunately, they do not last long. They clean themselves from the group and often carry a few light-minded followers wih them when they go.

Such persons cannot be trusted for any important labor or any important task.

13. There is another type called "shoppers." They come into the group to shop — to shop for girls, wives, husbands, friends, or even to sell their own products. The leader must be very careful to prevent the presence of such people because they may misuse the simplicity and honesty of many members and engage them in various troubles.

There are men who come for girls, and once they get them they pull them out of the group and out of the Teaching. The same thing is done by girls whose only intention is to find boyfriends.

Of course, friendship is noble, but only if it is based on the foundation of the Teaching.

I knew a few of this type who made girls pregnant and then disappeared. I know others who, after their physical satisfaction, told others about it and created vicious gossip and involvements.

The leader must be careful that personal interests are not pursued in the group and personal problems are left out of the group.

14. There is another type that can be called the "sneaky and separative" type. This type tries to use the group for its separative beliefs, religion, faith, dogmas, and doctrines. Such types are dangerous. They not only whisper into the ears, but they also spread literature and pamphlets to win people. Once they gain a certain amount of members, they act openly and fight against the rest.

Those who are members of the New Group of World Servers and are ready to be members of your Ashramic group must be inclusive, non-sectarian, non-nationalistic, and non-racist because if they are not, separative interests work through such people to destroy the Ashram or to make the Ashram their slave.

It must be clear to the members that the Ashram is inclusive in the sense that people resign from their separative interests and live in the light of the Divine Plan. Of course, one must love his race, his nation, his country; but he must recognize the rights of others to do so too. Those who cannot put the interests of humanity above their separative interests cannot be part of the Ashram.

15. There is another type of person that can be called the "all the same" type. These people do not have discrimination, and like trains they load themselves from each station without bothering about the quality of the Teaching. These people lack Intuition and they have no foundation. The foundation is built throughout centuries, and the foundation is the pure Hierarchical Teaching.

These people lower the standards of the true Teaching and spread words about the "sameness" of the true Teaching compared with other pseudo teachings. For example, they will not see any distinction between the works of Blavatsky, Helena Roerich, and Alice A. Bailey on the one hand and those who channel messages from the astral plane. There are mediums and channels who can repeat to a certain degree the words of Great Ones, but those who have discrimination will easily see their motives and the mixture of light with darkness and vanity. It is very difficult to build new foundations within such people without first destroying all that they have built upon false foundations.

It is better to admit those who have very little knowledge but pure and dedicated hearts than those who have well-loaded minds but are lacking discrimination.

The "sameness" types never engage themselves in any serious labor. On the contrary, they spread confusion and light-mindedness.

The leader must be very observant and record his observations in his diary. To know people is the first step in the success of the group life.

The leader must not negotiate or make reconciliations, but when he is aware of the facts he must act immediately with wisdom and tact. Chances must not be given to rattlesnakes to settle in and attack.

16. There is also a type who constantly jokes and uses the Teaching as a tool for humor. This is a light-mindedness that cheapens the Teaching and makes it seem commonplace.

17. There is also another type who seeks advice only to validate what he has decided. There are people who will come for counseling and then do exactly what they want to do. This is a very interesting phenomenon. Why

do they come for counseling if they do not want to change their minds or consider your advice? The reason is that they have already made up their minds, but they lack courage and need your endorsement for their decision.

How do they receive your endorsement? They present to you false data so that you give exactly the advice they expect from you. Thus, they mislead you and even create complications in your relationships with other people involved in the problem.

Let us take a very simple example. A boy comes and says to you, "My doctor told me to eat plums. There are none in the market. What do you think I must do?" He knows that you have a plum tree and that you care for him. You say, "Well, go to my tree and help yourself." That is exactly what he wanted to do.

A few years ago a young girl came and said, "My psychiatrist made a thorough examination, and he found that I must find someone who can really satisfy me sexually. I had a few boyfriends, but they were no good. What is your advice?"

Because I have had a few experiences like this before, I said, "Well, who is your psychiatrist? Can I have his telephone number?"

"Yes, I will bring it to you."

"Would you feel guilty if you didn't ask me and you followed your own plan?"

"Yes, I would."

"Why do you need my endorsement?"

"Because I don't want to do something wrong and feel guilty."

"If you do something wrong because you want to do it, whether I agree with you or not, what difference does it make?"

"I feel that I want someone to tell me to do it."

"That is why you are making up a story to lead me to the conclusion you want."

These are very mild cases. Be careful when you counsel people that you not only listen carefully to their stories, but you also see their motives and whether they have the intention to manipulate your authority for their own behalf.

Here is a heavier example.

A man came and said, "My wife has not made love with me for three years. She doesn't want it. She rejects me and tells me to find another woman for fun. What can I do?"

"I want to talk to you and your wife at the same time. Then I can try to help you."

He did not come any more. His wife came and said that he was interested in other women. "I am faithful and twice every week I am meeting his needs. So what can I do?"

"I want to see both of you."

She never came again. I found out accidently that she had a lover but wanted to keep her husband as an umbrella. It was true that she was also having sex with her husband, but her husband knew that she was going with another man and he wanted to play the same game.

A leader must be careful not to be trapped in such nets.

How does the leader handle a person who commits crimes or does stupid things and then comes for counseling to ask for peace, for forgiveness, or for ways to escape? Should the leader pity the person, or make him feel that his errors are not fatal, or try to inject some morphine in his mind, flattering or praising him? Or should the leader try to make him feel that he is innocent or that he can ignore his mistakes?

True guidance does not participate in the errors of those who consciously commit crimes or occasionally act against moral and other laws by making them believe that psychological exercises may make them free from the consequences of their deeds. Guidance must do the following things:

1. Make the person realize his transgressions or his errors as factually as possible

2. Make him see the possible consequences of his errors

3. Show him how to pay back his debts

4. Show him how to prepare himself so as not to repeat his errors

5. Teach him the true significance and meaning of repentance and true confession

Repentance is not only a clear realization of one's own errors and their consequences, but it is also a process of planning to heal the wounds he caused, or pay back the things he stole, or take responsibility for his violations.

It is possible through psychological exercises to patch the wounds, calm the consequences and the nerves, bribe and flatter the conscience, comfort the uneasy heart, and inject a certain dosage of energy and courage to make the guilty person run another mile with a wounded soul; but such remedies do not last long.

The guidance must emphatically make it clear that unless one goes through an experience of transformation and expansion of consciousness, no true healing can take place. Transformation and expansion of consciousness take place

1. When one realizes his errors and really feels sorry about them.

2. When one is ready to pay for the damage he did.

3. When one is ready to see how his mistakes and errors can produce a new generation of errors and how they can prevent his progress on the Path. Rationalization and self-justifications are the path which lead into the pit of self-deception.

4. When one is able to see a higher vision, the true destination of his soul, and make a firm commitment to stay in the light of his Higher Self.

The leader must not fall into the trap of a judgmental attitude. He should not fall into vanity nor play the role of executioner. The duty of the leader is to shed light on the consciousness of the person to enable him:

— To see his errors

— Not to identify with his errors, but to see them as destructive acts

— To raise his consciousness, so that he can deal with his life from a higher level of consciousness

Usually, those who have made errors seek pity or ways to escape. They use various methods to attain forgiveness. They forget their debts, and they continue to live on the same level. The leader must use his compassion, not his pity, with emotional detachment and with an attitude of non-identification. If any kind of punishment is needed, the leader must be very tactful so that the victim formulates his own punishment and the form of punishment. Any imposed punishment feeds the cause of errors.

Also, it is important for the leader not to let the victim get carried away in punishing himself. Over-punishment originates from a misguided consciousness.

10
Co-workers

Nothing can be accomplished in the Universe without the assistance of co-workers. The whole phenomenon of life is proof of this. An atom cannot do anything without the assistance of other atoms. A man cannot accomplish much on his own; he needs the assistance of other people, other co-workers. All life is interrelated, and the progressive part of life is always the result of a cooperative effort.

A solar system and a galaxy also stand on the foundation of cooperation with co-workers. Health is a phenomenon of cooperation. When all the parts of your body are cooperating, you have health. The success of groups, brotherhoods, and various organizations is also based on cooperation. Life and progress are the result of cooperating factors. As the field of cooperation becomes larger, you have greater success.

The idea of cooperation will be increasingly emphasized because man will surpass his present state of beingness only through creating co-workers who cooperate in reaching higher states of consciousness.[1]

Cooperation is the foundation of all group endeavor, and in the Future universal and Cosmic visions can only be impressed on those people who create a magnetic group aura due to their cooperation.

The term *co-worker* refers to those people who come together in the name of a great Principle, a great Service, a great Cause. Co-workers are those people who work together to bring greater Beauty, Goodness, Righteousness, Joy, and Freedom to humanity.

Co-workers do not cooperate to secure the self-interest of a leader but to actualize the vision, the plan of the leader. Cooperation means to have a principle, a vision, and to organize all your physical, emotional, and mental forces and efforts to actualize that vision or principle without having your personality interfere with that cooperation.

Co-workers are those people who collectively work for Beauty, Goodness, Righteousness, Joy, and Freedom; it is these principles that gather co-workers.

A co-worker is one who works under the direction and with the direction of the Hierarchy. In order to become a co-worker one must

1. Be permitted to do so by one's karma

2. Not create new attachments

3. Not scatter one's energies

---

1. See *The Psychology of Cooperation and Group Consciousness*.

4. Refine one's aura

5. Refine one's relationships

6. Reach a certain degree of illumination

7. Be aware of the Plan

8. Develop a sense of direction

9. Respect, protect, and not burden one's co-workers with one's personality problems, nor project one's troubles on others

10. Develop a bond with other co-workers which then makes them a group which assists greater Beauty, Goodness, Righteousness, Joy, and Freedom to penetrate into the world

11. Never belittle another co-worker, no matter on what level he works, but send steady blessings to him

12. Try to find co-workers in all fields

Co-workers are blooming flowers. As one approaches his Soul or raises his consciousness to higher and higher levels, he becomes a co-worker because he is in harmony with the direction of the Hierarchy.

In ancient times, co-workers were symbolized by dancers. As the dancers synchronized their physical, emotional, and mental movements to the music, they synchronized with each other for the Common Goal. Vision, understanding of the Common Good, and inner achievements are necessary requirements to be a co-worker.

Any responsibility given to any co-worker is carried on with the zeal of perfection and steadiness. A co-worker is dependable, truthful, and solemn. You know that by his actions, words, and ideas he will not embarrass and belittle other co-workers.

A Great Sage once gave an instruction to His disciples showing how a co-worker is created. He said:

The degrees of attainment are: alarmed; inquiring; knocking; hearkening; reminiscing; transmitting; sword carrier; puissant; lamp of the desert; lion of the desert; co-worker of the creative principles; creator.

Each degree is sub-divided thrice; the order must be passed gradually. He who strives attains swiftly, but the deserter casts himself down.[2]

One must graduate through these twelve stages in order to become a co-worker.

The first stage is the state of a person which is called **alarmed**. This is an esoteric word which means a man is suddenly awakened to a situation and confronts a decision. He has received a warning from his Soul, from his body, from his circumstances of life. He is horrified by some information, by some facts. He was horrified by a dream or by an experience, and now he is uneasy.

One must be "alarmed" in order to find the Path. No one enters the Path without being alarmed. Alarm is the moment when the human soul reaches the stage where his eyes are opened and he sees his situation clearly. He sees his karma, his slavery, the forces of materialism and darkness, and the danger of annihilation and destruction.

After this stage comes the stage of **inquiry**. The traveler begins to search for solutions; he wants to pro-

---

2. Agni Yoga Society, *Agni Yoga*, para. 107.

tect and free himself and those who are closely related to him. Here he makes inquiries. He becomes a question mark. He searches in religion, in education, and in philosophy to find ways and means to free himself from his state of alarm. He visits teachers, reads books, listens to lectures, and eventually reaches the conclusion that the secret of all these teachings is hidden somewhere within him. This leads him to the next stage.

This is the stage of **knocking**. Knocking means to gather all your physical, emotional, and mental aspirations into a focus and try to initiate yourself into a new state of consciousness where you will substantiate all that you have learned and dreamed. In this state you knock on the door of your Inner Guide. You do this by

— Asking questions

— Thinking

— Meditating

— Uplifting your heart and expanding your consciousness

— Cultivating virtues

— Transforming your life

— Committing yourself to sacrificial service

— Disciplining your physical, emotional, and mental bodies

— Exercising clear observation

— Exercising severe discipline of speech

It is through such means that you invoke and await evocation; you await an answer from the Inner Lord.

When the communication is established between you and the Inner Lord, your dreams come true and your inquiries find answers. Instead of being a man of ideas, dreams, and theories, you become a man of experience. Knocking leads you into experience.

After entrance into the presence of your Inner Lord, you prepare yourself for the next stage which is called *hearkening*. Hearkening is the stage when you are ready to load yourself with great responsibilities and tasks. You are ready to submit yourself to sacrificial service.

The voice that you hearken to may be the voice of your Inner Lord, it may be the voice of your Master, or it may be the voice of Christ; but you must hearken to it. The way to hearken is to close your ears to all those voices which speak about self-interest, vanity, pride, separatism, and greed.

Hearkening convinces you that you are not alone on the Path and that the Guides of life are watching your steps to the mountaintop. Hearkening is the stage where you come to the conclusion that you must live the things you believe.

The next stage is *reminiscence*. This is the stage in which the striving one remembers all his past; past lives slowly unfold themselves, giving him special understanding about his present and future life. This remembrance also clears up many factors hidden in his relationships with his family, co-workers, and those people who created problems for him. This stage is a clearing stage where, for the first time, the striving one knows why things happened to him the way they happened.

The next stage is called *transmitting*. It is after reminiscence that the striving one becomes a pure transmitter of wisdom. He becomes a Teacher who knows how to bring down the ideas and visions from the subjective world, from the higher realms, and formulate them adequately and pass them on to the people of the world.

He not only transmits wisdom but also energy: the energy of love, of light, and of beauty. A real transmitter inspires trust, confidence, and faith. People find the direction of their life when they meet transmitters who not only receive the Teaching as it is but also transmit the Teaching without distorting it through their glamors, illusions, and blind urges.

The next stage is called the *sword carrier*. Traditionally, this has three levels: On the first level, the striving one carries the sword of a Great One. On the next level, the striving one carries his own sword to protect the Great One. On the third level, the striving one carries his own sword for himself.

The sword is the symbol of

1. Pure discrimination

2. Power, might

3. Psychic energy

4. Fiery will

5. Law

6. Order

7. Fiery words

The sword carrier is one who is ready for sacrificial acts and is ready to carry on the command given to him by greater Centers. He is totally committed to the service and liberation of humanity. He is on the field of battle, and he is one who will never give up.

The next step is called *puissant*. The striving one, through his fearlessness, commitment, and sacrificial life becomes a tower of strength and power. His words, his acts, and his thoughts express power. He has power over his personality and over the forces and energies of Nature. He uses all his might and power for the progress and liberation of all living Sparks in any form. He radiates the fire of will. However, he is extremely cautious to use his power only to further the Purpose of the Planetary Logos.

The next state of attainment is called the ***lamp of the desert***. The desert symbolizes a state of consciousness which is aimless, goalless, fruitless, monotonous, meaningless, flat, isolated; a great vacuum, an emptiness. Those who live a meaningless life which has no purpose or plan, a life in which they are lost and do not have any direction live in a desert. It is such a life that presents the greatest temptation to those who, in the future, are going to be great co-workers.

The lamp of the desert is now a Teacher who brings meaning, beauty, growth, and life into the deserts of life. He gives vision and inspiration to those who were lost in the desert of a meaningless life. His life shines as a lamp in the darkness. His light gives direction and fills people with the sparks of purpose.

Sometimes people live in a "desert consciousness": when the doctor tells them that they have only a few weeks to live; when they lose a beloved Teacher or a family member or a friend; if suddenly they lose the things that they obtained with great labor, fear, and suffering; if suddenly they realize their worthlessness. Then life appears to them as a waste, as an empty, burning desert.

When you become a lamp of the desert, you begin to see new values in life. You see a great purpose behind your pains, behind your suffering and losses. You bring joy into life; you encourage people; you create striving; and you radiate your beauty as a service to others.

Because of your existence as a light, people find their direction toward their own spiritual destination. The desert blooms in your light because everything receives a meaning, a significance, a purpose.

Are we lights in the desert of crime, violence, deceit, hypocrisy, exploitation, greed, fear, and hatred?

When you have proven that you are a light in the desert, a lamp of the desert, you then pass to the next stage of evolution, which is called the *lion of the desert*. The lion is the symbol of power, protection, steadiness, endurance, beauty, victory, daring, courage, and fearlessness. The lion of the desert is subdivided into three degrees: the first degree is composed of those who make a breakthrough out of crystallization and fanaticism in any department of human endeavor. For example, Blavatsky was one of them. She attacked the merchants of materialism who were working in the field of science. She attacked the merchants of fanaticism who were working in the desert of religion. She made it possible for daring ones to expand the walls of science to Space and opened a new understanding between religious traditions and the mythologies of all nations. In the field of art and beauty, another great lion of the desert was Nicholas Roerich.

On the second level we have great religious leaders.

On the third level we have Buddha and Christ, Who were each actually called the *Lion of the Desert*.

Lions of the desert attack and try to annihilate all those barriers that stand on the path of human progress. They are fearless ones because they know that they are not bodies but living principles, living ideas; Beauty, Goodness, Righteousness, Joy, and Freedom. And because a lion of the desert knows that he is an embodiment of such principles, he is fearless and he is powerful. Fearlessness and power do not belong to you when you create slaves around you, when you exploit people, when you mislead people, when you try to kill their soul and conscience. Fearlessness and power do not come to you when your life is dependent on your possessions, positions, titles, lies, deceits, fanaticism, and separatism. All these make you a coward, a weak person.

Fearlessness and power are the virtues of those people who make themselves the embodiments of great principles, great visions, and great ideas.

When you read the lives of great lions of the desert, you see how fearless they were because they were fused with a divine principle. People could kill their bodies but never their visions and ideas; people could even distort and misrepresent their ideas and thus give them a second blow of death, but they could not touch their visions, the image they had imprinted in the souls of people.

Lions of the desert are protectors of the human race as a whole. When you reach such a state of consciousness, you graduate into the next stage and you become a ***co-worker of the creative principles, a creator***. You are now ready to cooperate with the creative principles of the Universe and become a creator.

The creative principles are contacted through the Hierarchy, through Shamballa, through the Zodiacal Lives, through the Lives of the Greater Zodiac, through the Lords of the Rays, through the Heart of the Spiritual Sun, through the Central Spiritual Sun. One becomes a greater co-worker of these seven Centers Who embody the seven Principles of the seven Paths of the Purpose of the Life in which all existence moves, lives, and has its being. The co-worker is now a conscious part of Life and cooperates with Life in Its creative efforts.

Can you imagine yourself cooperating with your Inner Guide and becoming Its co-worker? Can you imagine yourself cooperating with Great Ones in the Plan of the Hierarchy? Can you imagine yourself cooperating with the Lives Who are active in Shamballa? Can you imagine yourself being in contact and a close co-worker with higher and higher forces and Existences? What a glorious being is a co-worker. Instead of building our sand castles, or karmic prisons on our path, we can prepare ourselves to be co-workers of the creative Principles of Life.

A co-worker will never violate the principles for which he stands, neither through his acts, nor through his thoughts; neither through his words, nor with his motives. The gates of Hierarchy can open only to co-workers.

Co-workers have four characteristics:

1. They are without prejudice.

2. They are mobile in action.

3. They are young in spirit.

4. They are fearless of chasms.

1. A co-worker is *without prejudice*. When a man has prejudices, he works for the interest of his prejudices. He works for his separative interests, and he translates things through his prejudices and cannot stand on facts and on reality. Our life on the planet advances in great difficulty through suffering and pain because man created the barrier of prejudice.

A prejudiced person is intolerant; he relates on the basis of partiality. He misjudges people and situations. He is occupied with nonessentials and barriers. He misuses the essentials and opportunities. Such a man cannot be a co-worker because a co-worker cooperates with the souls of people, not with their failures and hang-ups. Prejudice is found in the minds of politicians, educators, philosophers, artists, scientists, religious people, and even in the field of economics. It is like a blind spot in the eyes of these people, and it plays a detrimental role in the work of cooperation and in the unity of nations.

Prejudice is separative and works only for self-interest. Prejudice is a mental disease which co-workers cannot have at all.

2. A co-worker is *mobile in action*. He cannot be lazy but must be rhythmic and active. Mobility means to be creative, to be in progressive transformation. When the creative forces and energies are filling your life, you must express them; you must manifest them in your daily living. This is mobility. Mobility is ever-progressing transformation of your life with new visions and new ideas, with new inspirations, and with new enthusiasm. If a man does not transform his life, he cannot be a co-worker because he lives as a personality. Co-workers are Souls.

3. A co-worker is *young in spirit*. He enjoys Nature; he loves the flowers; he plays with rabbits; he becomes friends with children; and he understands the psychology of youth. He does not think of himself as an old body but as a living spirit. He does not get tired of serving, learning, and creating. He does not live in the past and in obsolete ideas. He lives in the future, and those who live in the future, for the future, never become old in spirit.

Co-workers have the spirit of healthy youth — free, open, forgiving, playful, joyful, enthusiastic, and daring. Life for a co-worker is an opportunity, not a dead-end street. Life is a vision for him, and he is always young because he always receives higher, more universal, and fresh inspirations.

Those people who think they are old identify with their bodies and with the troubles of the bodies. A co-worker takes advantage of the process of the aging of his vehicle. A co-worker thinks young, and because of this he attracts the youth and prepares them for the path of discipleship. The youth like him because they see in him a man who understands them, loves them, and guides them. A man is young when he is identified with great principles, ideas, and visions and lives for them.

4. A co-worker is *fearless of chasms*. A chasm is the symbol of great disappointments, failures, betrayals, obstacles, enemies, catastrophes, ill health, losses, traps on the path through trickery. Even with all these, you cannot stop the co-worker. He goes forward toward his vision knowing that those who work with the forces of Light, Love, and Beauty are the victors.

In one of Nicholas Roerich's paintings you can see this fearlessness illustrated very beautifully. In the painting you see a chasm between two high mountains and a horseman is jumping over the chasm to hasten with a message entrusted to him.

Then we have a beautiful verse which talks about testing the co-workers:

> *... I advise you to begin the testing with a proposal to rest, not to work. Each one who is glad not to work is no coworker of yours. You may ask whether the services of the newcomer are recognized by ungrateful humanity. Each complainer is no coworker of yours. You may ask whether he himself is responsible for the past or others are. Your coworker will not impose responsibility for his past on others. Furthermore, note that, left alone, he does not move objects about. The man who is imbued with the importance of what is around him, does not disturb any process unknown to him. The man who knows something of*

the essence of objects, displays care with reference to your arrangement. Look after the silent ones especially sharply. . . .[3]

The testing of co-workers is very important. If they are not ready for great tasks, if they are not disciplined to meet great responsibilities, they ruin the work and cause great harm to people. Testing your co-workers is not an insult to them but is a protection for the co-worker and the work.

Those who are not co-workers waste your time, your energy, your vision. They even waste their own time and energy with their urges and drives, with their dreams and selfish interests. But the co-worker accomplishes the task given to him with a joyful, self-sacrificial attitude.

When I was principal of a high school, I used to observe the children. I made a list of the names of those who were self-sacrificial, full of the spirit of helpfulness and protection. Years later I found that these children finished their university education and became servers. But those who were selfish and self-seeking eventually found themselves in places which would not bring honor to them.

Co-workers must master inertia on the three planes and fill themselves with the fire of enthusiasm. Enthusiasm is a carrier of psychic energy which charges and recharges the mechanism of man when he is working for a great Cause.

The co-worker never complains, whether he is recognized or ignored. His work is not with those who like or dislike him; his work is with great Principles, and he tries to bring them into his life to water the gardens of

---

3. Agni Yoga Society, *Community*, para. 220.

life. When a co-worker complains that because of his studies and the demands of people he is deprived of television, baseball, his girlfriends, or other pleasures, he proves that he is not a co-worker. When he complains that he is losing out on his fun because of heavy work, release him as soon as you can because those who complain bring irritation and poison into the work. When a man puts his own personal interests over the interests of a cause, he loses the opportunity to become a co-worker.

Co-workers recognize their own failures because they have clear observation. Those who are not co-workers blame others for their own failures. Those who blame others for their own failures never improve and they do not live a righteous life.

A co-worker is a creative person, and he creates jobs for himself, even if you do not give him a job. He initiates work. He sees the need even if you do not tell him about the need. Co-workers are directed by their own Intuition. When one co-worker sees a need, they all see it, and they unite their efforts to meet the need.

It is very interesting to note that co-workers intuitively know their tasks. There is a minimum of talk in the circles of co-workers because they are telepathically attuned to each other. That is what makes them save time and energy and personality frictions.

The following extracts from the Agni Yoga books let us see the co-worker with deeper viewpoints:

> *Least of all do people understand success. Usually, when the success of a task commissioned by the Hierarchy, and imbued with the help of the Hierarchy, is attributed by the spirit steeped in selfhood to its own merit, the success turns into a heartache of the spirit. When a co-worker requires adoration of himself for fulfillment of the task*

given him, he closes by this very act the records of the space. The records of life passing on in all earthly glory reveal so many beggars in spirit! A co-worker who presents to the community the idea that the Hierarchy will act in accordance with the affirmation of the successful co-worker introduces truly a belittlement of the Hierarch. How difficult it is to introduce among the co-workers the true concept of success! Indeed, only humility of the spirit and the feeling of gratitude are appropriate. Who gave all possibilities? Who has given the direction? Who has manifested all good? Only the Hierarch, only the Leader, only the Forces of Light. Successful co-workers, examine thy armor; on each link is inscribed — Hierarchy. Not I, myself, nor mine, but Thine, O Lord!

Hence, on the path to the Fiery World one should remember that humility is the companion of success. Co-worker, pretend not to luck, for fiery energies are subtle, and crude egotism does not contain the fires. Thus, let us remember about humility when we wish to be truly successful.[4]

. . .Each co-worker can reflect upon the beauty of fiery daring, for it frees the spirit from all worldly chains. The daring one is not afraid of solitude, for in spirit he feels a bond with the Hierarchy of Light. The daring one knows that the joy of the spirit is contained only in achievement. The daring one is in need of no human recognition, for his achievement is a crown self-woven by labor and striving. Only the heroes of spirit know true

---

4. Agni Yoga Society, *Fiery World*, Vol. III, para. 52.

attainment. Thus, the daring one will be freed from selfhood. He knows true Service for the good of mankind. On the path to the Fiery World let us remember daring.[5]

... The co-workers must remember the first law, which affirms the first step — the expulsion of feelings of personal vengeance, for the feeling of revenge is a powerful manifestation of the unscrupulousness of selfhood. For the sake of personal vengeance the co-worker may give up that of greatest value. When a co-worker forgets, due to selfhood, the affirmation which he must forge in his spirit in order not to forget Service, the harm may become indelible. Primitive man lived and believed in vengeance, but the consciousness has broadened and man can no longer dwell with such black concepts. He who knows the meaning of Karma can understand that a man takes revenge only on himself. A co-worker will not become affirmed through selfhood and infringement upon the heart of his fellow-man. And a successful co-worker must not impose respect, but must merit it. A king of the spirit must first of all reveal himself in a small circle of life. The growth of dimensions proceeds from within, and the spirit may bedeck itself with all the crowns of human glory, and still remain a beggar. Thus let it be remembered by those who are diseased with selfhood and self-conceit. On the path to the Fiery World these chains are not fitting.[6]

---

5. *Ibid.*, para. 55.
6. *Ibid.*, para. 56.

11
Leadership and Co-workers

A Great Teacher says, "While building up the relations between the co-workers, you must not forget all the small workers."[1] This is very important advice for leaders. Leadership is right relationship with all those who are dedicated to an idea, to a vision, to a service. Through the network of right relationship, the leader becomes able to encourage and inspire his co-workers and synthesize their activities to fulfill the plan, whatever it is.

Once I read about one of the presidents of the United States. He used to greet the sweepers early in the morning on the streets and exchange a few words with them.

---

1. Agni Yoga Society, *Letters of Helena Roerich*, Vol. I, p. 36.

Imagine how a man works when his president greets him and says a few nice words.

Keeping right relationship with his co-workers, the leader is surrounded with positive energies, which in turn encourage him to work harder.

To be a leader means, in its true sense, to be an example, a path, a source of light, love, and power for others.

You do not need to have a group to be a leader. Your immediate environment, your society, and your friends are the field where you can practice your leadership. Whenever you encourage people toward light, love, striving, and perfection, you are a leader. You are a leader when people see in you a man of honesty, a man who can be trusted, a man who keeps his word; a man who discriminates between spiritual things and phenomenal things; a man who knows when to speak and when to keep silent; a man who is harmless and does not offend people with his actions and words.

Small workers need to grow, and their greatest nourishment is the example of the leader. Small workers also need to learn that the leader does not hate them when they fail, when they develop negative feelings toward him, even when they talk against him. A leader understands the workers' levels, their problems, and he does not offend them because of their weaknesses.

A worker turns into a co-worker when he sees a vision in his leader. Nobility, honesty, kindness, royalty, and solemnity always impress the souls of the workers, even if they remain indifferent to you in their personality reactions.

Leadership is a kind of life which inspires people to walk toward light and love, toward greater courage and greater beauty.

The leader must exercise total control of speech so that he does not even hurt the feelings of those who have negative attitudes toward him. It is a great test for the leader to see the good even behind the walls. Many great servers come from the ranks of those who have been respected by the leader, in spite of their disrespectful actions, words, and expressions against him.

Loving understanding has a great transforming power. A leader must be a transformer.

In the life of a leader, all his forces must move in the same direction. If it is a leadership group, all the forces of the members must move in the same direction. This is one of the greatest challenges of a leader or of a leadership group. All physical, emotional, mental, and spiritual forces must not conflict with each other. All expressions of these forces must be goal-fitting, going toward the same summit, though in different ways, by different means, and at different speeds.

No man and no group can be successful if they are divided in their goal and have conflict within themselves. "A house divided within itself cannot endure" and cannot be useful for the Plan of the Hierarchy.

A leader must teach and demonstrate in his life pure integrity. He must expand the consciousness of the group and let them see the need, the goal, and the vision without imposing his will, his ideas, his thoughts, his feelings, and his actions. No group can grow if it is subject to imposition in any degree. Only groups formed by free people can serve the world.

The leader must be careful that the souls entrusted to his care grow wings to fly. Groups of the Future are not formed by the presence of the will of the leader. They are formed around a vision, around a plan. The leader's job is to assist them to see the plan and the vision in the way they can, in the degree they can, and then take voluntary actions to serve the plan and to achieve the vision. Once they grow wings to fly, the leader must, by the power of his beauty, inspire them to harmonize their forces and labor to create a symphony.

The leader must always stand detached. The leader does not favor. He must not be too eager to increase his *followers*. Followers will increase his headaches. He does not need followers. He needs those who have a vision and want to work for the vision. It is the magnetism, the wisdom, the purity, the beauty of the leader that must attract people, not his personality or his "power."

Those who come for your personality will damage the growth of your service.

In any group meeting do not argue with those who come to you with personality interests. They will spread a low vibration over the group and obscure its light. Cut short such arguments and direct their attention to striving and self-improvement.

Do not talk politics in your classes. Do not discuss things you do not know. Do not try to impose your political opinions on anyone. Emphasize striving, service, goodness, and right human relations.

Do not ever attempt to make people conform to your religion, church, or ideology. Leave them alone; let them decide their own path. You teach them the Teaching of discrimination and enlightenment through service and meditation. Once they are enlightened they will find their own way that fits them. Do not interfere with their karma. Show them summits of achievements, and let them strive. *Summits create crises.* Crises eventually bring a person to the right path, to the summit. Discipleship is the response to the summit.

Leadership is not for a specific direction. It is inspiration, vision, plan, purpose. The rest must be decided by the individual. "With human hands and feet" the Temple will be built.

Leadership is creativity. The leader is creative; he inspires people to creativity. Creativity is the ability to unfold one's Self and to cause others to unfold their Selves. Creativity is the ability to find those new ways and means through which the Plan of the Hierarchy, the highest good for humanity, can find easy ways to materialize.

It is only creativity that conquers the world. When you are creative you are conquering your nature, you are conquering the world. Great Ones are Those Who were creative in Their lives.

Creativity means gradually, step by step, to express your Innermost Self. Man is not created yet. Man can be born if he gives birth to himself. We are living as physical, emotional, and mental bodies. Creativity is the gradient expression of your Divinity.

Great arts are the expression of the inner mystery in man. If that is not being expressed, all that is done is imitation. All art has one great goal: to bring out this Inner Divinity in man. Great Ones such as Hermes, Da Vinci, and Plato gave birth to their own Divinity.

The expression of your genuine Self is your art. Divinity is going to be born through you; this is the mystery of Christ. He was Divinity and manhood at the same time. Eventually the man is replaced, taken over by the Godhood.

Through creativity we make ourselves permanently shining lights through which the light can pour down. Only creativity can change the world.

Because creativity is related to our consciousness and its relation to our Innermost Self, we must strive to come into closer contact with our Innermost Core, giving expression to that Core through creativity.

Creativity is the expression of Divinity through any form.

The greatest creativity is to create yourself. Destroy what you are, and create yourself anew.

The Kingdom of God is the kingdom of blueprints, plans, purposes, and ideas. To enter that kingdom you must be born again because, until you are created anew, you will not be able to enter into that kingdom.

The leader or a leadership group must make a breakthrough in a larger group, and it will be possible to do this if the focus is on creativity, through penetrating into deeper meanings, into deeper and deeper visions.

A creative leader is a mountain spring. He is always fresh and pure. He brings the heart of the mountain, the refreshment of the heights, and the fragrance of flowers.

Creativity is the power of sublimation, transformation, and transfiguration. The leader's achievements and creativity inspire you and challenge you to unfold and be creative.

Our spiritual independence is achieved in the degree that we free ourselves from our personality interests. As long as we are slaves of our personality interests we cannot be independent agents of service; and one who is not independent cannot cooperate with the Hierarchical Plan.

The leader always stands for the Plan. The Plan is the Plan of love and light, increasing inclusiveness, harmony, unity, knowledge, experience, and Self-actualization in all departments of human endeavor.[2]

We must not have the feeling that the leader is a sweet, goody-goody person. He is stern; he is tempered by pain by suffering; he knows the depth of human misery; he is firm; he knows where the enemy can attack and how he attacks. But above all, he has faith in his destiny.

The leader conquers through his solemnity, through his strength, through his knowledge, through his magnanimity. In his presence people feel and realize their

---

2. See also *The Science of Meditation*, Ch. XXX.

vanity. They drop their armor because of the internal conflict which the beauty of the leader creates in them.

The leader is tolerant and forgiving, but the energy through which he tolerates and forgives turns within you into a source of turmoil, in which you eventually meet yourself in utter sincerity. Thus in fiery crisis you change your life.

The leader creates crisis within you, so that you meet your Self. You question yourself, and you open yourself to the sunshine and come out into expression as you are in your essential Self.

The progress of the human being is based on his ability to tune to the Divine Plan and the Divine Will. The Divine Will is the highest good for all humanity, and the leader stands for that Will.

Christ once said, "If anyone wants to find himself, he must lose himself." To lose oneself is to lose the attachments which tie you to your past and to the problems of the past. To lose yourself means to master all those urges and drives in your nature which work against your progress and perfection. In group formation the "wills" of these urges and drives must melt away to make the highest good of the group manifest, without violating your free choice or discrimination.

"To lose yourself" does not mean to surrender yourself to those who will exploit you for their own interests. On the contrary, a man "loses himself" to find his Self. He is a man who, because of being able to find his Self, is now able to see the traps of those who are anxious to exploit him.

"To find oneself" is a state of consciousness where a man is totally Self-actualized and Self-determined. No longer does his lower self rule him. No longer do the interests of those who are attached to their lower selves rule him. He has independence, and because of the purity of the note he sounds, he can be a part of the symphony.

A leader does not associate himself with a commonplace life. His time is very valuable; every drop of his energy counts. He resigns from many pleasures and experiences greater joy. He detaches from his personality reactions, likes and dislikes, and works for the Plan. Thus, gradually a true leader disappears in the labor of the Plan and turns into the Plan.

Christ emphasized this idea when He said, "Not My will but Thine be done."

The Teaching says,

> *The more ignorant a person or a nation is, the less cooperation is in evidence.*[3]

This can even be seen in the human mechanism. An ignorant man causes disturbances within his threefold nature by living a life against the natural laws. An ignorant man does not want to cooperate. He thinks that through cooperation he loses his grip upon objects. This is not true. We see in this age that through cooperation one grows because his individual labor is multiplied by the labor of many thousands of people. The enjoyment of the fruits of labor is greater in group formation than in isolation. The group provides those conditions in which the enjoyment of the fruits of the labor is perpetuated.

But again, cooperation is not possible when people cannot see the group or national welfare beyond their selfish interests, or the global welfare beyond national interests. Cooperation can be achieved with steady advancement in freedom from the past ways of life.

---

3. Agni Yoga Society, *Letters of Helena Roerich*, Vol. I, p. 47.

The Future is the age of group consciousness, group welfare — not groups of people but groups of nations. Feeling the inevitable labor of the great offering of the age, one must prepare himself to cooperate with the forces of the Future. This is not mysterious astrology. This is the demand of life. Life demands urgently the spirit of cooperation if the Planetary Life is going to survive and reach greater achievements.

The Teaching continues:

Each instructor must realize completely his responsibility for making a correct interpretation of the first principles.[4]

Principles are those foundations upon which the structure stands, upon which life continues and reaches a greater capacity for creativity. The esoteric Teaching emphasizes these principles before detailed instructions are given to aspirants. According to the Ageless Wisdom the following are the primary principles:

1. Life is one.

2. Life progresses in cycles.

3. Love nourishes life and gives prosperity and enjoyment.

4. Man can achieve through knowing and awakening into his own reality.

5. The Spark of Life within man is his True Self.

6. The Self is infinite and ever-existent.

---

4. *Ibid.*, p. 50.

7. All forms of life are related to each other through the substance called ether or electricity.

8. Service is the key to unfoldment.

9. Humanity progressively goes toward unity.

10. Harmlessness is the key to freedom and liberation.

11. The road to salvation is discipline and Self-actualization.

These are some of the principles which were emphasized throughout ages in most philosophies and religions. When the Teacher does not emphasize these life-giving principles, his students fall into the trap of satisfaction and into the feeling that everything will go well as long as they see the Teacher and listen to his knowledge. This is how religious organizations, which supposedly should be fields of self-discipline, striving, and self-sacrificial service, turn into social and political groups.

The leader is an "alarm" which calls others to the labor of self-perfection.

It is also necessary to manifest maximum discrimination when you give responsible positions to new warriors.[5]

The Teaching often uses the word "warrior." A warrior is a person who is armed with Beauty, Goodness, Righteousness, Joy, and Freedom and by the power of Spirit. A warrior fights against his own weaknesses and

---

5. *Ibid.*, p. 53.

against all obstacles which hinder his evolution on the Path. He risks his life to do the same thing for others, fighting against crime, corruption, hatred, and against all those conditions which make life a miserable field of destruction.

The warrior must be promoted very slowly so that he does not fall into vanity and wrong actions, hurting his life and the lives of others. The sense of responsibility, experience, and knowledge must go together if a warrior is going to stand for the welfare of others. Those who are promoted fast, without maturity, create a heavy karma for themselves. The Teaching must be presented in its purest form, and the life of the warrior must be an example of harmlessness.

In olden days warriors were tested in their punctuality, alertness, politeness, royalty, solemnity; in keeping their word; in their sensitivity to the need; in their courage, patience, and the spirit of gratitude. They were tested in harmlessness, gentleness, and respect. All were tested, year after year, until one was promoted into higher positions. This is how the Hierarchy works.

You cannot pass into a higher level of Self-actualization or Self-realization by cheating on your exams. Through each test you must prove your transformation. And the test is your everyday life and your every reaction to life.

> *Do not allow outsiders to criticize and condemn any of your co-workers in your presence. . . . Remember that as long as you are united you will be able to pass through all obstacles. . . .*[6]

A co-worker is sacred in the sense that he has dedicated his life to the Lord and to the Common Good. This

---

6. *Ibid.*, pp. 53-54.

does not mean that you keep yourself blind to some wicked weaknesses or failures of your co-workers. On the contrary, you must be the first one to know about them, but you must not allow people to influence your judgment, your actions, or your clear thinking.

Very often we hurt a co-worker because we listen to some criticism by someone who has a wrong motive, hatred, some desire for revenge, or jealousy. A warrior protects his friends because it is through the help of his friends that the spiritual mission can be accomplished.

The duty of the warrior is not do condemn, belittle, or criticize but to make his co-workers mature, bloom, and meet the standards of true servers.

> *Always try to find worthy words with which to stop evil-speaking and condemnation — for this you will receive respect.*[7]

This is exactly what a true leader does. He sees the beauty in his co-workers in spite of temporary failures. He emphasizes the beauty in them, stands by them, and encourages them to improve themselves.

> *Beware of co-workers with small consciousnesses, as the small consciousness will try to belittle everything.*[8]

A small consciousness is the mind with narrow viewpoints, a mind of selfish interests, a mind which has no ability to synthesize, to penetrate, to understand the larger issues of life. A small consciousness is always interested in himself. He is also the puppet of someone.

---

7. *Ibid.*, pp. 53-54.
8. *Ibid.*

A small consciousness has no capacity to meditate, create, research, or show endurance and patience.

A small consciousness is like a butterfly which jumps from one object to another, judging and condemning people with the measure of his own interests. A small consciousness is fanatic and cannot see existing possibilities beyond his stagnated pool of knowledge and information. Such people are dangerous people, especially when they are promoted into responsible positions.

In some organizations people are promoted to higher positions not because of their beingness or expanding consciousness but because of the money they give to the organization. This will have a detrimental effect on the life of the ideas on which the organization was founded. Those who cannot persist in meditation and show it in their creative life by manifesting Beauty, Goodness, Righteousness, Joy, and Freedom must not be promoted because of their donations.

Co-measurement is a quality which is most difficult and necessary to achieve.... [9]

Co-measurement is the requisite of a co-worker or a leader. A leader cannot exist without having the ability of co-measurement.

Co-measurement is an ability to have a balanced outlook about the realities and facts of life. It is an ability to measure things in such a way that you find the right solution to your problem. Co-measurement is the ability to handle people and use your words at the right time and in the right place for the right task.

---

9. *Ibid.*, p. 92.

Co-measurement is the ability to see the Divine Plan and the world situation, and to know exactly what steps should be taken to help humanity.

> ...Without it [co-measurement], it is impossible either to advance or to construct. The Teaching states that without the quality of co-measurement a person cannot be considered spiritual.[10]

Some leaders or heads of religious, philosophic, or educational organizations have an overprotective attitude toward their followers, students, or devotees. They think that their followers will be trapped in different beliefs or philosophies. This kind of attitude creates limitations in the minds of the followers and eventually makes them either fanatics or rebels.

The greatest protection a leader can give to his co-workers is to provide a central principle, a vision, a great beauty, a great human cause, a great value that can embody in itself the aspirations and dreams of those who want to study with him or try to be his co-workers. It is value that focuses the attention of the students and does not let them be trapped in values which do not satisfy their advancing soul.

The wise leader does not become crystallized in presenting the same value. As the students grow, the leader gradually expands the value and makes it a thousand-petaled Lotus, in which each petal stands for one value and the whole Lotus presents an infinite value for the aspirants. Such a leader never fails to affirm values presented by others. He teaches his aspirants the power of discrimination and leaves them free to find the value in its many expressions.

---

10. *Ibid.*, pp. 92-93.

A wise leader does not form a group or an organization for the worship of his personality or to entrap people within his own interpretation. He forms the group to serve more efficiently the Plan of the Hierarchy. He reveals or focuses the part of the Plan to be worked out by the group, if the members can see the goal and are ready for it. He explains the blueprint, the requirements for the laborers, and the time limit and cycle, and then waits for their understanding and approval. Once it is understood and approved, the plan and the discipline of the leader become the labor for everyone involved in the vision.

Plan is not vision; the plan is one part of the vision. The vision is capable of expanding and affecting the plan with new changes. If the plan remains static, it turns into a limitation.

Protection for the co-workers in the plan cannot be offered by outside means and warnings. The only protection is the sense of value, sometimes called "the esoteric sense," which means to see things as they are and the future effects they can have on humanity.

Leaders of Ashramic groups must be very careful not to encourage or allow people to join them with wrong motives. One of the wrong motives for joining is to create disunity.

As our machinery changes year after year, so the techniques of the dark forces change continuously. At the present they use three main techniques of which leaders must be extremely careful.

1. They praise your Teacher or your Master very highly to gain your confidence. Then after they gain your confidence, they slowly attack your co-workers, pointing out some of their weak points. Thus, they slowly and continuously create a subjective cleavage between you and the one to whom the attacks are directed. When this

is done, they secretly speak with the victim and try to create tension in him against you.

2. The second technique is flattery, which they use to gain your confidence or that of your co-workers. Once they see that you are weakened by flattery, they speak about your ambitions and stretch your imagination for greater work beyond your capacities. During such a process, they study your weaknesses and penetrate into your private life. Once they reach there, you will have a hard time to detach yourself from them.

3. The third technique is to approach with admiration for your Teacher and Teaching but slowly distort the Teaching with their words and writings and cause serious confusion in the minds of those who are not familiar with the fundamentals. These people use flattery, bribery, gifts, doubt, hypocrisy, and sex to trap you. They approach the Teaching on the surface, but in their depth they hate it.

Ashramic groups must watch for these signs.
Who are the Ashramic groups?

- Those who are led by a person who is a conscious member of one of the Ashrams in the subjective planes.

- Those who study the Teaching given by Great Ones.

- Those who are guided by a special Teacher for a special plan.

Dark forces literally hate such groups and want to disband them because it is these groups that eventually will terminate their existence on earth.

Dark forces have their agents everywhere on our path. This is why it is suggested that we be vigilant, obey the laws of the country, and exercise purity of mind, heart, speech, and action so that we do not open doors for them through our weaknesses. As long as we stand in the light of the Teaching and practice it in our daily life, dark forces cannot attack us. The only way they can attack us is when we weaken ourselves with our own weaknesses.

At the time of any attack, we are advised to come closer to each other, observe our daily meditation, attend the meetings, and exercise greater striving. These techniques must be carefully observed, and we must reject any kind of flattery, gossip, or closeness with those people whose intentions are doubtful.

A true co-worker manifests an urge to serve, to obey, and to keep his mouth shut. The greatest characteristics of a co-worker are service, meditation, and study.

Ashramic groups are precious to the Hierarchy, and one must be careful to help them grow, expand, and serve.

One of the fundamental rules in group unity is to protect your co-workers against any attack. Any belittling remarks, actions, or suggestions must be considered a part of an organized attack. The enemy does not, at the present, release wholesale attacks. Rather he attacks one-by-one not directly but through the hands of the co-workers. Once an enemy finds success in making a member belittle another member and creates doubts in his mind about the co-worker, he will attack the leader in due time. Doubt and criticism will weaken you, and the sneaky one will wait for the moment when you are confused.

If someone belittles your co-worker directly or indirectly, gossips about him, or criticizes him, you must immediately point out the ugliness that he has in his heart and warn him to try not to belittle himself in serving a dark cause. Sometimes it is necessary to keep silent to watch him and see how safe he feels to advance, but never affirm his remarks, criticism, gossip, slander, or malice.

Often it is important to recite verses from the Teaching at the moment of such attacks. For example:

> "The most powerful force which transmutes various energies is the magnet of the heart. All currents are transmuted by this magnet."

> "You know that Agni lives in the hearts of those who love the future."

> "People dream of freedom but in what a dungeon they keep their hearts!"

> "Let us speak kindly and scientifically."

> "Dust is harmful to the ears."

> "My shield is a refuge to the pure."

> "My arrows are wings to the faithful."

> "My sword is a Torch to the courageous."

> "My smile is the promised bliss to the wise."

> "My heart is the abode."

You can repeat such or similar phrases from the Teaching when someone tries to attack your co-workers, Teacher, or Teaching.

It is known that dark forces who use people to attack co-workers are terrified when they hear the words of a Great One because every word of a Great One, when rightly used, carries a tremendous fire that makes the dark force retreat and even leave you free forever. This was exactly the case with Christ. During His temptation, He used words of the Teaching to combat evil.

Some people think that group consciousness is achieved in communes or community living. This is an illusion. When a number of people unite with each other for their private interests, they form a commune.

Communes are separative, and they do not present group consciousness. Group consciousness does not allow a man or a group of people to disassociate themselves from humanity, from the world, from life.

Communes consider themselves better than other people. They separate themselves from the rest of humanity to save themselves, as if they were more precious than all other human beings who toil and labor and serve in their own fields with the sense of duty and responsibility.

The ultimate goal of the Teaching is the salvation of humanity. By escaping from humanity, no one fulfills this goal.

Communes eventually create in their members stagnation, egoism, and a hostile attitude toward the rest of humanity.

If people come together for higher education and spiritual practice, to perfect and make themselves ready for the service of humanity, such a group can stay healthy. It becomes like a healthy pool of energy which continuously receives new currents of light and releases light-bearers into the world to carry on the world salvation. Such a group works in a special field of human endeavor or, if it has the Teachers, it works in all seven fields of human endeavor to provide right leadership for each field. Such a group acts as a great university, open to all those who can demonstrate special qualifications.

Civilization can be divided into seven branches:

Politics

Education

Communication

Arts

Science

Religion

Finance-Economics

World salvation will not come through religion or politics only. It will come through all seven branches of human endeavor. Each of them is sacred and spiritual if their aim is to serve humanity and lead humanity into higher and greater achievements.

Communes cannot survive if they are not equipped to become places of discipline, learning, and preparation for service. There is no difference between a separative person and a separative commune. A separative commune eventually turns into a cult which worships itself or its own ideas and viewpoints and becomes "the only way to fly." When the members of a commune develop such an idea of being special, they fall into the trap of self-worship and separatism and look at other people as inferior. It has been noticed that such people have a very difficult time fitting themselves into any community if they leave their commune. Their adjustment is painful and full of rebellion and remorse.

The common person has a sound heart and right judgment. He looks on such "separative," "special," "chosen," or "bestowed" people with suspicious eyes because such people always, at any opportunity, try to exploit or use others for their own separative interests.

The motto of the world server is: "I belong to humanity. I will live with the joys and sufferings of humanity and will bring my share to the great labor of the redemption of humanity."

In working with co-workers, the Leader must try to do the following things:

1. Encourage them to improve things in their being after they see their shortcomings.

2. Give them hints to look more closely at their actions, words, and thoughts with the eye of an observer.

3. Make them understand that they must work for their own salvation with their own hands and feet and that no one can achieve mastery for them.

4. Let them see their vanities, show-offs, and forcefulness, as well as their exact level — what exactly they are and how the impositions of their personalities work against their spiritual progress.

5. Make them feel that they must gradually build their plan for their future field of service. Such a plan must not be suggested by the leader but must come from their own core. Through various ways and means, the leader must make the co-workers feel that he is also a traveler on the Path and that his relations with them are just to share the experience of the Path.

6. At certain times try to make them see the toys they are playing with and realize that they are no longer six-year-old children but adults. The leader must make them see how they cry and panic about things to which they are attached, just as children do. He must try to

bring them to the realization that they are adults physically and that they must have a parallel growth spiritually.

7. Try to evoke from their souls a spirit of obedience. The degree of the spiritual achievement of a disciple is equal to the degree of his obedience:

    a. to his Soul or the core of his being

    b. to his Master

    c. to the Plan, which reveals the need and shows the vision of the future

    d. to the directions of the Higher Worlds

Evolution as a whole is a progressive learning, understanding, and application of the meaning of obedience. The highest virtue on all planes is obedience to the pull of the Cosmic Magnet. It is obedience that brought out all manifestation. The path of return is also the path of obedience.

Obedience is the purest sensitivity to the directions coming from Higher Sources. Such a sensitivity is the result of agelong striving for obedience. When your fingers obey, when your feet obey, when your mouth obeys the inner directions, you are healthy. Otherwise there are cleavages in your nature.

In a complicated machine, the parts obey in exact detail the duties programmed for them, or else the machine either does not work or destroys itself. The human brain, the nervous system, and the glands are symbols of obedience. Imposition is not obedience because to be obedient one must develop the sensitivity to respond. We read that the members of the Hierarchy have a highly developed sense of obedience to Their Superiors, duties, and world needs.

8. Try to develop the sense of beauty in the co-workers. The sense of beauty is a spiritual sense. The development of this sense is urgently needed for the survival of the individual and humanity and for their ever-advancing transformation.

We have within us the sense of beauty. When it is developed and becomes active, it can discover beauty, create beauty, and enjoy objects or forms of beauty. Beauty is a form registered by our various senses. Beauty builds a harmonious relationship between the Purpose and Plan of life and the striving human being.

In each human being, a part of the Great Mystery is reflected. In considering beauty and expressing admiration and joy, one touches the sphere where the Plan exists and, through the Plan, the sphere where the Purpose exists. The sense of beauty finds the Plan and Purpose through beauty.

Beauty is a link between the Purpose of the Great Life and the striving Spark in man. Without beauty, man will not find the way out of the labyrinth of life. Without beauty, man will wander on self-destructive paths.

Beauty is recognized with our instincts, emotions, thoughts, and Intuition; but it is assimilated by the *sense of beauty*. Every contact with beauty makes us desire to strive higher than what we are, if we have developed the sense of beauty. Higher culture presents such a possibility.

Those forms which do not fulfill this definition slowly vanish after serving the vanity of their creators. Those forms of beauty which reflect Higher Worlds and evoke in man a striving last long.

Beauty in Nature, where no human foot steps, has its role, too. Intelligent Forces in the Universe enjoy creating beauty and letting it build links between the two worlds. Even a flower in the desert has a destiny to focus certain energies and create joy in Space.

The sense of beauty is a reflection in the astral and mental planes of the *sense of beatitude* existing on the first sub-plane of the Atmic Plane. When one occupies himself with beauty and discovers the reflections of the sense of beatitude in the emotional and mental planes, eventually he finds the way for direct communication with the sense of beatitude in the atmic vehicles. Slowly he feels the currents of bliss, exaltation, transcendence, rapture, and ecstasy coming from the sense of beatitude.

In reality, beauty is a condensed form of bliss, exaltation, and rapture.

9. Try to encourage co-workers to develop the sense of discrimination about the Teaching. Only after knowing the true Teaching can they dedicate themselves to the Teaching. What is the true Teaching? The true Teaching for our planet is filtered through the rays of the Sun. Its source is the Central Spiritual Sun.[11]

The true Teaching may be recognized by its fruits. "By its fruits you will know"

- Enlightenment
- Deeper love
- Inclusiveness
- Freedom
- Joy
- Cooperation, brotherliness
- Selflessness, the spirit of synthesis

---

11. See *The Psyche and Psychism* Chs. 41-43, and *The Ageless Wisdom* for information on what is the Teaching.

- Vision, future
- Practicality
- Harmony with the Hierarchical Plan
- Mastery

Enlightenment means to know better what you are, what you are doing, what you can be and do in the future; to have increasing awareness of the laws of Nature and an increasing ability to expand your consciousness through the study and application of these laws.

Deeper love means compassion and love expanding to all of Creation.

Inclusiveness is the ability to harmonize and orchestrate your thoughts in such a way that you use every possible "note" to build your symphony around the core of beauty.

Spiritual *freedom* is gained through suffering, joy, and labor. Freedom is the ability not to be used by separative and self-seeking forces, glamors, illusions, and vanities.

Joy is the ability to remain as a soul and look at things as your servants helping your evolution.

Cooperation and *brotherliness* refer to cooperation with Beauty, Goodness, Righteousness, Joy, and Freedom. You must have brotherliness especially with those who are on the path of self-transformation and service.

Selflessness is the spirit of synthesis. When people use the Teaching to advertise themselves, their self-interests, their racial or national interests, their "isms" and "ologies," they are thieves in the field. The Teaching has no purpose to be used for selfish interests. It is only for the benefit of all.

When a law or wisdom is used to advertise or make propaganda about a separative interest, it is called spiritual prostitution; this is a cardinal sin. The true Teaching does not produce such rotten fruits.

The true Teaching gives *vision*. People who have the true Teaching have vision; they have future; they have hope. Vision, future, and hope are the three energies of the Cosmic Magnet as far as the human being is concerned.

The true Teaching must be *practical*. It must cause changes and transformation in our lives, families, and environments. It must be able to be translated into the seven fields of human endeavor.

The true Teaching must be *harmonious with the Plan* of the Hierarchy. The Plan shows all the ways and means by which one can create the Highest Good for humanity and for its future.

Mastery is the flowering of higher powers...to be used only in the service of the Hierarchy.

The Leader should have the following expectations from his co-workers:

— Gratitude

— Solemnity

— The spirit of obedience to higher values

— Labor to serve and do something for their fellow beings in whatever way they choose, inspired by Beauty, Goodness, Righteousness, Joy, and Freedom, the five-pointed star of the Initiate.

12
Cooperation

Cooperation is a great discipline because in the process of cooperation we surpass our self-seeking ways, our self-interests, and our ego and we try to recognize the interests of the group as a whole. The principle of cooperation underlies all existence and pushes everything toward right and harmonious relationship.[1]

In cooperation, three or more people operate or work together to achieve a goal upon which they have agreed. Cooperation is the foundation of health, happiness, success, survival, and achievement on various levels.

Cooperation is an undercurrent which leads all forms of life to operate cooperatively to manifest potentialities within man and in Nature. Cooperation leads to

---

1. See also *The Psychology of Cooperation and Group Consciousness*.

integration, groupings, and alignment with higher sources of energy and guidance. It eventually makes people, groups, nations, and humanity transcend themselves.

Cooperation can be carried out in various ways and in many fields. Cooperation needs a common goal which is beneficial for those who cooperate and agree with it.

Cooperation needs a special skill and knowledge according to the field and the goal. The deeper the knowledge and the better the skill, the greater is the success of cooperation.

Cooperation needs concentration and focus, or dedication to the goal and application of skill not affected by personality interests.

Cooperation must be progressive as goal after goal is achieved.

Cooperation is a process of forgetting oneself in the group Self and group interest.

Cooperation cannot be carried on without firm control upon personal likes and dislikes, vanity, showing off, and hurt feelings.

Cooperation must be not only progressive but also inclusive. It must include larger and larger groups striving for the same basic goal.

In cooperation, everyone must have his own task and perform it within the vision of the whole work. Noninterference is a very essential attitude. In cooperation, encouragement is also a very essential factor.

Cooperation is a form of composing a symphony in which every note has its distinct position and its duty to complete the vision of the other notes of the symphony.

In cooperation, it is not the individual who is glorified but the group.

In every cooperative labor there exists a leader who attracts the co-workers by the magnet of a plan. As the work proceeds, he turns into a source of inspiration and courage. Eventually, when the goal is achieved, he tries to raise the labor of cooperation onto a higher level where more sacrificial and more focused labor is needed. A true leader inspires co-workers to lead themselves toward the goal through the path of the most essential.

On every level of development, cooperation is possible. But progressive and inclusive cooperation is possible only when the labor of cooperation becomes the outer manifestation of an inner process of cooperation.

The inner process of cooperation has four steps:

1. Integration between the physical, emotional, and mental natures

2. Alignment with the creative Source in one's being

3. Synthesis of one's actions, feelings, thoughts, ideas, goals, and purpose in life

4. Striving to contact planetary and solar group activities in order to cooperate with them

What Does Cooperation Do?

1. Cooperation saves time, energy, money, and matter.

2. Cooperation guarantees success.

3. Cooperation puts into action the potentials found in the group.

4. Cooperation teaches the science of adaptation.

5. Cooperation makes man progress and surpass his personality, personality problems, and attachments; it makes him grow into maturity and

achieve a certain degree of victory over his lower nature.

6. In the process of cooperation, one clearly sees the factors within himself which present obstacles for cooperation.

7. In cooperation there should be no pressure. No one must be forced by anyone to do his task. Cooperation rests on freedom. Co-workers must come together not by pressure of any kind but by the urge of their hearts and by the awareness of the plan and the need. Any display of force by any co-worker makes the spirit of cooperation impossible and creates resistance, cleavages, and other problems.

8. In cooperation, future mistakes, to a certain degree, are eliminated.

9. In cooperation, a magnetic field is created to draw new currents of inspirations and impressions.

10. In cooperation, the fire of the spirit is kindled and made a powerful agent to overcome obstacles and make new breakthroughs.

11. In cooperation, a fusion is accomplished between the etheric, astral, mental, and spiritual natures of the co-workers.

12. If cooperation is carried on for personality advantages, for selfish interests, or to please certain people, it fails. This is because in cooperation, four levels of man must cooperate and synchronize:

a) the level of purpose

b) the level of thought

c) the level of feelings and emotions

d) the level of action

Such a fusion provides the possibility of future cooperation in higher fields of human existence. Every organ in man is the result of cooperation between cells. Man is the result of the cooperation of many elements. Galaxies are the result of cooperation. Existence is the result of cooperation. Lack of cooperation is chaos. If cooperation is carried out in the right way, it eventually involves higher kingdoms or higher energy spheres from which come greater guidance and greater wisdom.

Cooperation is the meaning and energy source of evolution. Everything in Nature tends toward cooperation. Nature exists because of the cooperation of matter, energy, time, space, plan, and purpose. Nothing exists in the Universe which is not the result of cooperation.

Cooperation brings things into existence. Lack of cooperation becomes the cause of the chaos and destruction of things that exist.

The human being exists as a result of the cooperation of the elements of which he is composed. Atoms, cells, emotions, thoughts, plan, soul, and other factors cooperate and create the human being. No human being, no family, and no nation exists without the principle of cooperation acting within them.

The whole existence is the result of cooperation. If the whole does not follow the principle of cooperation, existence will vanish in time and space.

Progress, success, health, happiness, and great achievements are the results of cooperation. When a few people cooperate, there is success, prosperity, protection, and stability. If a few families cooperate, there is greater success. If nations cooperate, there is yet greater success and prosperity; but they need to learn one lesson: renunciation of their selfish interests in the interest of the whole of humanity.

Health is the result of cooperation of elements and systems in the body with the elements and factors in the environment. Health does not exist if there is no cooperation of the body with the emotions and mind. Diseases, ailments, and sicknesses are the result of lack of cooperation between the body, emotions, and thoughts.

If history is read carefully, it will be seen that the disintegration, destruction, and disappearance of nations has been the result of lack of cooperation — cooperation with Nature, cooperation with other nations, and cooperation within their own selves.

Cooperation must start within ourselves. We must try to create a cooperation within our systems and within our emotional and mental natures. Then we must make them a unit to cooperate with the goals we set and with the purpose in the vision of our Inner Guardian. We have a Trinity within us:

- The Inner Guardian
- The human soul
- The human personality (formed by our physical, emotional, and mental natures)

Those who have good cooperation within their whole system can be the cornerstones of groups which produce cooperation in the world.

You cannot really cooperate with other people unless you have cooperation within your system. Thus, an integrated and Soul-infused personality is a great powerhouse and foundation of cooperation.

If you bring three people together and observe the quality of their cooperation, you will find that those who have good cooperation within their own nature also have good cooperation with their associates and friends.

Once I was talking with a prison officer. I asked him, "What is your observation about the prisons in general?"

He said something very astonishing, "If you dig into the lives of the prisoners, you will find that the majority of them are coming from families or environments where cooperation between people was absent. A child who does not see cooperation at home will have a hard time learning it later in society."

Thus the foundation of cooperation is the cooperation between the parts of your nature. If you have such cooperation, you will create cooperation in your family, business, group, and society.

Cooperation can be developed if you try to think, feel, and act simultaneously. Most people think one way, feel another way, and act another way. This means that they have cleavages in their nature. To have cleavages in one's nature, in one's family and society, means that the unit is not healthy. The health of the three natures produces sanity and cooperation. Sanity is also pro-survival. Insanity is anti-survival.

A man was having trouble with his wife. His wife told me, "He is only a brain and muscles, or knowledge and action. He has no feeling at all, and I hate him."

I talked with the man and said to him, "You are going to develop feeling, or else your family life is in danger."

"Why?" he asked, "I provide money, food, sex. . . ."

"But you must also have feeling. Your wife needs to see that you are not a machine and that you have feeling."

He understood, and for six months I gave him a certain meditation to develop feeling for his wife, children, and Nature in general. After one year, he came to my office to say, "I have only one question for you. Can you tell me how I lived thirty-five years without feeling?"

"The answer is very simple," I said with humor, "you were dead, not alive. Now you are alive."

"I guess so. . . ."

All three parts of one's nature must be cultivated and balanced. I learned this by watching a girl who was having trouble making friends with many boys. She had a good head, a good body, but no heart strangely enough.

Only when you have cooperation within you do you have an impact on the world. People divided within themselves bring misery and death everywhere, and they vanish under the ruins of their destruction.

Society says that everyone must take care only of himself. Such advice has been given for a long time, and it led to bad results because it led people to self-interest. The new command will be that everyone must take care of one another.

You must not love your neighbor as you love yourself; you must love your neighbor *more* than yourself, if you want the world to survive. This is the foundation of the new race, the future race. If we love ourselves more than our neighbors, we will eventually annihilate the life on this unfortunate globe. This is where we are now.

Cooperation makes the planetary creative and constructive forces help you; but if you do not cooperate, you will fight against these forces. Eventually these forces will grind you and turn you into dust to be used for other kinds of future pottery.

Integration and fusion with your Soul reveals the goals of your body. But when you try to cooperate with the Divine Presence, you will know about the purpose of your life. Why do you need integration, health, happiness, joy, and freedom? For what purpose? You will find your purpose in the light of your inner, Divine Presence.

If you do this, you will be a purposeful human being. You will evoke purpose in other human beings and help them live a purposeful life. Unless one finds his purpose, he is lost.

In cooperation every group has its own goal, but groups must come together to find the common purpose of all goals. It is only after the common purpose is defined that cooperation between all groups is possible.

Without purpose, goals will conflict. Without goals, people will fight against each other or inertia will prevail. Unless the goals are beneficial and meet the requirements of the Common Good, no cooperation is possible. This is very important. The first guarantee of achieving a success in any goal is that the goal must be really good for all human beings, everywhere.

Of course, one will not expect to have the cooperation of the enemies of mankind, but the final victory belongs to those who really formulate goals that are for the whole human welfare. Partial goals, partisan goals, goals based on separative interests, do not survive very long. Whatever was built under these conditions will fall upon the builder's head.

Personality cooperation is *materialistic*. Personality and Solar Angel cooperation leads to extremist activities. Personality and human soul and Solar Angel cooperation creates progressive, balanced cooperation. Cooperation between people and groups must follow the same procedure: There must be three or more in order to create cooperation.

It takes ages to bring together the personality and the Soul. After they contact, for ages the personality is fanatic, or the human being lives a "spaced" life. Until the third factor emerges, there will be no equilibrium. The third factor is the human soul, which takes birth within the cooperation of the personality and the Inner Guide.

There are millions of groups in the world with millions of goals. Each goal is a different direction and can be an antagonistic or conflicting goal in relation to the others. This is why we have so much unrest in the world: revolutions, wars, massive exploitation, and crimes.

The ultimate destination of cooperation is to create a common goal for all these goals. This goal is called the purpose. Unless people see the purpose existing beyond their goals, they cannot grow further.

This is like climbing a mountain: hundreds of people climb the mountain and use different paths to reach the summit. If reaching the summit is the purpose, they will all meet on the summit.

First, people must have goals in order to start learning cooperation. The purpose is the highest magnet which brings goals together to make them cooperate with each other. If there is no purpose, goals can culminate in global tension because they cannot see the vision; they cannot see what they are going to accomplish.

This is the situation in the world today. Every nation has a goal, but they do not have the awareness of the purpose. The purpose is the Common Good without any exclusion.

It is not enough to have a goal for cooperation. You need skills or knowledge to fit yourself to that goal. If you have a goal but no knowledge and skill, you destroy the goal which you are trying to actualize.[2]

In order for any cooperation to be successful, you need to take your personality interest out of it. If you are building a goal and cooperating with it only for your self-interest, the cooperation will fail because others will

---

2. See also *The Purpose of Life*.

either not tolerate your actions or they will do the same as you are doing.

Cooperation is renouncing your self-interest and working for the interests of all who are laboring for that cooperation.

Discipline is related to getting rid of the ego, which seeks only his own interest at the expense of the interests of others. By working in a cooperative spirit, we eventually see the following factors and ask ourselves:

— What are those things in me which are creating obstacles for cooperation?

— Are these factors mental? Emotional? Physical?

— Are they a lack of knowledge? A lack of skill? A lack of interest?

Any group or any committee is successful when the people in the committee or the group keep their self-interest out of the work and focus on the interest of the group as a whole — which includes the individual interest. People can fit together and work together only if they renounce their self-interest for the good of the group and for the purpose of the group.

Many businesses fail because people act in ways that profit their own separate self rather than the business. We can also see this in the international field of politics. For example, many nations try to exploit the United Nations for their own interest. The United Nations is not yet successful in the desired degree because many nations are not forgetting their own self-interest in the interest of all nations and of all people.

The goal is to cooperate with each other to bring understanding and reach the purpose of cooperation — which is prosperity, health, happiness, freedom, joy, and universal peace. This is accomplished by forgetting separative interests in the all-inclusive interest of all nations.

Cooperation works in atoms, cells, forms, families, groups, nations, and stars. It is the undercurrent of progressive achievements on all levels. This can be very clearly seen in family formation. If one family member is selfish and therefore cannot cooperate with other members, that family suffers and fails.

Cooperation means to find a common denominator in which everyone shares the benefits without imposing self-interest, superiority, expectations, or separative goals. The hindrance of all committees or groups trying to reach a goal is a member who forces or imposes himself with a motive of self-interest. That self-interest is either to gain position, recognition, or the emotional satisfaction of superiority in showing off.

Discipline means to cooperate in self-forgetfulness and act in harmony with the goal of the group, family, or nation. You can see the best cooperative drama in the configurations of stars and galaxies. Not one of them violates the space of the others; if it does, it brings destruction to itself. Cosmos means that everything fits everything else for a common purpose.

Cooperation must be progressive. This means that cooperation must go deeper into the emotional, mental, and spiritual realms of those who cooperate with each other. This makes the whole group very powerful and extremely successful because it cleanses all obstacles existing in its threefold nature.

Cooperation must also become inclusive. Success and power are very dangerous energies unless they are shared by increasing numbers of groups.

Thus we see that in the history of humanity successful families formed a successful nation. Successful nations must form a successful united nations; successfully united nations must form a global humanity. But each expansion is carried out by the renunciation of a certain amount of self-interest. Every nation is created by families who tried to find a common goal.

Cooperation works in all departments of human endeavor. Any success in any field is the result of cooperation. For example, communication is a great cooperative effort in the world. Through communication, we see how distant nations and areas come close to each other and how everyone becomes aware of what the rest of the world is doing. Thus communication makes us realize that the cleavages between all nations must vanish through cooperative efforts.

Religions were created to teach people to cooperate with each other and with the message or the will of the Creator or the Illuminator. But they became islands within themselves. Religions have had their goals — economic, political, and spiritual goals; but what is the real goal of religion? If religions find that common goal or the Supreme Purpose of all religions, they will create international or global cooperation and thus achieve a greater result than what they could achieve before with their non-cooperative attitude.

In the past, religions hated each other. At the present, there is a strong effort among religions to see each other's values and cooperate for a common goal. Religions have goals, but the purpose of *religion* is to be one — to make all people communicate with the Source of Light, Love, and Power.

In the future, if a person is going to move even a stone, he must study the influence of that move on the common interest! Everything done against the common interest will be counted as a severe violation of the law.

Every human being and every nation should have the privilege to survive, to be prosperous, and to be enlightened. This will not be possible until cooperation is established in our consciousness. Thus, in cooperation we eliminate all those factors which do not fit the Common Good.

Cooperation is like a gearing process. If a gear does not fit, there is something wrong with that gear, and it must be modified or removed so that all the gears can function. All forms of creation are separate gears. Cooperation is the science of adapting these gears to each other so that the One System of the universal gear is in operation.

In the universal gear, all will share each other's labors, and their needs will be met abundantly because in cooperation there is economy and economy is the source of abundance.

In all forms, the principle of cooperation is a progressive movement toward the future and toward greater achievements. Health can be defined as the result of cooperation between all that is the body, emotion, and thought. Every sickness is the result of lack of cooperation. Hospitals and prisons are nothing else but inefficient efforts to execute the principle of cooperation. To behave properly means to cooperate with others for the Common Good.

In cooperation, you see your needs and the things that are lacking in you to make cooperation successful. Thus, cooperation challenges you to educate and cultivate yourself so that you can be useful in higher and higher fields of cooperation. All your weaknesses will come to the surface when you start to cooperate: your jealousy, selfishness, inferiority or superiority complexes, your vanities, prejudices, etc. If you eliminate them, you will see how the labor of cooperation is bringing you joy and prosperity.

Later we will learn to cooperate with Great Ones in Their plans. Imagine how much greater skill, knowledge, and purity we will need in order to cooperate with Them and not create disturbances in Their great labor.

Once a Christian boy came to me smoking marijuana and asked whether he was saved or not. I said, "You cannot cooperate with Christ with that marijuana in your mouth"

Cooperation is a science, like physics and chemistry. In the future, a book must be written about the science of cooperation. Because we did not teach this science in our schools and colleges, we created a world of competition and exploitation instead of a world of sharing. We see now where this negligence is leading us.

The science of cooperation is like the science of chemistry and physics in the sense that it has its laws and its effects. You combine certain elements to produce another element. The same applies in cooperation. You cannot put this man with that man in a committee and have a good result unless they fit together or adapters are used to make them fit.

Certain elements cannot cooperate with each other until a third element intervenes. Christ gave a scientific formula when He said, "If three of you come together in My name, I will be among you" There are the three persons; there is His name, which is the goal; and there is Christ, the purpose. These three are the representative of light, love, and willpower. These three elements are important for successful cooperation. Three elements must come together with a goal which will lead them to the purpose, symbolized by Christ.

If you have light and willpower only, you become very destructive because you use your knowledge, information, or mind with power without considering the interests of others — which love reveals.

If you have willpower and love only, you become a blind, forceful person with great power behind you. You need light to balance yourself.

If you have love and light without willpower, you will not be progressive and productive, which are the gifts of willpower. Thus a trinity must be formed by the representatives of these three factors. This is why in almost all religions we see the Trinity in different forms to carry out the will of the One in cooperative efforts.

The three energies of light, love, and power create a field of magnetism which makes the group inclusive. Success will come if the number of the members in the original trinity increase in equal proportion and do not disturb the equilibrium of the group by increasing one aspect of the triangle of light, love, and willpower. This is the secret formula of success.

Light is knowledge, skill, information, reason, and logic. Love is magnetism, the bond, the Intuition, the heart. Willpower is the driving force which opens new paths and overcomes hindrances and difficulties on the path of cooperation.

Light synthesizes the arts, science, religion, and economics. Love synthesizes the fields of education and communication. Power represents the field of politics. Thus the triangle is also the symbol of the seven fields of human endeavor. The middle point of the triangle is the Christ, symbolically, the purpose of all seven fields.

As we said, cooperation saves money, energy, time, matter, and suffering. If people cooperate, they will eliminate all duplicate efforts and save time, matter, and energy. Actually, big companies are swallowing small ones or merging with each other in order to survive and be economical. What about if other fields — politics, education, communication, arts, science, religion, and economics — serve only humanity in close cooperation with each other? Billions of hours spent will be saved; energy and matter will be saved; and most of all, those weapons that are sucking the blood of nations will be eliminated as the guardians of self-interest will be eliminated. Once this burden is taken off the shoulders of humanity, we will see the dawn of a superior civilization and cultures never dreamed of before.

Cooperation between nations will save not only money, matter, energy, and time but also precious lives of human beings and of nature. The same is true for families.

Once I was talking with a man who had a wife and three teenagers. I said to him, "If you cooperate with your family, you will save money and avoid lots of misery." He gave a big laugh, but a few months later his wife divorced him because of his drinking habit.

After he was divorced, he visited me and said, "You were right. We spent eighteen thousand dollars fighting for our divorce. And I feel miserable. We lost the respect of our children, and we even lost the children themselves. I guess cooperation would have been less expensive."

Of course, it is also better to save four hundred million lives and massive destruction by creating cooperation among nations rather than entering into a war.

13
Leadership and Assistants

The leader must be very discriminative in choosing his immediate assistants. One of my Teachers used to say that a leader must choose his immediate co-workers after a long time of observation, prayer, and thinking so that he does not regret it later.

For the leader it is a great test to choose the right person for the right duty. He must especially see that the following main characteristics are present in his co-workers:

- Fearlessness

- Peacefulness, or absence of irritation and anger

- Selflessness

- Health

- Absence of flattery

- Honesty

If these characteristics are evident, the individual will make a good assistant and may carry on the work of the leader. The leader must be very alert to change his immediate assistants if he sees any questionable behavior or lack of striving.

Fearlessness helps people see the real issue outside and inside of the group without illusion, exaggeration, and distortion. Fear distorts communication and does not allow contact on reality levels.

Peacefulness is a great quality in which the mind has control of the emotions, interruptions, unpleasant and pleasant impressions, and physical urges and drives. Unless the mind has such a mastery of the emotional, physical, and lower mental planes, there will not be peace. Only a peaceful person can communicate with the leader on the level of facts and realities. If any assistant is disturbed emotionally or mentally, communication will suffer and he will mislead the leader in his contacts.

Selflessness is another quality. Many leaders cannot do a good job because some of their immediate assistants block their direct contact with the public, or distort the communication directed to them, or use various opportunities for their own personal advantages.

Selflessness creates an open channel for the leader to see his field of service as it is and receive communication as it is. Due to self-interest, some assistants do not transmit to the leader the information given to them. They keep some of it for themselves for future use. Such actions make it difficult for the leader to make a decision and take right action.

The leader must have persons around him who can act as pure channels between himself and outer contacts.

Health is also very important. The leader must try to choose assistants who have healthy bodies. Healthy bodies are in most cases reflections of healthy thoughts, emotions, and motives and are indicative of past good karma.

Healthy people increase the efficiency of the service of the leader. Sick people bring in negative moods, depression, tension, irritation, distorted viewpoints or opinions, and hinder the work with their absences.

Absence of flattery is another characteristic. Flattery is a great danger for the leader. Often the advanced leader yields to flattery, especially at times when his energy level is low and burdens are heavy on his shoulders. He must be careful to avoid those who like to flatter and use flattery for self-interest.

Whenever we listen to flattery, we lower our standards and independence and follow the hints of the flatterer.

Flattery, when accepted, turns into vanity in the leader. When a leader is contaminated with vanity he can no longer be used safely in the Plan.

Flatterers are dangerous in the sense that they can be easily influenced by bribery and flattery and eventually cause many complications in the life of the leader and the group he serves.

Easily influenced people are like holes in the boat of the leader. Outside forces can reach him easily through the weak ones.

Flattery is a subtle means to make other people surrender themselves to our selfish interests.

Honesty is a sum total of many virtues, for example loyalty, sincerity, truthfulness, morality, integrity, and so on. An honest person is like a fortress or a treasury for the leader. He is one on whom the leader depends and places his trust. Also, it is the honest assistant who helps the leader keep his equilibrium in daring times.

There are also many negative characteristics about which the leader must be watchful, for example:

— Jealousy

— Depression

— A scattered state of mind

Jealousy creates great tension between the leader and his assistants. The assistant who is jealous continuously sends negative energy to the leader. Eventually he desires the position of the leader or the possessions of the leader. To satisfy his desires a jealous assistant distorts the facts, causes trouble, and creates hindrances to the leader in subtle ways.

A jealous person tries to possess the object of his desire. If he cannot possess it, he tries to destroy it. Jealousy develops greed and ambition. A leader is in danger if he has a jealous assistant. Jealousy in the assistant polarizes the leader negatively. When the conflict comes to the surface, the jealous assistant uses every kind of dishonest means to take over the position of the leader, even at the expense of destroying the field of service he created.

Depression brings great harm to the work and to the magnetism of the leader. It saps the energy produced by the service of the leader. Depressed people channel tamasic force, produce repulsion toward the work, and distort the beneficial currents pouring into the field of service.

Depression leads to irresponsibility and indifference. When an assistant loses his sense of responsibility and interest, he turns into a burden on the shoulders of the leader.

Enthusiasm is a divine fire with which every assistant of the leader must be charged.

A scattered state of mind brings great harm to the work and causes delay, waste of time, energy, and matter. A scattered mind cannot see the overall plan of the leader. Neither can the scattered mind use the technique of service to a satisfactory degree. Once a Sage said that a scattered mind is a basket in which you cannot keep the water of wisdom and knowledge.

A mind which is able to concentrate and focus itself on the given task renders a great service to the leader.

Test your assistants again and again until they prove that they have the six main characteristics and have mastered the three main weaknesses before you promote them to higher levels of responsibility.

One of the most important things a leader must do is to avoid those people who are trying to make a leader depend on them. When a leader is dependent on his workers he easily can be influenced by them, pressured by them, or even controlled by them.

The leader must have three or more people trained for every job so that none of them, by taking advantage of his position, influences the decision of the leader or uses his position for his own interest.

Let us take a secretary who knows all aspects of the office work and rejects anyone else who wants to learn all that she knows. Such a secretary gradually imposes her thoughts and desires upon the leader. She thinks that the leader is forced to keep her because no one else can do her job and the leader has no time to train anybody else.

The leader must be careful that all his co-workers are willing to share their knowledge with others so that in case of vacation, sickness, or resignation the work will not suffer but will go on without interruption.

The leader must impress on the minds of the people that the workers are not as important as the work and, for the work's sake, the leader can sacrifice any worker.

There is another way that a worker can exercise pressure on the leader. Beyond the regular and routine job, he creates different jobs and tries to do all of them to please the leader. The leader, seeing that this one man is doing three or four jobs, feels pleased and becomes careful not to hurt him in anyway. Once the worker feels this, he tries gradually to force his will on the leader.

For example, there was a man in a group who could do almost any job. He started with gardening. After planting many trees, he planted vegetables; then a vineyard; then he tried to build various rooms. Then one day he said, "I need to rest because I cannot do all these without payment." After receiving a good payment, he expanded his field of activity, and it reached a point that the leader could not do anything in that field unless the man was present. Eventually he became the chief director of the leader, and the leader lost his independence.

Loading the leadership with work that is not directly related to the plan of the leadership wastes the energy of the leadership, diffuses its focus and direction, and makes the leadership fail in the "most essentials."

The leadership must be very careful that the expansion of the group or organization is very gradual. First people must be trained for certain jobs, and then the jobs must be provided for them. But if the job is expanded and the workers are not ready, that is the moment when failure starts.

You can make a man fail by loading him beyond his capacity. The same thing can be true of a group. The leadership must be very careful not to be caught by its ambition in work that group members create but are not able to carry out.

Sometimes a group slowly heads toward the waterfall like a boat that moves down the current so slowly that no one can perceive it. A leader who is truly awake must stop the boat when he first feels the danger.

Another mark of a leader is readiness to give up people and sacrifice money to save the group from greater failure and greater expenses. He must not wait or tolerate what goes on if he sees the future danger.

Sometimes pity can play the most dangerous role. Pity makes you forget the interests of a larger number of people in the interest of a single person who is able through his emotional games to arouse your pity.

A leader must be careful not to have any personality relations with his co-workers. He loses his power, his freedom, and his independence once his co-workers are trusted with his personality life secrets. He must not have even business transactions with them. He is there for the work. His co-workers are there because of the work. All relations must be kept on the level of the work. If the workers need help in their personal problems, he can guide them as much as possible but without creating dependence on him.

The leader must be extremely careful not to impart any personal issue of any co-worker to another member or co-worker. Any such act weakens the power of his leadership. He must be a big ear but have a silent mouth. In all ages the enemies of the Teaching were those who were related to the Teacher very closely, not because of the Teaching but for their personal interests.

Christ referred to the same fact when He said, "Man's enemies shall be those of his own household."[1] And the prophet David said, "Yea, mine own familiar

---

1. Matt. 10:36

friend, in whom I trusted, which did eat of my bread, hath lifted up his heel against me."[2]

Personality-level relationships must be reduced to zero if a leader wants to accomplish a great service for humanity.

A leader becomes vulnerable due to his own failure to stand above personality level relationships.

When you are charged with the virtues, you will transform people because then your words will have power. But when you are not charged with virtues, you cannot lead other people into a higher life through your words. People do not obey words. They obey the energy and electricity that touches them through the words.

If you are awakened, you can awaken people. If you have energy, you can give energy; and you can have energy only when you are united with your Transpersonal Self or when you become your real, Divine Self. Energy pours out of you when you are united with your Self. It is your beingness that causes transmutation in other people.

The everlasting value of the Great Ones is not in Their knowledge but in Their beingness. The greatest value that a man has is not his knowledge but his beingness.

A leader is necessary until he teaches you how to lead yourself. The greatest guru is the one who awakens in you your own guru. The greatest responsibility of a guru is not to impart knowledge to you but to lead you to yourself. If a guru is leading you to himself, he is a false guru. The true guru is one who works with you to make you your own guru. The moment you contact the Divinity

---

2. Psalms 41:9

within you, he must leave you free to be your own path, find your own truth, and create your own life.

No disciple can achieve mastery until he rejects all dependency. When you depend on your guru, or if he makes you depend on him, he is a false guru and it is better for you to stay away from him.

14
Leadership and Inspiration

There are leaders who, before building the foundation, try to build the roof, or before the baby can walk, they prepare an Olympic race for him.

One of the best ways to prevent right unfoldment is to present visions which the subject cannot achieve. Visions must be given in the right dosage. When the vision is too high, it creates depression.

For example, if you make a decision and say, "I am going to be a Master in one month," you will end up in depression. But if you start with little improvements, with little goals, your enthusiasm will grow and you will increase your joy as you go forward.

The leader must give vision, but it must not paralyze people. The vision must move forward and higher as the aspirant, with better preparation, goes toward the vision. The distance between the goal and the person must be kept the same, but the speed of moving on must gradually increase.

The leader must organize the procedure of progress in such a way that the aspirant can record daily achievement. As he achieves, his courage and daring increase.

The aspirant usually rejects all that is imposed on him or forced on him. The capacity of the aspirant to understand the Teaching must be clear in the mind of the leader.

If you give a cup of water to someone, he will drink it with joy; but if you want him to drink a bucket of water, you will create rejection and anger in him. If you want him to drink a barrel of water, he will fall into depression.

As with quantity, so with the time. A speed which is too fast will create rejection or inertia; a speed which is too slow will disperse the interest. The right speed will keep the interest and striving alive and fiery.

The goal must be presented by the leader. The speed must be decided by the aspirant. He must prepare his own momentum. Any imposition of speed will retard the progress of the aspirant.

If the goal is kept at the right distance, the speed will adjust itself to the goal.

On the path of progress the leader must encourage the aspirant and make him search and find, but he must not force either his standard of speed or the quality and the level of the Teaching. He must wait until the aspirant asks for more. The wise leader will even neglect the demands of the aspirant for more light in order to accumulate in him a greater urge to know and to be.

Forced teaching creates hypocrites and puppets.

The leader must not give deeper Teaching until he sees transformation in the life of the aspirant. Without transformation of life, the Teaching degenerates and serves selfish ends.

Learning takes less time than transformation. If the transformation is speeded forcefully, it does not take place, and instead of wine you end up with vinegar.

The leader is the trustee of the Plan; he is the trustee of wisdom accumulated throughout the ages within his Chalice. His success depends not only upon his knowledge, experiences, love, and sacrifice but also on his immediate co-workers. Co-workers have a grave responsibility to protect and support the leader and to carry on his sacrificial labor for one humanity.

It is very important to be aware that the dark forces try to use the leader's immediate co-workers to make him fail. This has happened throughout time. This happened to Blavatsky, to Nicholas Roerich, and to many others. When the selfish personality element is not defeated within the co-workers, this element is stimulated by the beauty and closeness of the leader to such a degree that it overpowers sanity, vision, and dedication and leads the co-workers into acts of betrayal. Jealousy, hurt feelings, bribery, and health problems are often the first sign that the co-workers cannot see beyond their own noses.

Co-workers must be extremely careful not to be caught in any act of betrayal because not only will they burn the petals of their Chalice, but also, when ages later they step into the path of leadership, karma will catch them in various ways, thus creating unbearable tensions in them.

At the time of an inner crisis with co-workers, the leader must fix his soul on his vision and let everything else go in the fire of the vision.

If the betrayal was the result of the leader's past karma, past deeds, he will be tested in all his points. He will either make it or give up. But if the betrayal is organized by dark forces, it is a sign that he is confronting a major initiation.

A very important point to remember is that co-workers must be extremely careful so as not to be caught by the dark forces which are attacking the leader. If they are caught and agree to help the dark forces against the leader, their karma is darker because they have associated themselves with dark forces. For millions of years they will not be able to free themselves from the grip of the dark ones and will serve as their slaves.

Co-workers must not occupy themselves with the shortcomings of the leader but, instead, dedicate themselves to the vision of the leader, to the vision that they hold within their hearts.

The leader is loaded with an immense responsibility, but co-workers are also loaded with a more serious responsibility. If they fail to support the leader, not only may the leader fail but also the Plan and the whole group of co-workers may fail. This is why each stone in the building must stand faithful to the building. The building depends on the firmness of each stone.

Esoteric tradition says that no fate is more awful than the fate of a co-worker who betrayed the servant of the Plan. A co-worker must be awake every moment to avoid falling into such an abyss.

15
Choosing Students

When you accept students, as far as possible you must see them in person and observe them closely. All leaders at the present do not have clairvoyant eyes, but they can detect things through close observation. For example:

1. The leader must observe the applicant's clothing, the color, the shape, the materials, etc.

2. He must observe the movements of the applicant, how he walks, how he uses his hands and arms, his lips, his eyes, his face. Does he have any involuntary movement, such as moving his feet or fingers or eyelids when he speaks or talks?

3. The leader must also observe the logic behind the conversation, the vocabulary, the voice.

All these factors may reveal many points in the character of the student.

The leader must take only those who are ready for discipline and teaching.

4. There is a fourth factor which is given in the Agni Yoga Teaching. The Teacher says,

> *You have already seen how I put questions to a newcomer. From the replies it was possible to form an opinion about the qualities of the newcomer. Each one of you will be obliged to teach those who come to you. If they begin with a question, reply with a question of your own. You know how the quality of a question gives direction to the next question. It is inadmissible to allow inexactness to creep into the essence of the question. . . . And first of all ask what has drawn him to you. And then ask him to tell when for the first time he felt the worthlessness of contemporary life; and then let him relate how the first conception of the Teacher arose in his consciousness. Let him tell how he understands achievement. Does he feel the difference between the evidence and the reality; and can he realize the community within his consciousness?. . .*
>
> *. . .You must exclude all questions about former family life. . . .*[1]

---

1. Agni Yoga Society, *Community*, para. 209.

5. Postpone his acceptance. This sometimes reveals secret corners in his nature.

During your conversation he must not feel that you are accepting him; neither must he feel that you are not accepting him. You must try to put his mind in suspension.

This often clears his glamors and vanities, and if he is not ready he will never knock at your door again. But if he is ready you will see him visiting, calling, and writing to you.

6. Do not try to increase your students for the sake of numbers. Also, do not feel pity. Try to be very factual. If he can go with someone else, let him go, or encourage him to find another Teacher. In no event must you build attachment. All you should do is to feel the Plan of his Soul and cooperate with it.

7. There are a few questions that you can use in your conversation:

   a. Do you have time? What do you do with your time?

   b. When did you start to be interested in the spiritual life?

   c. Do you have strong guilt feelings?

   d. Did you ever attack someone and want to hurt him? How? When?

   e. Are you interested in the welfare of humanity?

   f. Do you feel unhappy if an injustice is done to anyone?

   g. Have you had moments when you were really sacrificial? What were they?

Such questions reveal the hidden sides of the applicant, and you can more wisely approach his needs and give better spiritual direction.

After you admit a student, watch his behavior. See if he likes to use others for his advantage or if he gossips, criticizes, or belittles people. These are really bad signs about which you as a leader must be aware.

The esoteric leader strongly emphasizes that promotion must be done very slowly, and if negative signs come, the applicant must be suspended for a long time.

The Teacher has a very heavy influence upon the student, and the student may have a positive or negative effect upon the Teacher.

Before the Teacher chooses the student, he must have reliable information about the state of the student's personality vehicles and motive. Will his influence be constructive for him and for his environment? A premature charge can damage the student or put the student in such a condition that the environment rejects and hurts him. The Teacher's intention is to prepare a spiritual hero. . . with as few problems as possible.

The Teacher also knows that certain students will create problems for him. This is why he must choose them with clear discrimination.

The Teacher cannot waste his time with the petty affairs of the student. He knows that

1. The thoughts, the thoughtforms, and the imagination of the student affect the aura of the Teacher.

2. The student's life becomes a part of the karma of the Teacher.

3. The inertia or the striving of the student creates changes in the aura of the Teacher.

4. The relationship of the student with living beings or entities beyond the physical plane affects the Teacher's life. If the student is related in some way to certain undesirable entities, the student becomes a door through which entities attack the Teacher.

5. The relationship of the student with various exoteric or esoteric organizations creates pressure fields in the Teacher's aura if the relationship is not on the level of Beauty, Goodness, Righteousness, Joy, and Freedom.

6. The condition of the centers of the student affects the Teacher's aura if the student is very active in certain centers. These centers try to upset the balance of the Teacher's centers.

The Teacher is a very sensitive instrument. Whatever happens to the life of the student — joy, grief, violent emotions, or depressions — are registered in the Teacher's aura, and his time and energy are sometimes wasted in cleaning his aura and restoring his peace and balance.

The Teacher is very cautious that his work does not suffer from the wrong activities of his students. The Teacher has committed himself to a certain service, and his focus is disturbed if the student cannot live in a level of harmony with the Inner Plan.

There are many other factors that make a Teacher very cautious and discriminative when he chooses his students.

All the above is information to try to explain what transpires when a new student is admitted into close contact with the Teacher. Those Teachers who are trained along Hierarchical lines seldom take students. They wait to see

- The sincerity of the student
- The depth of his devotion and dedication
- The health and the karma of the student
- The degree of the unfoldment of his senses on various planes
- The purity of his striving
- His sensitivity and discrimination
- His commitment to serve humanity

The student must be ready to bring his offering to his Teacher before he is admitted. This offering is not flowers, money, body, material articles but higher Treasures such as various *talents* that can be used for the work; various inner *achievements* that profit the efforts of the Teacher; *silence* and the control of speech which does not create disturbances in the aura of the Teacher and which can be used for service; various *virtues* that can be used in the labor of the Teacher.

The student must be somebody. He must have something to offer. This is why he is left for a long time by himself. He must prove his sincerity, his aspiration, his willpower, his striving, his gratitude, his labor, and his service.

The Teachers I met were very discriminative. They had very penetrative eyes and clear Intuition. They were never moved by any showing off or phenomenon, but they registered every melody that passed through the hearts of those whom they thought of taking in. To find out all this, the Teacher watches his students-to-be. He watches them very patiently before he commits himself to them.

A Teacher is also a leader. A leader not only teaches but shows in a practical way how to live the life of discipleship. Once the student is totally committed to the path of perfection, the Teacher changes into a leader for him. For a few years the leader's instructions must be very clear to the student so that he develops a certain degree of Intuition.

Clarity is one of the great signs of a true leader. He must make his plans clear and his words clear. Often it is better to make the plans clear in writing in order not to create any confusion in the minds of those who will carry out his plans. Also, he must clearly understand the decisions of others, so that he has no doubt about their attitude and behavior. This clarity works in two ways:

1. He must make clear all that he orders, plans, and asks for.

2. He must be clear about the responses of his co-workers.

Most clarity is related to time, location, numbers, names, duties, tasks.

Time. Exact time. You must be sure that the subject is clear about it. Make also clear whether you are referring to A.M. or P.M.

Location. Repeat and spell the name. Make a map. Tell about the streets close to the location and how far it is from other certain locations.

Numbers. Do not say "few." Say "five," say "seven," say the exact number.

Names. Make it clear. Who is it? Give first and last names. Even mention his office, for example Charles Folly, the president of the school, the fellow who brought you a mirror, etc. If there is another fellow with the same name and, if the one you are mentioning is clear in his mind, do not mention it. Mentioning two names may confuse him.

Duties. Be very exact and clear. Who is doing what? Write it down. Make the time, the location, and the specific work to be done clear. Mention advantages and dangers involved and special cautions to be observed.

Tasks are not duties. They have personal involvement. Duties must be done exactly as told to you, but in tasks only the final goal is emphasized and the ways and means are left to your choice.

The leader must be very careful that his words are thoroughly understood.

16
Leadership and Decisiveness

One of the virtues of the leader is decisiveness. Decisiveness is the ability to make a decision clearly and at the right time.

One can develop decisiveness in daily life by trying to be decisive and clear in all his actions. One must not only develop decisiveness, but he must also work to increase his

- Clear vision
- Courage
- Willpower
- Detachment

- Indifference to personality reactions
- Sense of values
- Discrimination

The would-be leader must, by all means, develop the above virtues. As he develops them, he will become aware that the power of decisiveness is growing within his soul.

Indecisive people spread harmful effects upon themselves and upon other people. For example, an indecisive man:

— Loses time

— Makes other people or circumstances control him

— Delays his own evolution

— Brings harm into the field where he works

— Creates tension in his own system

— Creates confusion in the hearts of his followers

— Loses opportunities

Decisiveness is a sign that you have a ruling center in your nature which is dominating all the rest. This ruling center can be your body, your emotional nature, your mental nature — each separately, or all together as a personality. It can be your Soul, or the Soul-infused personality, or it can even be your Spiritual Triad.

There can also be other decision-making centers within you such as a strong urge or drive, a strong emotion or fixed idea, an entity in your aura, or an entity that has remote control upon you.

Decisiveness grows in the right direction when you begin to notice all that is violating your inner freedom and forcing you to formulate your decisions. But if the above-mentioned seven points are developed, there will be no chance of falling into the hands of negative forces in you or around you.

You may also notice that whenever you are indecisive, there is a conflict within you.

Sometimes it is more dangerous to avoid a decision than to follow wrong decisions. Negative forces win many battles by making you become confused and avoid decisions.

Of course, one must take his time when confronting serious decisions and search for many viewpoints, but, in the meantime, he must know that time is an important element in making decisions.

The safeguards for making right decisions can be given as follows:

1. Harmlessness

2. Beauty

3. Goodness

4. Joy

5. Righteousness

6. Health

7. Unity, synthesis

8. Non-violation of the rights of others

9. Right motive

When these nine rules are observed in your decisions, it is most probable that your decisions will be right and there will be no chance left for the lower centers to control you.

There are also other factors which must be considered.

At certain times our consciousness is elevated, and in the light of our elevated consciousness we make certain decisions; but two hours later we cancel our decision or take an opposite decision. This happens when our consciousness falls back down to its normal levels where the values are different. This shifting of consciousness creates inner conflict between the Higher Self and the personality and sometimes leads to depression and inertia. This is why a leader must not believe the promises of people but look only for the acts and deeds.

A leader is promoted not on decisions and promises, but on labor and sacrificial service.

Decisions given by the personality bodies cannot be taken seriously because as their moods and climates change the decisions change. The conditions of the personality vehicles are responsible for such decisions, and they are not valid.

Our traditions and moral codes, our religion, our financial interests, our vanities, prides, and illusions also control our decisions. Illusions exercise such control over us that we hardly can escape their power. An illusion is a distorted truth which is accepted as a fact.

Illusion is also created as we read fiction. In the religious and spiritual fields especially, there are thousands of fictitious stories which create a great thoughtform in the mental body of the race. The Forces of Light struggle and fight to the end to wipe out such illusions.

Significant victory has yet to be achieved to eliminate such fiction.

It is true that some of their contents and indications are highly beautiful and moral. But fiction has no place in Space. It contradicts the laws of Nature and creates psychic turbulences which affect the health and sanity of the human being.

Fiction, especially in the religious field, prevents the progress of light. Higher light cannot proceed and reveal deeper truths and facts as long as these thoughtforms exist. This is one of the reasons why the morality of the race has not advanced far. In fact it has degenerated to a great degree.

People have great admiration for fictitious stories about angels, about God, about prophets and saints, about the human soul and the souls of the dead. Since these stories are not based on pure experience, pure reason and logic, or pure scientific fact, they are obstacles on the path of human progress. They block the mind, prevent expansion of consciousness, and make it impossible for the human soul to see things as they are, as they exist.

Every deviation from reality obscures the mind.

Higher forces cannot reach a mind which is clouded by illusions or by distorted facts or truths.

Scientific thinking is an effort to see things as they are without the distortion of prejudices, superstitions, or illusions.

One of the most innocent fictitious characters is Santa Claus. This character occupies a large territory in the minds of children. Such a fiction is a distortion of truth, and it must not be allowed to occupy the minds of children if we want them in the future to see things as they are and live in the field of reality.

One wonders how much territory of the mind is already occupied by fictitious television programs as the child watches them with intense concentration and involvement. There is no method yet to burn out such illusions which, like a curse, sap the sanity of our youth.

It is very difficult to expect right decisions when a person is obsessed by such illusions and does not have a clear mind to formulate a decision which is inspired by Beauty, Goodness, Righteousness, Joy, and Freedom.

There are two kinds of fiction. One is made up by our own imagination and inspired by our blind urges, drives, and desires. The other is a fiction in time, but it is a reality in Space. These things exist as fact in higher realms, in archetypal planes, and reflect on certain minds who present their reflections as fiction.

Thus, a great genius writes a fiction which years later manifests as reality. It is possible that the genius cannot reveal clearly all that he can *see*, but at least partially he can reveal whatever he *senses*. It is also possible that through a strong imagination a man can affect thousands of minds and build a fictitious thought-form which eventually manifests on earth. The difference between these two is that the first one brings greater achievements for humanity, but the second one brings retardation and even degeneration.

One of the greatest aids for humanity is to clear away illusions and establish factuality, reality, and common sense.

Decisiveness must come from your Inner Core, or else it does not work. For example, you say, "I am not going to use alcohol any more." But if deep in your heart you do not believe what you are saying, your decision is false and it will never work.

Decisiveness is experienced when there is no division within you. When you are integrated and united, your decisions have a great influence upon others. To make a decision means to fuse oneself with a source of high-voltage energy.

People cannot give orders or influence people if they are divided and are not decisive.

In the coming age disciples and initiates will be more decisive. They will have more willpower, greater Intuition, and purer minds to formulate and express the decisions made in the light of Intuition.

Indecisiveness is a state of conflict within you: two or more forces are confronting each other and keeping you in a condition of confusion. A decision puts an end to confusion. Confusion or inner conflict affects your nervous system and creates psychological and physical problems.

There is also family indecisiveness which causes permanent damage to the children. For example, mother says to her son, "Go to sleep; it is late." Daddy says, "Let him watch the next television program."

The boy is caught between two forces, and he can use either one of them. Either he obeys his mother and goes to bed or he denies his mother and stays and watches the next program. Thus conflict in the family creates unhealthy situations. Divorce contributes heavily to the state of indecisiveness in the children and often leads them into confusion.

In your daily life you can learn decisiveness through mechanical means. For example, if you cannot decide to go to a movie or not to go, take a coin, choose either the head or the tail, and flip the coin. If the tail is to go and it appears, hold the tail in your hand and go to the movie. If not, sit and read or whatever, but don't go to the movies.

No one can be a real leader if he is not decisive or if he changes his decisions continuously.

Decisiveness is willpower. And those who do not have willpower can be used by the maya, glamors, and illusions of others.

A changeable man is an unstable man. An Initiate is an example of stability. Unstable people cannot create faith or inspire hope. Psychic energy evaporates from them; they cannot create aspiration in others. People cannot aim the arrows of their striving at an unstable target.

Decisiveness creates stability, and stability inspires respect and certainty. Certainty is one of the elements of mental health and success.

One must try by all means to make the right decisions, and if he fails he will learn from his failure. Decisiveness makes you the master of your life. A successful life is a succession of right decisions. An indecisive man is like a piece of lumber floating on the sea on which you cannot stand. You cannot trust a man who is always indecisive.

A decisive man has strong arms to stretch the bow and release the arrow.

Decisiveness creates contact with higher realms and higher frequencies. Indecisiveness blocks or distorts impressions coming from higher sources.

Some people justify their indecisiveness under the veil of neutrality. Neutrality is a hidden hypocrisy, fear, and self-worship.

Creativity is decisiveness. Life is not a neutral force but a creative flow.

Neutrality is a hidden support and engagement with the forces of destruction. One of the techniques of the dark forces is the creation of neutrality. Neutrality is used as an intense field of activity by dark forces. It is through neutrality that help and assistance is prevented from reaching the creative forces.

Decisiveness develops the sense of intuitive perception of the right direction. Decisiveness eventually leads you into the light of your Inner Guide. In this light you always decide rightly.

17
Impersonality

There is a pseudo impersonality cult which must be understood.

The Self is divine. There is nothing wrong if you say, "I wrote that book and it is really beautiful and far superior to many others." There is nothing wrong when you say you are a disciple. There is nothing wrong if you say, "I am mastering my three bodies and achieving great results." There is nothing wrong if you use similar expressions.

It becomes wrong and selfish only when

1. You have a vanity about it

2. You want to humiliate others

3. It is a lie

4. You have hidden your motives

5. You expect praise

There is nothing wrong if it is true. Christ said, "I am the way, the life and the truth." A Great Teacher says, "I said it, twice I tell you I said it." These were human beings. There is nothing wrong in Their statements because They *are* — They are reality.

As far as a man knows his real value and states it for better understanding and communication, there is nothing wrong.

Actually, it is false humility or impersonality that hides the facts. Behind such false humility and impersonality lie many poisonous serpents and scorpions that can only be discovered in critical times when suppressed lies reach the surface.

When a man knows his Self, the Real Self, and observes everything through the eyes of the Self, he does not make mistakes when he speaks about himself. Such a man does not lie, does not have vanity, does not boast, does not exploit; but he speaks about the facts if necessary.

There is nothing wrong if you say, "I discovered this. I wrote this. I am a creative writer. I am beautiful," etc. But all these expressions must be the real reflection of your being.

Impersonality does not mean to hide your personality or not to feel yourself as a Self. It means to recognize and love all human beings as *Selves* from one source; it means not to misuse them because of their ignorance and weakness for your own separative ends; it means not to project your glamors and illusions as being your Self.

One who knows himself as divine has no fear of speaking about himself; he is an expression of Beauty, Goodness, Righteousness, Joy, and Freedom. Why should he hide it? Such people know that just as they surpass others, others will surpass them, and when they do, they recognize them as greater ones who did greater things.

"You will do greater things than I did," said Christ. This is the true spirit of One Who knows the Self.

They do not say, "I am beautiful, but others are ugly." They say, "I express beauty now, at this time, but it does not mean that someone will not be able to express more beauty than I do at the present."

He says, "I wrote this book and it is really the best." But he does not mean that others cannot surpass him. On the contrary, because of his true sense of values, he rejoices and believes that all those who surpass and "win the prize" are those who are becoming more divine and entering into greater recognition of the One Self in all Selves.

Great Ones rejoice for the success of others as if They were rejoicing for Their own successes because every greatness makes Them greater.

People hide themselves if they are not sure what they are. People are afraid to talk about their deeds because they have doubts about their deeds. But if you know exactly what you are and what you did, why will it be wrong if you show it? Only those who have fears, doubts, inferiority complexes, and many hidden vices hide themselves behind the veils of impersonality.

Of course, it is wise not to speak about yourself and your deeds until you know yourself and you know your deeds. The world needs people who speak about themselves and prove what they speak.

An inferior person can only see selfishness in any true expression because only his false self responds like a broken glass to that great light.

No true statement can veil a vision; on the contrary, through all true statements the reality comes in contact with life. That is why Christ said, "Let your light shine."

Inferior people who preach pseudo unselfishness and pseudo impersonality see only their own motives and read only their own preconceived ideas in the expression of Great Ones and Their disciples. This is a great glamor which must be overcome. There is jealousy behind it; there is absence of love and a terrible feeling of frustration or an inferiority complex behind it.

You want to prove that he is bad, he is wrong. You want to humiliate him in order to feel safe in the presence of greatness. This only brings your true wretchedness to the surface and creates a fever of criticism. But those who know what they are, what they do, and why they do it walk on like elephants while the dogs bark.

There is also nothing wrong in recognizing the greatness of someone in speech or in writing, if you know that he really did a great job and served sacrificially. But this must be done, of course, without flattery. In the Teaching we read:

> *Great is the contempt of a flatterer when he sees how easily we fall for his sometimes rather crude strategems. . . .Nothing lowers and destroys a person so much as his acceptance of flattery. . . . A person who is guilty of flattery, or one who accepts it, can never become a close co-worker.*[1]

Recognition of the greatness, recognition of virtues, and proclamation of the values of others are acts of gratitude and signs of greatness. Only a noble man can

---

1. Roerich, Helena, *Letters of Helena Roerich*, Vol. I, p. 102.

do these things without flattery and without expectation. A small and narrow consciousness enjoys condemnations. The Teacher says,

> *Beware of senseless condemnation. . . . The injustice of condemnation, like any lie, weakens the already insignificant consciousness of the self-appointed judge; thence issues extreme harm for him, whereas the one who is unjustly judged only gains through strengthening his magnet by the attraction of new auras.*[2]

There is a concept in pseudo esoteric groups in which the "leaders" speak against the idea of leadership to foster their own wrong concept of leadership in the consciousness of their followers.

Leadership is your specialization, your level, your experience, your knowledge, and your wisdom. Leadership is authority. You cannot take a leader and make him follow a group of people who know nothing about the purpose for which they have come together, and who know nothing about the ways that must be used to reach that purpose.

It will be disastrous if great scientists are put on the level of their students and waste their time arguing with students who know nothing about the subject. It is stupid to make a leader follow the ignorance of his followers.

No matter what you do, you are the follower of the one who knows, is, and has wisdom. To try to kill the idea of leadership or the idea of authority is to create anarchy — social and educational anarchy.

---

2. Agni Yoga Society, *Heart*, para. 89.

This does not mean that a leader is a tyrant or a totalitarian. If he is, he is not a leader. The real leader stands there to lead people toward their True Selves, or toward the object of their achievements. Once the group of students or the followers reach his level, then the leader no longer leads them, unless he has worked on himself and gone forward and ahead of them.

The leader is greater light, greater love, and greater beauty to the lesser light, lesser love, and the lesser beauty of the followers and students.

Democracy is not an effort to wipe out leadership and authority. It is an effort to create those conditions in which everyone can unfold and bloom without the pressure of false leadership and false authority. False leadership and false authority belong to those who are swayed by pride, vanity, illusion, and glamor. They do not know, and yet they want to teach; they are blind, and yet they want to guide.

The Aquarian Age will give us great leaders in all fields. The Christ is a great leader. Initiates in all fields of human endeavor are powerful leaders. Leadership is the ability to shine your light and inspire people to come closer to their Inner Light.

Leadership is not imposition; leadership is beauty, inspiration, and expression of your knowledge and beingness as a service to others.

True group unity does not mean not to have a leader, not to have a principle, not to have a greater light or experience. True group unity means to have a purpose and work harmoniously to manifest that purpose through self-forgetfulness, harmlessness, and right speech.

The Guardian Angel is the great leader in every man. In all organizations and fields of human endeavor we have real leaders of knowledge, beingness, and experience. On the planet, we have Christ and the Logos. In the Aquarian Age all mountains of achievement are not going to be flattened into fields. This would be disastrous! You will always have spearheads leading you toward greater light. This is what the chain of the Hierarchy means.

I remember once a boy said to me, "This is the age of the destruction of the concepts of authority, leadership, parenthood, kingship, presidency, chairmanship."

"Then who is going to guide us until we begin to walk on our own?"

He laughed and laughed and cynically said, "Well, as we destroy these authorities we can be like animals; we can do what we want to do."

He did not know that even animals would be in worse conditions if we annihilated our respect for authorities and leaders in all fields.

People climb mountains because the heights challenge them.

There is an interesting phenomenon in human relationships which is called imposition. Imposition is of two kinds:

1. Exoteric imposition

2. Esoteric imposition

Exoteric imposition means to make other people do what we want them to do, to make other people think what we want them to think. This is a totalitarian attitude, and it is found in homes, in offices, as well as in governments. Such an attitude fosters revolutions, wars, and hatred and creates unnecessary and intolerable difficulties on the path of human evolution.

Esoteric imposition is very different. To be able to impose yourself on others esoterically, first you must present an achievement of high degree. Esoterically, to impose means to evoke responses from others identical to your achievement. For example, if you are a rare beauty, you impose on the minds of others the image of your beauty. Your image of beauty creates in them a striving toward beauty.

If you are a great talent, you impose on others your talent, and people feel the urge to speed their evolution. If you are a great leader, you impose on the minds of people the image of your leadership, and they make efforts to develop leadership in their lives.

You can impose your values on others not through forcing yourself on others but by becoming the embodiment of certain values.

Every kind of beauty is evocative. In reality, esoteric imposition is not an act of violating the free will of others but an act to evoke the Divine Will to engage in self-improvement.

In every human being there is the source which can create all the values that you yourself have. Your effort is to evoke that source into activity by presenting to the source your own achievement.

In esoteric imposition there is no forcing, demanding, or dominating but an attitude of revealing your own beauty. The Sun imposes its rays on life forms and becomes the cause of growth. Thus, one can shine and let his rays carry nourishment to every living form.

In esoteric imposition it is not the person who imposes; it is the value that imposes itself, and often the strongest imposition is carried on in total selflessness, self-forgetfulness, and indifference to the reactions of others.

Some people think that gang leaders, leaders of organized crime, and racist leaders are always to be considered leaders. True leaders do not occupy themselves with crimes, destruction, and separatism. They stand and work for healing, for construction, for synthesis and unity.

False leaders are under the influence of their separative interests, glamors, illusions, posthypnotic suggestions, hatred, and fear. Real leaders are above these things.

The intention of the real leader is to free human beings from everything and from every level of slavery and provide those conditions in which such freedom can be perpetuated. False leaders also build and become successful, but their construction and success eventually become their worst enemies. They build only to be buried under the building when it falls upon their own head.

False leaders work for separate interests. True leaders work for the one body of humanity. Every success and achievement gained at the expense of the success and achievement of others is a sickness in that body. Sooner or later Nature will eliminate the sickness and the causes of it.

Leadership is not the result of knowledge, education, and specializations but of direction and self-mastery. No one can be a leader without integrity and self-mastery. History shows how all false leaders wounded the body of humanity through their insanity and selfish, self-destructive actions.

True leaders are living examples of Beauty, Goodness, Righteousness, Joy, and Freedom.

Many false leaders not only follow their personality interests, glamors, and posthypnotic suggestions, but they are also faithful servants of separative interests and slaves of those entities who possess them and lead them into destructive activities. Obsessed and possessed leaders fill many pages of history. Their true nature is revealed to humanity through the effect they leave for future generations.

People often think that leaders are free to do anything they want. This is wrong. A true leader has self-imposed restrictions, which are the guidelines from his Higher Self. They are his principles. He cannot violate such restrictions and principles without endangering his path of leadership.

18
Leadership and Obedience

Those who are learning on the path of leadership must remember that there are two main types of leaders. One is called the ego-centered leader, and the other is called the Core-centered leader.

The ego-centered leader obeys his urges, drives, desires, wishes, glamors, illusions, vanities, and pride. The Core-centered leader follows his own leader's commands and indications with deep understanding and cooperation until he develops his soul nature and begins to be impressed by the Spiritual Triad.

True leaders are those who have found the way into the Spiritual Triad. Only in the light of the Spiritual Triad can a leader receive impressions from the Purpose and the Plan and synchronize his thoughts, words, and actions accordingly.

The ego-centered leader eventually fails on the path of leadership because he not only cuts his relations with his own Core but also becomes a servant to his lower self. He lies; he flatters; he gossips; he serves his vanities; he loses his punctuality; he deceives; he follows the directions of his lower self. Such a leader eventually becomes a tumor in the body of leadership. He creates his own selfish ways, his own methods, his own interests, and his own goals.

Leadership is not egocentric. The ego must be transcended and the *Center* of the galaxy of Leadership must be found. The Center is the group Spiritual Triad from which the inspirations, impressions, and directions reach us; the Center is truly Shamballa. Until one has definite contact with Shamballa, or the Spiritual Triad within him, he must learn the laws of occult obedience and tune himself to his immediate leader and follow his directions in detail.

Eventually the ego-centered leader not only destroys himself but also causes great damage to the field of spiritual service. He becomes more dangerous as he is promoted to higher positions.

The true characters of future leaders cannot be revealed until they pass through tests.

The ego-centered leader knows how to hide his true face under many veils. It is even noticed that he tries to hide his face from his own Soul. This is why responsible leadership so often does not judge by appearances and puts people through tests.

It is even possible to see a Core-centered leader acting and appearing as an ego-centered leader on the path of probation or learning. Once a responsibility is given to him, he reveals his true nature and disperses the veils of appearance. This is why the leader in training must pass through continuous tests before higher and Hierarchical responsibilities are given to him.

An ego-centered leader can overcome his limitations by working against the demands of his lower self and developing *detachment, cooperation,* and *group-consciousness.*

The ego must be decentralized before one can understand the meaning of Core.

An ego is not a Core. An ego is a trapped human soul who is serving as a slave to the interests of the glamors, illusions, and maya of the lower self. The ego serves the glamors, illusions, and maya of that which has power over him.

The Core is a totally different phenomenon. It is like a seed which contains a plan, the urge to develop the plan, the creative energy to unfold the plan, and the sense of direction which puts him in contact with the central Core of the planet, solar system, and galaxy.

The intention of a Core is to unfold the prototype impressed in *his heart.* The intention of an ego is to manifest the vanity, glamors, and illusions of his owners.

Before one leads himself to the path of leadership, he must clearly understand through his own life experience the differences between the ego and the Core.

Ego-centered leaders are separative; they tend to misuse people and exploit them. They have the urge to ignore the rights of other people and destroy their efforts to protect their own rights. They work by means of imposition, and they are highly trained to take advantage of the weaknesses of others and use every opportunity for their own interests. For them a group, a church, a nation, or even humanity is only a field which exists only to satisfy their unending exploitation.

On the other hand, the Core-centered leader is a part of the Cosmic Symphony. He works in the line of the Laws of Economy, Love, and Synthesis. All that he thinks, speaks, and does is to serve the great Purpose of redemption, freedom, and synthesis. Even in the smallest details he obeys the command of his leader.

It is possible to feel many kinds of reactions and rejections toward the directions of the leadership. This is very normal and instructive. It is normal because the synchronization of the wills has not yet taken place. Second, it is instructive because the leader-to-be has a chance to observe himself and find out the source and cause of his rebellion. Often this is very beneficial because the neophyte of leadership finds out exactly where his hindrances lie and how he can handle them in the right way in order to proceed on the path of leadership.

The path of leadership is a continuous way of self-confrontation. The leader-to-be must keep himself watchful and notice those intruders who try to sneak in with all possible veils and in all possible ways.

A great protection for the neophyte is his obedience to the rules of leadership and his obedience to the command of leadership, in spite of his personality reactions. The Ancients used to say that the future leaders are those who learn the lesson of obedience.

Of course, no leader is an infallible person. But in his own field and in his own position he sees farther ahead than those who have not yet the needed training, experience, and wisdom.

In some training centers for leadership there is even a period of strange training during which the leader gives you illogical, awkward orders or suggestions in order to break your ego-centered constructions. For example, he may say to a student, "When I am giving the lecture, stand up and dance in the class and bear the consequences." Such a method is not acceptable to our modern hypocrites, but it works because it destroys the vanity on which the ego is built and liberates the subject from certain hindrances.

The real leader must destroy all that is false in you and reveal all that is real in you.

On one occasion our leader told us to cross the river by swimming and walking through it instead of crossing it by a bridge which was hung from cables. Most of us, although wondering, crossed the river by swimming and walking through it, but some of the students went across by the bridge. To our surprise the bridge fell down, and those boys had a very hard time reaching the shore.

After everyone was on the shore the leader asked, "What was the order?"

"To cross the river but not by the bridge."

"Well, did you see what happened?"

"Yes."

"Present a paper for next week with your observations and thoughts, and explain why this lesson was given to you."

Fourteen people read their papers in the gathering. They were full of ideas and observations. One of the boys wrote, "Until wisdom, insight, and foresight is developed, one must obey those who have wisdom, insight, and foresight. Obedience is not slavery but understanding of the ideal and synchronizing our efforts to the ideal presented by the leader."

I remember other times when we were ordered to go to our bedrooms through our windows, or write a beautiful letter to someone we hated.

Later when I was in the mountains with my Teacher, I asked why he had ordered us to cross the river by swimming instead of going by the bridge. I added, "Did you know that the bridge was defective?"

"Yes," he said, "we made it defective to teach a lesson." Through the conversation he explained that such a way of teaching is extremely dangerous in the wrong hands. If the dosage is not watched, it creates machines or robots instead of independence. He added,

"But first we must help the student to establish contact with the center of leadership, confidence, and faith and dispel many vanities before we lead him into independence."

There are cycles in which the student is left totally alone to decide for himself; there are cycles in which he has no need to make a decision but only obey. The cycle of self-decision must start after the cycle of obedience to the leader is far advanced and is done in such a way that blind obedience slowly decreases and conscious independence increases until total synchronization with the goal of the leader is achieved.

Ego-centered leadership is very dangerous because it serve the glamors, illusions, and vanities of the ego-centered leaders. Such leaders lead nowhere, except toward enslavement and exploitation. The ego-centered leader traps himself in his own vanities and builds a network of imprisonment for others.

In true leadership, vanities must be overcome through the painful method of obedience. For certain students, such a kind of Teaching was great fun. They used to look at it as an exercise in obedience or as an opportunity to see different ways or viewpoints in doing things and, in the meantime, as an opportunity to develop confidence in their Teacher and gain the trust of the Teacher. Those who gained the trust of the Teacher advanced faster because they were given more opportunities to develop themselves. A closer relationship with the Teacher increased their wisdom.

My first test of obedience occurred when I entered an organization and the Teacher told me to take off my clothes and jump into the cold river. For one second I questioned it, but my Soul rejoiced and I immediately jumped into the river with joy.

The Teacher mentioned that event often and told me that it impressed him and from that moment on, he had a deep trust in me. Years later, after going through many disciplines, I asked him, "It is very strange. I have a great sense of obedience to you, but for a long time you have let me do things my own way."

"Well," he said, "we prepare leaders to do things in their own way after we see that vanity is totally destroyed in them. You learned the secret and occult meaning of obedience, and your egocentric tendencies were dispersed."

Imagine an office where the employees do not follow the orders or instructions of the boss. Imagine an army where every soldier acts according to the way he feels or wants.

Freedom and independence grow as the knowledge and understanding of the situation and ways to handle it grow.

Egocentric people must be decentralized before they begin to build their Core-centered life. A Core-centered life is defined as a process of life which is in harmony with the highest that one is, with the highest that everyone is, and with the highest keynote one can sense in the Universe.

Once, while my Teacher and I were working in the vegetable garden, two boys came and asked if they could be accepted as students. The Teacher watched them for a few minutes and said, "Are you tired from traveling six to eight hours on horseback?"

"Yes," they said.

"Well," he said pointing to one of them, "go to the town and buy some parsley seeds for me."

"But," said the boy, "it is late afternoon. I can go tomorrow."

"Oh!"

The other boy said, "I will go, and I have some money."

"Okay," said the Teacher, "hurry." And he told the other boy to go and rest under the trees.

While we were working I said, "Now what is your decision?"

"Wait and see."

Close to midnight the boy came back, and we opened the gate. The Teacher said to me, "Give a room to this boy and go and tell the other boy to leave the monastery immediately."

While I was taking the boy to the gate he asked, "Why is my friend admitted and not me?"

"Because," I said, "he was able to respond to a need and obey the Teacher."

That was a great lesson for me which gave me a new insight into the art of leadership. Only after you find a *real* Teacher can you see the value of obedience, and obedience becomes the fastest way to get rid of your ego and proceed toward independence.

One day my Teacher was installing a new electrical wire. He was showing me how to do it and explaining to me how dangerous it was to make any mistake. Then he added, "Until you completely learn the laws of electricity and the techniques of applying them, I will never give you a chance to do such installations by yourself because you may kill yourself."

This is exactly what the leadership is. You need a long time to obey and wash out your ego and your ignorance before you earn a leadership position. Leadership is often a process of sacrificial obedience to an ideal or a vision.

The leader must not give up his labor of transforming egocentric people into Core-centered people.

Some leaders think that they should only deal with those people who are ready to be led. If every leader thinks so, no progress will be recorded. Progress is achieved when leaders are able to help people make breakthroughs and transform their life. This was the secret behind the words of Christ when He said, "Great joy is felt in heaven when a man turns his face toward the Kingdom of God."

This does not mean that one must try to squeeze water from a stone. There are cases when the leader hands a man to the currents of his karma. This is why it is imperative that the leader develops his Intuition and does not waste his time and energy with those who will progress faster in their daily labor and struggle than in the classrooms of the Temples.

On the path of discipleship *readiness* is required, or else everything runs against the aspirant's interest.

Those leaders who are Core-centered act in a balanced manner. Egocentric leaders have no balance; they are one-sided and they act in extremes.

The duty of the leader is to know the real motives and the character of those whom he is training, but his responsibility demands that he not be caught in the weaknesses and shortcomings of the people in training and reject them because they are not what he wants them to be. His responsibility is to take risks to help them enter the path of Beauty, Goodness, Righteousness, Joy, Freedom, and simplicity.

Thus, the leader must know, but also he must have compassion to overcome the negative things he knows.

Of course, caution is necessary when the defective side of the applicant is very heavy. Special measures must be taken to transform even a Judas but, if possible, without letting him betray the sacred work.

Responsibility is not an attitude that accepts a rotten egg and expects a chicken from it. Responsibility is Intuition, understanding, and sacrificial action to protect the work and the persons involved in the work. Responsibility is even a permit for the leader to step on the head of a serpent and to put on his shoulders an elephant to save its life.

Thus, the leader keeps the balance between what he knows and what he should do. His Intuition must lead him in his task, not his pity or emotions or even self-interest.

The innermost Core of the leader acts as the fulcrum of balance.

The leader must also observe the behavior of people to see what motivates their actions.

The ego can motivate people. The Core can motivate people, and also hidden guilt and crime can motivate them. For example, when people attack others through their gossip, slander, and malice, you can clearly see that they are trying to suppress within themselves crimes committed by their own hands which are bothering their own consciousness. If thorough investigation is carried on within the lives of such people, many hidden crimes or planned crimes can be eventually revealed.

The law is very simple: People attack others to cover up their own crimes. A man without any crime in his life and nothing bothering his conscience will never engage in an unhappy labor of malice, slander, and gossip. People reveal themselves by what they do to others.

There is also the other side of this behavior. If a man has guilt feelings and sees that people similar to him are under attack, he feels a release and even tries to justify the attack on the other man, no matter how unrighteous it appears to him. Not only individuals but also nations often behave in this same way.

There is another phase of the same psychology. People usually hate those who remind them of their pain, suffering, and failure. The hated one may not even be related in any way to the sufferings, pains, and failures of these people, but he attracts their hatred because in certain ways he reminds them of those who afflicted them.

A leader must know about such behavior and try to reveal the facts to the subjects to end the unconscious battle growing between them.

Hatred can perpetuate itself under the veils of darkness.

Ego is the most vicious obstacle on your path. It prevents you from meeting your True Self and becoming your Self. The greatest secret to becoming a leader is to renounce your ego. As long as you serve your ego, you cannot serve others or the Common Good.

Those who have ego use servility to pretend that they are exercising obedience. They do this under the pressure of conditions or under the pressure of their selfish interests.

Servile people are the most dangerous traitors. Through the appearance of obedience they gather information and secrets and eventually use them against you to gain their "freedom." It is only a slave who aspires to such freedom. An obedient person's freedom is to gain harmony with the higher command or authority or law.

Once a person falls into the trap of servility, it will be very difficult to pull him out of his ego and hypocrisy. It will take ages for such a person to overcome his ego and enter the path of leadership. If a servile person occupies a position of leadership, out of habit he will yield and be the servant of those who flatter and bribe him for their own interests.

Real obedience is the ability to understand intuitively or consciously the purpose of the given commands and act according to the instructions. In true obedience, you raise your power and dignity. In true obedience there is integration, alignment, and fusion. The results are bliss and health. In obedience you let your ego drop away.

Ego in leadership leads toward imposition of the personality will, to self-interest, and to a life controlled by personality reactions. A leader must have total control over his possible personality reactions. Justice can be carried out only when one operates in the clear light of his Soul to respond to people and events. When ego rules, you are dealing with an ambitious person, not with a leader.

Leadership is closely related to the idea of obedience. When people hear about obedience, they instinctively feel uncomfortable because they have been taught that obedience is submission to the will of another person and means losing one's own free will. Of course, there is some truth in such an approach, but real obedience is the ability to appreciate the sources of knowledge, power, wisdom, or experience and to engage oneself with that source to save time and energy and to be protected from possible mistakes and their consequences.

For example, if you are working with an electrician and you are only a beginner in that field, it is better for you to obey your boss in detail while handling and connecting the wires. If you obey the commander in your army, you may save your life or do a great service. If you obey the principles of Beauty, Goodness, Righteousness, Joy, and Freedom, you may develop spiritual powers. If you obey the law, you can save yourself from many problems and headaches.

Obedience is not obedience to personality desires and interests but obedience to principles, experience, authority, and wisdom. It is obedience to your conscience, to your Soul, and eventually to the good of all.

There is nothing wrong in benefitting from the wisdom of others and using their insight and foresight. Obedience creates humility, cooperation, and accumulation of knowledge and experience; it saves time and energy.

You obey not to be a slave but to benefit from the power and wisdom of the one with whom you work. Of course, one must obey a Higher Authority and in a way disobey those who oppose the Higher Authority. The Higher Authority is beyond one's own logic and man-made rules and laws.

Obedience is not blind submission to the will of those who lead you into darkness and corruption. Obedience is conscious cooperation with the Divine Will and with all those who are functioning in that Will. That Will is defined as

- Beauty, harmony
- Love, goodness, compassion
- Light, knowledge, wisdom
- Unity, synthesis

These are the four principles of the Divine Will.

Through obedience, you expand your consciousness and beingness into the One Who embodies the Divine Will. Victory, success, and prosperity are the result of obedience to higher principles.

There is also obedience to one's duty and responsibility. Karmically, we have certain responsibilities and duties. We must obey them and do our utmost not to fail to meet our duties and responsibilities.

It is interesting to know that the greatest leaders were those who were able to learn the lessons of obedience.

People think that obedience is the easiest thing to do and that everyone who wants to can obey. This is false. To obey, one must have a very advanced sensitivity of heart in order to be able to tune to the essence of the leader. Second, one must have a great amount of freedom from self-pity and posthypnotic suggestions. Third, he must have a great degree of control over his mechanical nature. Besides these, his chemistry must be in tune with the one he is going to obey.

In obedience one does not become an inferior being. On the contrary, he becomes superior to what he was. He proves that he is not an idiot but a person of understanding and that he is free of self-interest.

In certain esoteric schools, a drastic method is used to bring to the surface the latent qualities required for obedience. They order you to do things which

a. you know or think are not logical to do

b. hurt your feelings

c. reveal your ego and vanity

d. test your fearlessness, courage, and daring

e. Are difficult to do

You are ordered to do these things at an unexpected time when there is the least expectation of your obedience. It is after you learn the lesson of obedience that the Teacher makes you a candidate for conscious cooperation. This stage takes years. When it is done, the candidate becomes a co-worker, then a Teacher, then a leader.

These steps are called the "five golden steps of mastery of the field of service." It is through the tests of obedience that the whole nature of the candidate for leadership is revealed.

The command or the order also has its subtleties:

1. Direct command or order

2. Indirect command

3. Suggestion

4. Example

5. Hint

The candidate for leadership must clearly respond to these forms of command to prove his alertness, sensitivity, and sharpness. These five forms of command have different shades and magnitudes. The whole purpose is to make the candidate totally awake, conscious, and tuned to the leader.

Maybe a few words are necessary to explain number four, "example." The leader and the student go for a walk. The leader shows how to climb, rest, breathe, and walk without any explanation. The student is supposed to learn by example. The Teacher handles different situations. The student must learn.

To give another example: The Teacher and the student work together. After the work is finished, the Teacher continues to do other kinds of work, while the student has a tendency to rest. Here the Teacher introduces another technique. For example, he says, "You rest; I will work. You sleep; I will read. You eat; I will fast," and so on. The student at this stage is expected to learn by example, not by following words.

Words are spoken to please your personality. Examples are given to your soul, and the Teacher wants to see which one is active in you.

For some Teachers, such training is a highly developed science. Through such a training, they create integration, alignment, sensitivity, and Intuition in the student to prepare him for leadership.

Students express different moods through obedience. For example:

— Some of them are rebellious and angry.

— Others feel happy but do not understand the spirit of the training.

— Others are mechanical and indifferent, but they obey.

— Other strive by all means to obey in detail, and they feel joy.

— Others inwardly know the purpose of obedience, and they are always ready to obey.

One can benefit by watching and observing the reactions and responses of the applicants. Sometimes their bodies and their bodies' contents are assets. The Teacher observes whether it is the mechanism or the motivation of the candidate that is creating the hindrance. Sometimes "operations" are needed to release the student from his self-made traps.

Some students have a great capacity to pretend obedience, but they cannot pass more subtle tests of obedience. In advanced training, the Teachers very carefully design conditions in which the very goal of the candidate to become a leader does not exist, and instead there is a goal which seems very common. Teachers believe that the training of obedience must not be taken in order to climb five golden steps and become a leader.

Obedience is not a means but a goal, and the student must understand this. When the student thinks that he must learn obedience to become a leader, a whole new diplomacy is used with him to make him forget about leadership. If the student leaves the training of obedience for that reason, he will prove his bankruptcy. So the Teacher trains him and watches him, to see if an ambition or fever of leadership is growing in him, or if he is absolutely indifferent to such a goal and does not consider it as a requisite for his spiritual destination.

The Teacher must be convinced that the student is totally uninterested in being a leader while he is passing through the training of obedience.

To some very successful students a very humble task is given after they graduate from the Teaching position. For example, they are appointed chief gardener or supervisor of the kitchen, book indexing, or bathroom cleaning, and they are watched by the Teacher who hears their joy or complaints. If they survive such "humiliation" tests, they are raised to leadership.

Humiliation always precedes an unfoldment and advance on the path of service.

In dealing with the preparation for leadership, there is also more subtle training given during the stage when the Teacher himself is passing into a higher leadership position. This training is related to the chakras of the etheric, astral, and mental bodies, to their unfoldment and coordination with each other, and to their correspondences on higher planes. For example, in the stage of Teacherhood, the leader-to-be must experience the feeling of energy in various centers while he is reading, meditating, or talking — in class or privately.

Advanced Teaching is written by the charge from higher centers to vivify and awaken the higher centers of those who read it. The Teaching will not be understood and assimilated unless the corresponding centers in the person respond through fragrance, vibration, or emanation of light.

Most reading is a storing process; it is not a process of understanding or assimilation. Assimilation comes when the corresponding center is affected; the more deeply it is affected, the greater will be its capacity to assimilate.

A similar thing must occur when one is in meditation. Unless the heart, throat, and head centers are involved in simultaneous vibration and attunement with each other, very little light from Space is contacted.

Higher Guidance needs to develop in a person in order for him to have such experiences. The Inner Fire of man must contact and fuse with the Fire of Space if he expects to be a transmitter of higher ideas, visions, and revelations.

While speaking, the leader must direct his conversation through certain centers, according to the need of the one to whom he is talking. Some speakers have no idea about such a factor, and they fluctuate from one to another center, creating confusion in the being of the listener.

The same applies when giving a speech. During the speech, either the head, heart, or throat center must dominate. In rare cases, the ajna center may dominate, if command and clear directions need to be given. But the head, heart, and throat centers must keep the speaker in balance, providing him energy, will, purpose, plan, magnetism, love, light, creativity, and applicability of ideas. A conscious leader can, in rare cases, use other centers to impress an idea even more.

Advanced Teachers think that one cannot have Inner Guidance until he proves that he has understood the value and the subtlety of outer guidance by a Teacher or leader. It is only after one fully cooperates with outer guidance that the Inner Guidance makes an effort to contact the candidate.

Outer guidance is programmed in such a way that the candidate becomes ready to be sensitive and receptive to the Inner Guidance. Only after a very long training with outer guidance can a person be ready to become finely tuned to the Inner Guidance. Before the training through outer guidance is assimilated, one cannot consciously benefit from the Inner Guidance.

The student learns the science of obedience from his outer Teacher and uses it to understand the Inner Guidance. After he learns how to obey the Inner Guidance, the real education and training of leadership start.

19
Leadership and Impulse

A leader works under spiritual impulses. Spiritual impulses are communications received by the leader any time he needs to take action.

Spiritual impulses will be replaced when the human soul penetrates the sphere of Intuition and prepares his mind to translate intuitive impressions accurately and instantaneously.

Spiritual impulses can reach the leader any moment of his life and call him to take action.

In the Teaching we are told about external and internal commands. External commands are given by spoken words, by writing, or by gestures. Often these commands create pressure, rejection, animosity, and karma.

Internal commands do not refer to suggestion, hypnotic suggestion, or hints but to impulses coming from inner sources.

There are also commands coming from our glamors, illusions, urges, and drives. But real commands come from our soul or from our Inner Guide and act as impulses. Esoterically, an impulse is a command of the human soul or Inner Guide, the reason for which is not yet comprehended by the mind. When the command is carried out, then the reason for the command is understood by the mind.

Impulses are in harmony with the Plan of love, light, and beauty. As the human soul enters greater illumination and develops greater sensitivity to the One Will, his external life is carried out under spiritual impulses.

Impulses also create certain frictions with glamors, illusions, and maya, but these can be overcome easily because impulses control the inner centers which do not yield themselves to such formations.

To help people act under spiritual impulses is to give them the pure Teaching, to enlighten their minds, to reveal and expose the needs of life, and to show the direction of evolution. This will give them the opportunity to use their impulses and cooperate with those Forces which work with evolution.

When, through Intuition, the leader develops direct guidance from his Master, spiritual impulses still remain but their source changes. He receives impulses from higher sources such as from the Tower, from Zodiacal Sources, or from still Higher Existences.

The spiritual leader must continuously strive to synchronize himself with the line of command coming from higher sources and reaching him from his Soul, or from the Master of his Ashram. Only through developing sensitivity to this line of command does the leader keep his direction right and inspire his co-workers with the vision of future achievements.

A true leader never receives any order from any medium, channel, or so-called guide or psychic. Because of his victory over illusions, glamors, and maya, he cannot allow himself to be trapped by those psychics who work in the shadow of illusions, glamors, and maya mostly inspired by astral entities or dark forces.[1]

True leaders follow divine direction, confirmed and affirmed by their Intuition and logic.

The first step to develop the sense of direction is regular, daily meditation. Meditation is a continuous progress toward your innermost Reality. Meditation gradually wipes away the accumulated illusions and sets you free.

Meditation is a conscious withdrawal from your physical, emotional, and mental natures. Through meditation you will be able to see your thoughtforms, illusions, superstitions, and prejudices and make your mind your machine to use and develop for higher and higher services. It is after such an achievement that the leader gains the right to penetrate the fields of higher contacts. Meditation creates cooperation between thought and action.

Cooperation is agreement between action and thought. Inner impulse is created when the will is guided. Then, when the command is given, impulse comes into action with the conscious cooperation of the receiver of the order. The will is guided when it is tuned to the frequency of the guiding one. The guiding one uses thought power and shows the necessity of cooperation.

---

1. See *Breakthrough to Higher Psychism,* and *Other Worlds,* especially Chs. 37 and 38.

This is a subjective operation in which the will is enlightened and direction is shown, but no pressure is put into it.

The command is given externally when enough time has passed to allow the formation of the impulse. An impulse is like a mechanism waiting for the combustion of the order to gear it into action.

Impulse comes into action through the agreement of the consciousness. Because of this the guiding one is left free from karma as he does not exercise any imposition for action.

One must remember that *will* is the direction of the energy set by the decision of the human soul. It is possible to enlighten the human soul and help him make a decision and put the energy into action for that decision. Will is energy plus direction. Energy and direction create impulse. Impulse is put into action through the command.

After the impulse is created, the consciousness is engaged in action to cooperate with the impulse. This is exactly the opposite of hypnotism. Hypnotism blacks out the consciousness and puts commands into the mental body. Any such command creates an impulse, a posthypnotic suggestion which controls the man without his conscious cooperation.

In hypnotism the decision is not made by the human soul. Energy is not put into a certain direction by the decision of the human soul, but the will is created by the decision of the hypnotist and by the direction given by him to the energy.

20
Leadership and Religion

Many people break their former religious or traditional limitations and begin to open their sails on the oceans of new interests. They enjoy their new adventures for a long time, generally until they are sixty or sixty-five years old and in some cases only until they are thirty or thirty-five. Then they slowly return to their former interests, religion, traditions, or the habits of their childhood.

An average man in his seventies usually reflects the habits and mentality of his childhood when he was seven years old. This is the result of beliefs or traditions having been imposed. Converting people to your religion or traditions is the best way to create conflict within your church or group in the future. If the converted ones are in the majority, or if they are a powerful minority, and they are reverting to past beliefs, they will take over your church or group and translate your religion or tradition in a way that agrees with their former faith or habits.

How does this work?

Childhood impressions are the strongest because the vehicles are pure. The young mind does not have the disturbances or turbulences of adulthood, and the incoming impressions are almost carved in the deeper consciousness of the child. These impressions are not gathered there through logic or reasoning but by *faith*. Faith is total acceptance.

Logic and reason are ways of dialogue or negotiation. Early adulthood is a time of exploration and interaction with ideas. As a man grows older, his reason and logic weaken and his faith grows stronger.

Childhood faith stands there as part of his being. As he becomes older, his beingness becomes his only refuge. Man takes refuge only in those things which he believed without any doubt in his mind, things which he accepted on faith.

Doubt is the substance of disintegration. Whenever a man doubts some logic or knowledge, that logic or knowledge does not last long. Curiously enough, dogmas, doctrines, or beliefs impressed upon the child through his faith are the factors which create doubt in all things that he tries to study in the future. As such people grow old, they have less trust in other people of different faiths or traditions.

The cure for all this is to impart to children universal principles without dogmas, doctrines, and beliefs. Universal principles will be the foundation of future right relationship with all traditions which have universal principles in them.

Superstitions engraved in childhood will not lose their power over a person until the person clears his superstitions and illusions through the expansion of his consciousness and the transformation of his life through the fire of Intuition. Outer pressure to change superstitions, illusions, deep-seated convictions, and beliefs proves to be a failure.

There are three important factors in the psychology of man: knowingness, beingness, and adaptation.

Knowingness is a manifold formula by which man solves his problems of survival.

Beingness is formed in a moment of admiration, exultation, and ecstasy — when the light of Intuition shines and transforms the man, making him more spirit and less matter. This is Self-actualization.

Adaptation is related only artificially to knowledge and beingness. Adaptation is done under the pressure of fear, bribery, flattery, or when the person is in a semiconscious state of mind.

Adaptation is a method by which information is received without question and incorporated as an artificial part of our beingness. The information can be superstition or truth. If it is superstition, it stays in the sphere of beingness and acts as a rejector of light. If it is truth, it slowly becomes part of the beingness of the man but carries with it impressions of fear because it is artificial.

Adaptation can be cleared only through the growth of the inner man. The inner man can be fed only through his Intuition or experience. Intuition and experience nourish and build the beingness of man. They help man grow spiritually and drop all that is not truth in his nature.

As man becomes more spiritual, or as he evolves toward greater achievements of Beauty, Goodness, Righteousness, Joy, and Freedom, he does not limit his life through any separative interest or any particular religion or politics. Instead he expands his life within those principles which tend to synthesize and unite.

Converting people to other faiths in most cases creates internal conflict and tension. Internal conflict and tension affect their social behavior, their relations with their family, and their health.

Believing their way would change the world, religious zealots have tried to convert people for centuries. In the process of doing so, they attacked and destroyed old traditions and manuscripts and wiped away in many places the precious culture of the so-called pagans. But despite all this we still have a world full of crime and rejection of religions. One crime cannot eliminate another crime.

All religions have their Divine inspiration. And each one is a path to reach higher beingness and Divine awareness. We do not need to convert people but to show them the beauty of their own religion, the divine principles in their religion, and encourage comparative efforts in religions without any criticism.

Christians think that Christ is the custodian of Christian churches or of Christianity. The fact is that He is the Spirit of Unity in all religions and the ideal toward which all aspire in their Essence.

Each religion has a distinct message, and all of them complete the message for human conduct and relationship. We need to cultivate tolerance, understanding, and respect and not force people, bribe them, or threaten them into accepting the things we believe.

It is a crime to convert people into your own beliefs by force or by bribery of any kind.

Shine your light and let people see your light. Express your own faith in a graceful way, but do not make it the only way to fly.

When you attain illumination, *religion will not limit you*; dogmas and doctrines will not limit you. You will not be caught in any scripture, but you will base your life on principles and laws and above all on your experience with the God within and the God in the Universe. You will never boast about your religion but will shine out your light of Self-actualization and God-realization.

To try to create uniformity in religions is a futile effort. No two men have the same faith or belief. Even in one religion there are many conflicting interpretations or disagreements. Our effort is not to create uniformity in religions but harmony between religions and cooperation between religious people "based upon a true mental perception and a sound idealism."

We must create or reveal the Common Good for all and invite all religious people to work for that Common Goal. Any effort to create religious hatred is an action against the future unity of mankind.

People must enjoy their religious freedom. Religious freedom means to respect the religions of others. Only through respect can we begin to understand each other's religions and proceed toward cooperation.

People sometimes force their religion on their children. A forced religion first creates fanatics, then hypocrites, then disbelievers. If you want your child to hate your religion, force it on him. Such children will act totally against the moral codes of their parents' religion in order to take revenge upon them.

The best way to encourage your children in your faith is not with Sunday School and forceful lectures but through a life of beauty. Only beauty can lead your children toward the treasury of your religion.

A religion is like a flower. It reveals itself petal by petal, or level by level, as you proceed on the path of virtues, on the path of transformation.

People can understand their religions through their level. It is useless to impose a higher-level revelation on a person of a lower level.

Degeneration in religious teaching starts when levels are mixed or confused.

Religion has seven levels:

1. Physical level

2. Emotional level

3. Mental level — laws and rules and disciplines

4. Intuitional level — on which the hidden side of it is revealed

5. Actualization level — on which your beliefs become experience

6. The level of sacrifice — on which the Divine inspiration makes your life a shining light for the world

7. Divine level — on which you contact the Spirit that inspired the religion

It is impossible to impose higher levels on people who are still wandering in low levels, or to force your level on people whom you want to convert.

As we go to higher levels, disagreements in various religions disappear. This means that religious harmony cannot be achieved by imposing dogmas and doctrines but by transforming our life through the suggested levels.

21
Promises

A promise is considered very sacred. In Asia, a Sage formulated a saying which emphasizes the importance of a promise. It says:

One would rather die than to make a promise, but if he promises, he must fulfill his promise even to his death.

Our promises cause certain patterns in people in relation to their time, daily work, feelings, thoughts, plans, motives and in their relationships with other people. Let us imagine such a pattern as a set, electrical pattern in which things are done automatically according to how it is set. As long as the promise continues, things go as they were planned to go, but when the promise is broken, the whole pattern of set activities of the physical, emotional, and mental levels and the set patterns of relationship are disturbed.

Many physical, emotional, mental disturbances and states of confusion are the result of broken promises, whether it was a promise formed with a friend, a mother, a father, or your own promise to yourself.

People do not pay attention to this subtle factor, which plays a great role in our health, sanity, and behavior. Promises from others or from our own self considerably damage our health and sanity if they are not met and fulfilled.

During childhood, unfulfilled promises by parents, teachers, and friends have such an effect on our system that we may even wait for the fulfillment of the promises for seventy years and run our life in accordance with the thoughtforms of the promises given us long ago. Thus, a promise builds a prison around us and does not let us take self-activated actions.

Throughout our life, whenever the promise is attached to any circumstance or event, we go through acute crises, depressions, and failures.

A promise forms a special thoughtform in our mind and a strong expectancy within our emotional vehicle. Sometimes even the awareness of the futility of the promise does not annihilate such thoughtforms, and the expectancy of the lower mind brings in many rationalizations and lets us hang on to the promise.

Great depressions, disillusionments, inertia, and apathy are the result after the thoughtforms and the expectancy melt away. In such cases the best way to help is to find the promise and the one who promised it and dissipate the promise through analytical logic, replacing it with a spiritual challenge. It is also helpful to analyze the one who made the promise and search for the motives behind the promise and the circumstances which were related to it.

It must be remembered that the moment of the dissolution of the promise is a moment of pain and suffering. Once this phase is over, joy will be witnessed by the observer.

It is very interesting to note that the promiser builds a thoughtform within his mental sphere. If he fulfills his promise, this form melts away. If he does not fulfill his promise, no matter how lightly made, it bothers him in subtle ways, creating confusion in his mind and behavior.

If the promise is forgotten by him, the thoughtform still exists, and it is registered as a defect in the mental computer which does many things wrong because of this invisible defect.

The thoughtform of a promise can be restimulated either in the mind of the one who promised, or in the mind of the one who was promised. Every time the thoughtform is restimulated, it takes away the clarity of the mind and creates minor or major disturbances in it.

In certain cases, one promises but for a while does not carry it out. Later, he wants to meet his promise but cannot find any opportunity to fulfill it because of many circumstances. But the thoughtform of the promise remains in his being as a sore spot until it is analyzed and dissipated.

Some people make false promises. In this case they have a weak thoughtform of a promise in their minds. This thoughtform gradually grows and bothers them because the one who was promised nourishes the weak thoughtform by the force of his expectation. The thoughtform of a false promise not only becomes a promise but also a hated thoughtform within the man. It is mostly such thoughtforms that weaken the memory and the clear thinking of a human being.

It is very helpful to do a review to find your promises and either dissolve them consciously or fulfill them if possible.

A promise has a form element in it. It has etheric, astral, mental elements, and willpower. The melting process is almost impossible left to itself, but through logic and analysis it is possible to dissipate it, paying some taxes in the meantime for the delay.

Promising to oneself is also a very serious matter. In most cases, a person promises when he is in a higher state of consciousness or is Soul-infused. A promise made from such a level evokes positive polarization from the lower vehicles, but when the promise is not carried out, the positive polarization changes into negative polarization. Then the man on the personality level does exactly the opposite of what he promised in his inspirational or uplifted moments. This eventually creates an intense inner conflict.

A related situation also creates problems. Many people make various promises to their Higher Self and when they do not carry them out, they try to hide from the light of the Higher Self and keep themselves busy with lower activities. But promises made to the Higher Self can never be forgotten because the Higher Self eventually will create those crises in your life in which you recollect yourself and meet your promises through painful experiences.

It is also true that we promise on various levels with our false I's. Because we change our levels very often, we create conflicting promises within our nature. On each level we see things from different viewpoints; we have different interests and also different relationships. All the factors combined force us to make various promises to ourselves and to others which are often conflicting. Conflicts created in these ways do not contribute to our serenity and growth.

Expectations are not promises. In expectations, you form a thoughtform which may obsess you gradually if you feed it with your imagination and thoughts. Generally, expectations fade away when the source of inspiration does not show the evidences of support for your expectations.

It is very beneficial to clear your mind of the thoughtforms of expectations because they consume a great amount of energy from your mental, emotional, and etheric nature. They create diffusion in your mind, which makes you take unreasonable actions or attitudes.

Vows are of a higher order. They not only have etheric, emotional, and mental forces and the energy of the will, but they are also associated with devas and higher beings. The violation of vows creates serious disturbances in man's subtle bodies and in his relationship with subjective forces.

As we go higher, our words, promises, and vows are taken more seriously because they are connected with speech and thought. On higher levels, speech and thought are agents of creative forces which bring into manifestation and objectification the things about which we talk and think.

In breaking your vows, you start a destructive process within the forms and relationships which you have been building with your vows. This destruction affects your higher and lower vehicles in many ways.

It is possible to break vows if they were taken under pressure or in a state of unconsciousness, or if the vows interfere in your relationships with greater principles, laws, and service. If this is the case the vows must be analyzed, brought into the light of your present consciousness, and cancelled. At the cancellation ceremony, the vow must be read exactly as it was and then the cancellation form recited as a resignation process.

A vow is a promise to higher beings. Once this promise is made, they firmly expect you to follow your vows. Breaking your vows creates disturbances in their planes and in relationships with higher forces.

Decisions are related to promises. If they are done mentally, without letting another person know about your decisions, you have a less complicated labor. Decisions are related to various levels according to your state of consciousness and interest. They build thoughtforms in various intensities. Mental decisions are less complicated than when they are related to your emotions. Decisions can be made in private — that is, done in secrecy, individually, between two people, or even within a group. As the decision is known to a larger field, the possibility of its fulfillment increases *if* the people concerned are in favor. It decreases and dissolves if they are antagonistic, jealous, or not in favor.

In esoteric circles, decisions are sacred, and only the leadership formulates them and nourishes them within its own heart and mind. The leadership may also share decisions with those who will bring greater inspiration and vitality to them.

Decisions are thoughtforms. If they are exposed to people whose level does not allow them to understand and cooperate, the thoughtform suffers and even passes away. This happens because of those thought-currents and emotions which come like static or distortions and affect or infect the thoughtform of the decision. That is why decisions and plans should be kept secret until the time when their power is so great that no serious damage can be done if they are exposed.

Continuous change or breaking of decisions produces a great amount of substance of dissolved thoughtforms within the aura. Such a substance can block the passage of psychic energy and prana and create various mental and health problems. The disturbance is greater when a great amount of people are involved in the decision. Sometimes the one who breaks the decision is the object of many hostile arrows coming to him from various levels. All this suggests that promises, vows, and decisions must be made with extreme carefulness in the light of one's reason, logic, and consciousness.

Expectations must be minimized until they totally fade away. Expectations cause weaknesses in our system, and they must not be allowed to grow and occupy space in our mind. Expectations project thoughtforms into the minds of those who are the object of our expectations and cause disturbances whether they are aware or unaware of our expectations. Such disturbances mostly take the form of irritation, which eventually causes an unhappy relationship between the people concerned.

If a man nourishes an expectation and sticks to it strongly, he may force the object of his expectation to take actions without his agreement. There is thus created a great amount of irritation and emotions of secret refusal, which in due time spoil the relationship.

We must start to practice living in the light of our Soul and see things as they are.

22
Leadership and Self-Confidence

The leader continually needs new energy. He must transmit energy; he must direct energy. If he lacks energy he should not lecture, he should not hold responsibilities, and he should not write letters or communicate with people until he is totally rested.

A leader loses a great amount of energy if he concentrates his mind upon his past failures and begins to condemn himself.

One of the great characteristics of the leader is self-confidence. He is his own source of courage, his own support, his own inspiration. He never condemns himself, even if he often does not like things he does. His failures or mistakes cannot hinder his path. He casts a sharp look upon things he does not like and continues his service with self-confidence. He is self-confident because he is in contact with his True Self — and at the very moment of failure he withdraws himself and fuses himself with his True Self.

This is the reason why the criticism of people does not hinder his path or slow his speed. Actually, he does not need to know the criticism of others because he already knows before they do if it was his failure. . .or his planned action and expected results. In any case, he is not influenced by the criticism except that he learns in their criticism the mechanism of reaction and its reasons.

When the leader concentrates on past failures, he loses energy and eventually identifies with his lower self.

The leader must act always from the Soul or from the level of the Spiritual Triad. He must learn to detach himself from the three worlds and withdraw to the Inner Sanctuary whenever he sees a danger of identification with the lower self and its failures.

A leader is mostly occupied with his vision. He keeps the personality under his constant watchfulness. He knows the weak points of his lower nature and keeps an eye upon them so that they do not distort the beauty he wants to express through his leadership and service.

No one can defeat a leader except himself. It is always beneficial to remind oneself:

> *More radiant than the Sun,*
> *purer than the snow,*
> *subtler than the ether*
> *is the Self,*
> *the spirit within my heart.*
> *I am that Self.*
> *That Self am I.*

When a leader condemns himself in front of his co-workers, he deprives them of a living example of inspiration. This does not mean that the leader boasts, shows off, or makes claims, but he continues his service in the best way he can, with humility and harmlessness.

If at any time failure is noted by his co-workers, he gives a supreme example of how to overcome his failure and proceed on the way of perfection and service.

The leader does not build thoughtforms of failure in himself or in his co-workers. Often such thoughtforms attract a great amount of emotional substance and become like obsessive entities. Such thoughtforms are difficult to destroy. They heavily influence the co-workers and the leader, preparing the way for disintegration.

The leader tries not to build such thoughtforms. He controls his imagination, his words, and his manners and courageously comes out of the traps of his personality life.

One of the major concerns of the dark lodge is to discourage leaders by infusing them with self-condemnation, guilt feelings, and images of failure.

The leader does not live for himself but for the great service, and he knows that the great servers learned from their failures and never identified with them.

Instead of self-criticism or self-condemnation, the leader observes his actions very carefully and leads his personality into right action as much as possible. But he never gives up if the personality does not respond to his will in complete obedience. He observes, finds the reasons of failure, and tries again, enriched by the experience.

A disciple does not stand for himself; he stands for the labor, for the needs of others, for the call, and for the cause.

To serve the needs of others is more important than to sit and lament your own failures or your own lost prestige or position.

The Rays of the leaders condition their actions in different ways.

When a First Ray leader on the personality level fails, he becomes destructive to himself and to others. He isolates himself and develops heavy depression, self-criticism, and an inferiority complex. On the Soul level, a First Ray leader observes his failures with detachment, finds the causes of failures in order not to repeat them, and continues his service in any form possible. He pays back the damages he did to others with an indifferent attitude but with the consciousness of justice.

On the personality level, a Second Ray leader is very critical of himself at the time of failure. On the Soul level, he has great understanding and tolerance of himself and of those involved in his failure. He receives a great lesson from his failure which enlightens his mind.

On the personality level, a Third Ray leader presents many forms of rationalization at the time of his failure to escape admittance of his failure. On the Soul level, he clearly sees the reasons for his failure and in a philosophical attitude overcomes his sense of failure and penetrates into greater ideas.

A Fourth Ray leader on the personality level condemns himself and others. Like a pendulum he blames others and himself. On the Soul level, he sees greater wisdom received from his failure. He thinks that his failure was a subjective success.

On the personality level, a Fifth Ray leader analyzes all that transpired before, during, and after his failure. He finds mostly physical reasons. On the Soul level, he accurately sees how the failure developed, and he takes cautious action to secure his future success.

A Sixth Ray leader on the personality level prays for forgiveness of his sins and conflicts and becomes very active. He wants to confess and be forgiven. On the Soul level, he introduces new causes in his life and enthusiastically grasps new ways of effort and service. He invokes the help of supernatural powers.

A Seventh Ray leader on the personality level ritualistically deplores his failures. He drinks, smokes, and wastes his time and energy to forget his failures. On the Soul level, he takes his personality into discipline, harmony, and order to prevent future failures.

In cases of success and achievement, leaders act according to their level. They either enter a state of pride or a state of humility.

The road called pride says, "Now I know everything, more than the books and more than my Teacher. Everybody admires me. I am really something; from now on I must show everyone my power, and they must listen to me," etc.

This path leads eventually to refusal. People reject you, and for a while you try to use any kind of force to impose yourself, which again leads to failure. In such a state the vision is lost and the leader begins to worship himself. We are told that Hierarchy forsakes those who lose their humility and the sense of proportion or relativity.

The second path leads to humility. The leader sees that the words of praise coming from many directions are actually threads of the trap. He sees that he is very far yet from achieving the vision which his Soul holds in front of him. He sees that many things he thinks he knows are the registered thoughts of others which he repeats without any actual realization. He tries to learn more, to be more, and to become more interested in the needs of others than in his own achievements.

Every time you do something great, try to remember the needs of the group members and their problems. Remember the problems of the world. Remember the increasing crime, exploitation, hatred, and separatism. See what you have done to decrease the problems of the world and how successful you have been.

Remember yourself and see how limited you are, how limited your heart and mind are, how limited you are in your creative power. Remember the things that you did but do not approve. Remember your past errors, mistakes, and failures and look to the future. Build a vision for yourself and see how much of it can be actualized.

Thus after each victory, defeat the voices of pride within you, renew your vision, and take new steps to progress.

Do not be flattered by the praise of your friends, nor be discouraged by the attacks of your enemies. Do not listen to the voice of your personality. Perform your duty as if you were the servant of the Lord.

The leader must be very careful to take action at any evidence of showing-off or pride. Such action is composed of the following steps:

1. Do not give any chance to the person until he learns the lesson of humility.

2. In certain cases catch him at the point of his failure and make him realize it.

3. Your duty is to crush his pride but encourage his Soul for further striving.

4. Give him duties in which he will face his own shortcomings.

5. Do not encourage his personality, and be hard on him.

6. At the right occasion, humiliate him in front of the group.

Consider also that the leader must be very careful in praising his co-workers. A little extra dosage of praise can ruin a co-worker's life and make him the slave of his glamor for a long time. Praise must be given in a way that the co-worker is encouraged but challenged to a greater striving. A leader who praises and admires everyone loses his power of guidance.

Magnanimity is a virtue of a great leader. He praises people by giving greater responsibilities and greater sacrificial tasks. Real co-workers are not nourished by flattery or praise but by heavier duties and heavier responsibilities in which greater wisdom, silence, honesty, and selflessness are needed.

The leader's duty is to lead his co-workers from the field of self-interest and self-worship to the field of human service — service which is rendered in a deep, sacrificial spirit. One of our Teachers used to say to us after we performed our duties, "May God increase your energy so that you work harder."

23
Self-Defeat and Self-Victory

It is very difficult to defeat a man who is not separated within himself. We call such a man a *holy man*, a man who is one with his True Self. It is such people who bring great changes in the consciousness and life of humanity. All the hatred, jealousy, neurosis, madness, and brutality of people come like huge waves and break upon the rocks of such individuals. Even if they are the objects of hatred and crimes, their light shines forever in coming centuries with increasing brightness and beauty.

The secret of their power is the integrity of their Self and personality. They are shielded by faith, hope, striving, daring, and courage. Their deeds are the manifestation of their Selves. Their emotions are the fragrance of their hearts. Their thoughts reflect the Will and the Purpose of the Supreme Life.

Self-defeat is the result of a divided inner condition of a man or a woman. Whenever a man acts, talks, or thinks against his own conscience, he creates cleavages within himself and weakens himself. Whenever a man acts, talks, or thinks against the interests of the spiritual reality of other people, he creates cleavages within himself and weakens himself. Whenever a man acts, talks, or thinks against the welfare of Nature, he creates cleavages within himself and weakens himself.

Inner cleavages breed fear. Fear produces poison. This poison gradually spreads over the nervous system and paralyzes the thinking process, then the mechanism of speech, and then casts a deep inertia all over the body. Defeat is inevitable when cleavages come into being.

Cleavages occur, also, when one increases his karmic debts. Stealing, gossiping, criticizing, nosiness, using things which do not belong to you, living at the expense of others, using other people for your own personal interests all create cleavages within yourself. Cleavages bring in fear; fear produces poison.

People become sick and die prematurely because of their cleavages, fear, and poisons. Immunity is developed through integrity and wholeness. Mixed measures do not build a strong temple.

It is interesting to note that sometimes criminals and those who work against the interests of their fellow human beings, causing great difficulties in their lives, have healthy bodies and live a long life. Such people have "integrity," though it is a negative integrity which gives them strength. They act as a unit in their physical, emotional, and mental life. They do not have cleavages.

The reason that they do not have cleavages is that they have their own standards, and they believe in their standards no matter how far their standards are from the standards of righteous and holy ones. They keep their "integrity" and build a personality crystallized on the lines of negative or anti-evolutionary force.

This continues until the Soul sends a beam of light into the personality and creates an opposing thought-form, which later will serve as the base for evolutionary forces. As the influence of the Soul dawns and increases in the personality, the problems of the subject increase and multiply. He confronts physical, emotional, and mental problems, as if all the creditors were coming at once and demanding their payment. The reason for this is that the inner "integrity" is distorted, and no form can exist for long without inner unity, inner harmony or integrity.

There is also another condition in which the subject thinks that he is not living by his highest standards, though he is living with the standards of society. The Soul's standards may be very high and ahead of the standards of society. Thus he has conflict between these two standards. This also leads to an inferiority complex, a guilt complex, and defeat.

This type of person suffers long and lives a very difficult life, because he attracts higher energies into his system through his higher standards, creating chaos in his threefold system. Many highly developed mystics live such a life. They condemn themselves and feel that they are great sinners, trangressors, and violators of the Will of God.

There is another type of person who, though he lives within the standards of society, always has the opinion that he is doing something wrong and that everybody knows about his faults. Such a man lives in constant fear, which causes cleavages in him and leads to self-defeat.

Such a person probably has many imported suggestions and commands from his parents, superiors, teachers, or friends who on certain occasions did not approve of him, not because he was wrong but because they had a different standard. In adopting other people's standards, the subject creates conflict within himself because, instead of measuring himself by his own standards, he measures himself by the imported standards.

There is also the possibility that certain people act as the agents of karma and appear to others as persons without higher integrity. If they are unconscious agents, it is possible that they accept the attitudes of others and judge themselves by the judgments of others, thus creating cleavages within themselves.

There are various ways to solve inner conflicts and to bridge inner cleavages.

1. Make sure that all your deeds, words, and thoughts are based on your *convictions*. If there is any doubt in your mind, it must be handled before the action is taken.

Those who act from the ground of their inner convictions develop integrity, influence, and power, plus health. If their inner convictions are based on divine principles such as Beauty, Goodness, Righteousness, Joy, and Freedom, they become invincible.

Immortals are those human beings who were able to solve the problems of cleavages within themselves and to reach the highest unity on progressive levels of their evolution. Such people, being focused in their Divine Self, are not affected by the temporary actions of their personality vehicles.

2. Another method to heal cleavages is to remember your *Self* and to meditate on the mantram of "The Self."

> *More radiant than the Sun,*
> *purer than the snow,*

subtler than the ether
is the Self,
the Spirit within my heart.
I am that Self.
That Self am I.

Such a meditation helps to heal the cleavages and releases energies from the Self. These energies eventually purify those elements in the lower bodies which act as contributors to cleavages.

3. Another method is taking occasional retreats during which you create your own standards in the light of your highest vision and try to live your standards through all your inner and outer relationships.

It is not others who defeat us. It is we who work out our own failures. A man on the path of integration and at-one-ment draws great wisdom and energy from any kind of attack, whether it is based on his mistakes or on the hatred, jealousy, greed, or ignorance of others. Such attacks pull him together and make him focused and more creative in bringing greater beauty to the world.

Such people even admit failures but do not admit that these failures were their own. After recognizing and admitting them, they grow into greater integrity. This is why the wisdom of the Ancient Sages emphasized achieving peace within. They prescribed various methods:

    a. Confession and absolution

    b. Forgiveness

    c. Understanding

      d. Sacrificial service

      e. Devotion

Confession is a method to make you aware of the cleavages. After the awareness, the healing of the cleavages takes place. The formula which the Church has used has led millions into greater integration.

> *In Him we have salvation, and in His blood, forgiveness of sins, according to the richness of His grace.*[1]

> *...that He might sanctify His people with His own blood....*[2]

The Church built a thoughtform of Christ Whom they believed would forgive them and sanctify them from their sins if they confessed them and recognized them. This is a very potent method to heal cleavages for those who have faith.

Forgiveness, if done in the light of realization of both parties, leads to greater integration and unity. Revenge creates cleavages or perpetuates them. Forgiveness heals cleavages and gives a chance for progress toward greater integration.

Understanding human nature and the threefold mechanism of the personality leads us not to condemnation but to revelation. You understand why and how the cleavages occurred. You understand the way the forces of Nature function. You understand the chemistry of thoughts, emotions, urges, drives, and many hidden

---

1. Ephesians 1:7
2. Heb. 13:12

pressures collected throughout your lives. You try to heal and not condemn and perpetuate the cleavages.

Those who widen or increase the number of cleavages in others, through their condemnation, criticism, and punishment, prepare future criminals. Most criminals are those people who sought understanding but did not find it, and they were unable to heal the cleavages within themselves.

Sacrificial service for a greater cause brings in a high-level integration, not only within the personality but between the personality and spiritual spheres.

Sacrificial service releases the fire of will, which cleanses the impurities causing cleavages in our system. In the meantime, sacrificial service acts as payment for all that was taken from others consciously or unconsciously.

I met a great Teacher once who used to work in very difficult conditions, dedicating his life to the many needs of his students to such a degree that he was able to forget his own life and interests almost totally. Once I asked why he was so dedicated to his work. The answer was short, "I am paying back".... "Paying back" is a method of high integration.

One-pointed *devotion* to an ideal creates integration in your nature and brings higher influences into your life. Devotion prevents cleavages or heals them. It creates polarization and harmony within your system and opens the resources of light, love, and power in your higher centers.

Man is not created for defeat. His destiny is victory, synthesis, unity. Nature provides all the ways and means to make a man victorious, no matter how and where he failed.

The karmic law sometimes is understood as the law of punishment. Actually, it is the most beneficent law which paves the way for a future of greater and greater integration and of greater and greater victory.

It is suggested that we do not think about dangers but try to fulfill our mission the best way we can.

What does it mean not to think about danger but to live in danger? To think about danger means to preoccupy oneself with the consequences of danger to such a degree that one paralyzes himself and makes himself unable to find ways and means to face the danger.

Danger, in reality, is not factual but is only a possibility. Thinking about danger makes the possibility a reality for us. The power of danger does not come from its possibility. It comes from the fact that we make it a manifestation within our imagination.

To live in danger means to realize that anything can happen anywhere and anytime. If this realization is clear, one does not waste his time thinking about any particular danger but thinks how to live a life that makes all dangers a "ladder" of achievement.

It will not be an exaggeration if we say that creation is a field of dangers. Dangers are considered as "propelling forces." They are also the best doors of opportunity. A great success comes after mastery of a greater danger.

People must not dwell mentally on dangers but must forge ahead using the dangers as a propelling force.

24
Leadership and Failure

A leader must inspire his group with an image of nobility and honesty and an ideal image of leadership in order to win the trust of people and organize them for the service of the Plan. He must try hard to exemplify an image of a true leader in his actions, emotional reactions, and thinking.

Some leaders emphasize their failures and forget about their achievements. Such leaders slowly develop doubt about their leadership, and gradually people lose their trust in them.

A wise leader must not only try to exemplify the ideal leadership, but he must also teach people with examples and words how to develop successful leadership. One of the secrets of this path is to avoid strongly emphasizing his own weaknesses and personal failures and instead to emphasize and demonstrate the techniques of success.

A true leader is a Higher Self in tune with the Plan and with the needs of the time. It is possible, however, that he may fail temporarily and identify himself with the lower self. This sometimes happens when his focus for some reason goes down to the personality. But when the personality fails, he does not admit that *he* failed because it was not his failure but the failure of the personality. If he had good intentions, even if his personality failure appears as a failure, in the long run it is not a failure but a cause of great success.

One admits *his* failure only if he is identified with the lower self or the failing one. A real leader is not identified with his lower self, and he can detach himself from the lower self and see why and how it erred.

Identification with the lower self develops guilt feelings and hinders the great service the leader is going to perform. Many would-be leaders were destroyed because they identified themselves with their petty failures. Dark forces work very hard to exaggerate our failures and lead us into dismay.

One can admit that the lower self apparently made a mistake, but the lower self sometimes acts under the programming put into it in past lives. When the programming is activated, the result may appear wrong to some; but when it was programmed, it may have been done for a right purpose.

If the leader's intention is good, no failure brings bad results; it works in some way for the good of the group.

Many so-called leaders in all areas have a custom of talking about their failures and shortcomings, thinking that it is a sign of humility. They excuse themselves for their failures by confessing them to people, but actually they create distrust in the hearts of their co-workers.

The leader must inspire faith and trust and must actually try to inspire people by his noble character and deeds. But when he talks about his failures and impresses people with how weak is his leadership, he loses his magnetism and the influence he had on people.

This happens not only in esoteric fields but also in all fields of human endeavor. If a teacher of mathematics talks about how many mistakes he makes in his calculations, the students will turn away from him. Leadership is the inspiration of trust.

When a leader is accused of doing something wrong in a large organization, the leadership, after examining the situation, often raises his position to inspire in him self-trust and to evoke the trust of the group. This does not mean that the leader is ignorant of what his lower self did, but he cannot destroy his opportunity to serve because of his occasional mistakes or personality mistakes.

Sometimes if we are strongly impressed by the image of our failures, we become incapacitated. Some parents and other people in authority do this to us often. They tell us how nasty we are, how great a failure we are, and gradually we believe them. This affects our whole life.

Wise leaders do not take your failures seriously, except in the case of treason. They try to make you understand that you can still be successful and learn a great deal from your mistakes which, in turn, will bring you greater success.

Failures done under obsession and possession are considered fatal, and must be dealt with properly.

A wise leader will explain to you that as long as you are under the control of your personality, you will have failures. To be under the control of the personality is in itself a failure.

It also happens occasionally or in rare moments that you fall under the control of your personality or the personality of someone else. These are the moments of failure. But it is not your failure; it is a failure of identification.

Failures are of different sorts:

1. Failure because of identification

2. Failure from the viewpoint of those who have different standards

3. Failure because of time and lack of means

To define failure, we may say that *a failure is an act by which you make yourself and others incapable of continuing to strive toward perfection.* As long as you or others are identified with your failures, you will not be able to strive.

The duty of a leader is to stand above his failures and make others stand above their failures by making them understand that it is the *persona* or the false self that makes mistakes — not the Self. This means that it is only the personality that makes mistakes, not the Self.

A leader does not make mistakes as long as he is conscious of what he is doing. For example, if he is doing something nasty to reveal to you how obnoxious you are, he is not doing anything wrong. Making you awake about yourself is the first step to free you from your limitations.

When a leader does things unconsciously, he may fall into traps. But if he immediately becomes aware of the traps and sees how he trapped himself, his failure changes into a victory.

Every leader must have a committee of Elders, or a leadership, supervising the work. He must have occasional meetings where he can discuss his personality failures and ask advice to overcome them. Of course, the leadership will try to make him feel the seriousness of his mistakes and also the fact that he, as a Self, did not err. This is important in order to make him continue to strive.

The ideal of leadership must always be demonstrated, even if the leader cannot meet the details of that ideal.

Once my Teacher tripped on a branch and fell. When he got up, he said with a smile, "I felt I should kiss the blessed earth for a moment!" In a split second, I saw the ideal beyond him, which he was trying to uphold even in his momentary failure of observation. The ideal was the *One* who never did anything without a good reason.

Of course, the merchants of the Teaching can play similar games to cover their intentions and poverty and appear with robes of authority, but the discriminating heart reveals the facts.

Once there was a great painter who was exhibiting his paintings in a gallery. While he was observing people's attitudes and interest in his work, a shoemaker approached him and said, "Master, you did something wrong with the shoe of the man in that painting. If you please, I will explain to you why."

The painter listened to the words of the shoemaker and admitted that he had made a mistake. He told the shoemaker that he would correct it. But after this victory, the spirit of vanity entered the heart of the shoemaker and he said, "By the way, the eyes of this lady and the flowers also need corrections."

After examining the suggested points, the artist turned to the shoemaker and said, "Stay with the shoe, and don't go beyond it."

Thus a leader must not tolerate vanity and belittling criticism from those who are unqualified or trapped in their spirit of criticism. It is often necessary in leadership to put people in their right place and not give them an opportunity to go beyond their shoes.

Once in a certain monastery, the graduate students went through certain tests by which the leadership would determine whether or not it would give the last blessings to the graduates. One of the tests of a certain student was to carry a bowl filled to the brim with water carefully for a distance of two hundred meters to the Board of Teachers, exactly at an appointed time. On the way, some Teachers would hide, waiting to throw pieces of wood in the student's path or to trip him with a rope.

As he was walking, the student stumbled on one of the pieces of wood and the bowl fell and broke into pieces. Leaving behind the pieces of the bowl, the student walked to the hall of the Board and announced, "I am here."

One of the Teachers asked, "Where is the bowl?"

Without hesitation, the student answered, "It tried to cause delay, and I broke it into pieces."

He was allowed to sit on a chair in front of the Board, and the president of the Board said, "You are here exactly at the right time. We graduate you because you did not admit an imposed defeat." And each of the Teachers hugged him and congratulated him on his graduation.

This will seem like a hallucinatory game to contemporary teachers who hand a diploma for book-knowledge to hundreds of students waiting in a row for the support of a piece of paper.

After establishing a great deal of trust in the hearts of their co-workers, some leaders play a very disturbing game. This game is intended to dismiss those followers who are gathered around the leader because of their personality interest or security, or because they want to feel comfortable in their purposeless life. The game is often very successful in identifying those who have developed discrimination and trust, and those who have superficially and with self-interest attached to them.

The game has many names, but its essence is as follows: The Teacher does seemingly obnoxious things, creating a storm in the minds of his followers. Seemingly he steals, lies, and reveals his egotistic intentions and past transgressions. He seemingly involves himself with prostitutes or gamblers, etc. In doing all this, he patiently and firmly watches the reactions of his followers. Some find an opportunity to take revenge on him, using malice, slander, and treason. Others feel desperate, hopeless, and lost. A few keep their trust, love, and adoration.

This game is sometimes called the "game of separating the wheat from the chaff." The majority of the followers are thus scattered in various places. Some see their own weaknesses in the purported weaknesses of the Teacher. A minority moves closer to the Teacher.

A similar "game" was played during the Crucifixion of Jesus. It was seemingly His worst defeat when only a few disciples followed Him to the Cross. May God save those who throughout centuries played at religion, turning their backs on their Master!

The drama of the Crucifixion ended with the reappearance of the triumphant Master to those who were faithful and did not leave Him in His apparent defeat by the forces of darkness.

25
Leadership and Faith

One of the greatest virtues and protections of a leader is *faith*. Without faith a leader cannot go too far. It is possible to say that there can be no leader without a strong, abiding, fiery faith.

To have faith means to have contact with those who have been shaping the destiny of humanity for millions of years. To have faith means to be under the protection and the guidance of those who are subjectively supervising the work of the externalization of spiritual values and the fulfillment of the Divine Plan.

Faith gives strength, courage, daring, and endurance through difficult cycles. It unfolds the spirit of patience, which overcomes the obstacles created by the adversaries of the evolution of humanity.

Real faith is an intuitive contact with subjective realities. This intuitive contact must be present if a leader is going to act in harmony with the Divine Plan, charged with the energy of the Custodians. This intuitive link transmits the wisdom, the love, and the beauty of the higher realms. This is why a man can be unconquerable if he has faith with which, as Christ said, he moves mountains.

Hierarchical work is very discriminative and sensitive work. The leaders of the Future must prepare themselves to be accurate and up-to-date, and reject all activities that are not inspired by the principles of Beauty, Goodness, Righteousness, Joy, and Freedom.

Before "leading" other people, a leader must lead himself into a new dimension of sincerity, honesty, renunciation, dedication, and deeper faith. It is very important that a man transform himself before he tries to transform others.

Your subjective achievement will take the role of leadership. Not your vanity, your desires, your ambition, but your inner achievement will pave the ways for others.

Leaders are those people who were led into the spheres of Hierarchy, into the spheres of the Plan, into the boundaries of Shamballa. The first striving of the leader-to-be is to exert himself and lead himself into such dimensions. Once he is in contact with such higher spheres, he will magnetically attract those people who are anxious to release themselves from the slavery of life.

People ask, "Why is that man or woman magnetic?" The answer lies in the fact that they initiated and led themselves into higher levels of consciousness, into new spheres of spiritual values, into higher states of awareness. That is why they are magnetic, and they are leaders in virtues.

Often leaders help you without your awareness. Their presence and contact with you, like a magnet, create new formations and configurations in the atoms and cells of your bodies. These new configurations slowly become constructive for your spiritual energy, which gradually flows down to your vehicles and causes a new awakening, a new sense of values, and a new enlightenment within you.

Without faith you do not have the urge to strive. Once you are charged with faith, you do not identify yourself with the failures of your personality. No matter how many times your personality has failed to live up to the standard required, you will press forward and say, "I will try again. I will teach, serve, sing, and write again even if people have destroyed my reputation and the result of my long labor."

No one can conquer a man if that man has faith — faith in the Self within, faith in the Great Ones, faith in the One Life, faith in the inner resources of beauty and creativity.

Some leaders develop a very high degree of the sense of purity, justice, and honesty, but because of many personal and social conditions, they often fail in their practical life. They make little mistakes here and there; they say words which they do not approve; they take actions which they condemn. These little things accumulate in their conscience and eventually become so unbearable that they decide to quit their duties and responsibilities and hide or disappear and work on lower levels of life.

It is only faith that will help them stand. Sometimes the greatest light, the greatest success comes to those who endure a long tunnel of failures and humiliations. With patience and faith a new dawn starts for them, and they enter a field of greater service of which they never dreamed.

Many of our failures are karmic debts. It is better to pay and get rid of them because until they are paid you are not free for greater labor.

Again faith, courage, endurance.... A leader must keep on going. Even if everything fails, he will keep going with the victory of spirit and faith.

A leader is one who has learned to identify himself with his True Self instead of with the weaknesses of the vehicles.

When we read the lives of great leaders, one thing shines out in their life history. They could not be so great if they did not meet great dangers and problems every minute of their life. Their greatness is equal to the dangers and problems they passed through.

It is very interesting to note that dangers and problems help leaders by spreading their ideas and creating greater creative tension in them, which will be used to raise the level of human beings.

How to obtain faith? We can obtain it from those who have it. Faith is very contagious. It is electrical; once you receive it, it charges you for a long time.

We can obtain faith by following the history of our life and seeing the dangers and troubles we passed through with invisible help. We can consider how an invisible hand guided us to the right places, to the right people, to the right conditions in which we grew.

We can obtain faith by living a life of service, sacrifice, and purity. We can obtain faith by reading the lives of Great Ones and pondering upon their Teachings.

We can obtain faith through steady, regular meditation. Steady, regular meditation takes us eventually to the spheres of Intuition where faith starts. When the Fourth Cosmic Ether, or the Intuitional substance, penetrates our etheric, emotional, and mental bodies, we feel charged with faith.

Faith enlightens the consciousness and opens the gates of the future.

Faith creates a symphony in your thoughts and actions. Faith evokes willpower from higher sources. The regeneration of the world will come at the hands of those who are charged with faith.

Follow Me. Strive to Me. Only thus can you understand the future. What could be preferred to the Forces of Light? One's faith can be renewed as an immutable force. Faith that does not guide one's entire life is worthless. I indicate the countries that have lost their path; the machine is still in motion, but without a regeneration of the consciousness there is nothing on which to exist. New consciousness can come only from the spirit. The new force can be strengthened only through knowledge of the higher worlds. The accumulation of such knowledge will strengthen life. One may reject the most essential if one fails to consider the future! One must accept all transitions as improvements. A single flight of thought can transport us across the abyss. Even that which seems most inevitable depends upon the quality of thought. The affirmation of thought can even alter the return to Earth. The Subtle World is regarded generally as a passive state, but it need not be merely passive; it can be active as well. If it has been said, 'As in heaven, so on earth,' this means that there, also, conditions exist for higher achievements. We should not judge only by average measures. If the average period between incarnations is approximately seven hundred years, there can also be spans of seven or even three years. Karmic conditions themselves must yield to the hammer of the will. Thought itself is the best fiery guardian. Thought is unconsumable! Even on Earth, a man suffused with faith and thought loses weight. Thought also leads to the higher worlds. When thrown off balance, a man requests a moment's respite. This respite affords an accumulation of will. Without will there is no faith. Thus We arm people with weapons of Light.[1]

---

1. Agni Yoga Society, *Fiery World,* Vol. I, para. 340.

26
Inspiration and Impression

Sometimes we live four or five previous lives in one life, and often the seeds of problems of these four or five lives germinate in that one life, causing great pressure on the soul to face them, handle them, and keep going on the highway of his evolution. This is one of the reasons why we must not judge when we see a man traveling on the highway of his evolution, while at the same time demonstrating various personality problems and struggling with them.

In our daily life when we see a man striving to stand up, we do not kick him down but extend our help and lift him up.

One day a Teacher said to his disciples, "If I had never failed in my life, I would never tolerate what you are now at the present." The spiritual leader sees in other persons his past, his efforts, his failures, and he waits patiently to see his victories in them.

True leadership is not imposition of ideas, ways, or means upon the followers. Actually, a true leader does not work to create followers but people who know how to lead themselves in the right direction. Everyone has his own level, needs, karma, and goals. Everyone must have his own way to do things. Leadership does not mold all people into a unified form of activity but creates harmony between all ways and all forms of unfoldment and progress so that the subjective unity is realized in objective diversity.

Leadership creates spiritual tension. Spiritual tension is created when leadership presents those same goals and visions that your Inner Guide is trying to project upon your mind. Leadership creates the polarity between your Inner Guide's visions and goals for you and the ideal expressions of the visions and goals in actualization.

Between these two polarities tension develops. This tension is creative in the sense that the visions and goals of your Inner Guide are drawn out into objectivity in the field of your mind, and striving is created within you to carry them into actualization. The striving is carried out through firm decision. In true decision one uses his willpower to overcome any interference that hinders his steps from reaching his goal.

The vehicles of man are put in harmony with the Monadic intent in four ways:

1. Through inspiration

2. Through conscious love

3. Through illumination

4. Through impression

Inspiration is a flow of energy which carries with it a purpose and a plan and puts the mechanism of man into action in a certain direction. Inspiration can come from the etheric planes or from the higher Cosmic Ethers. It is not censored by the mental body, and it activates the etheric centers.

Some spiritual books were received through inspiration, for example the *Koran*. Mohammed was an illiterate man, but He spoke the most practical and esoteric language. The *Koran* was given through Him without the conscious collaboration of his mind.

Inspiration reveals the purpose of any object and of life as if a light were thrown on the object and you could see the reason why it was created.

It is very interesting to know that one can be inspired by dark forces and follow their path. But it is very rare, if not impossible, to be *impressed* by dark forces. This technique of communication, which is called "the communication technique of impression," cannot be applied by dark forces because the receiving agent is too far advanced to be deceived and misled.

Inspiration by dark forces is an act of obsession and possession to hinder the progress of evolution. Inspiration by higher forces is an act of harmonization and vitalization of the vehicles to enable them to take constructive evolutionary actions.

Conscious love is the light of the Inner Guide which, when absorbed by the human soul, produces wisdom. Man draws knowledge and guidance via the beam of conscious love emanating from the Inner Guide. Love evokes the hidden treasures within the human soul and brings the soul into a flowering process. Great poets created their masterpieces through such a love. A classic example is Jalaluddin Rumi, the great Persian poet.

Illumination is the result of a light thrown into the mind to make man able to see the laws and principles of life and solve the problems on the Path.

Illumination leads to holism.

Impression in its highest form has to do with the Monad. It is a Monadic communication with the unfolded human soul who is in control of the totality of the mental plane.

Esoterically we can say that impressions reach the human soul from his own core, the Monad, and from higher centers on the planet, the solar system, and beyond.

An impression is an idea, vision, instruction, direction, or symbol projected from a greater center upon the *soul*, which receives the projection as if he were a photographic plate on which the impression is projected exactly as it is. Telepathy is the first step toward the science of impression.

There is a very subtle difference between inspiration and impression. Inspiration uses your etheric centers for certain activities. During inspiration there is even a moment in which you observe yourself doing things as if you were pushed by a current of energy. In inspiration you are almost forced toward a certain direction in certain ways.

If the subject is sufficiently prepared, he acts synchronously with the power of inspiration and, in the meantime, *translates* or interprets the inspiration to the level of those to whom the inspiration is related.

In impression you are given the exact plan, the exact purpose, and the ways and means to fulfill the plan and the purpose. A poem can be impressed exactly in your mind, and you just write it down. A whole book can be impressed on your mind to give to humanity as it was given to you.

In impression you know the source; you know the instruction; you know the destination. It is just like a complete blueprint of a building which you can read, understand, and begin to build stage by stage.

In inspiration the idea and the energy is given to you to use according to the need. It is possible that after the inspiration is put into action and actualized, your mind begins to analyze it and plan activities based on the inspiration.

Impression can change into inspiration when, for any reason, your vehicle of registration is not clear or is not in operation. In such cases, inspiration changes into drives and urges in the lower vehicles. If you contact any source of inspiration prematurely, it creates blind urges and drives within your system and generally works in destructive ways.

Inspiration is energy charged with a direction. Impression is energy plus clear instruction, subject to the voluntary and conscious cooperation of the person.

Inspiration is not created by the person. It depends on the decision of higher forces to inspire a person. But one can learn the science of impression and use it by his own choice.

Inspiration is conditioned by your background, the state of your physical, emotional, and mental bodies, and your environment. All these influence the inspiration, to a certain degree, in its process of manifestation. But an impression stays as it is and is not conditioned by the forces emanating from your personality or environment, although you have the freedom to adapt the impression to existing conditions.

Some people use the word impression in its exoteric sense. They say, "I had an impression to do certain things, but it was not clear." If it is an impression, it is registered clearly in its exactitude and vitality. For example, an individual is impressed by a diagram related to Cosmogenesis, and he puts it out exactly as it was given to him. If it was inspired, he can only produce a diagram with his own interpretation.

Inspiration creates varying results on different planes of the personality. Impression remains the same on all registering planes. It may become darker on the lower planes, but it does not lose its exactitude.

Inspiration can be transmitted by Shamballa, by the Hierarchy, or by your Inner guide. But if you do not have the appropriate equipment to translate the inspiration consciously on the level it was sent to you, you do not even bother to translate it until after it is manifested.

In inspiration you are taking the energy and using it according to what you are. The same energy of inspiration might be translated by you as a painting, by me as a symphony, and by others as a dance, etc. But in impression you do what the source of impression wants you to do, with the utmost exactitude.

Inspiration is like giving you some fabric and asking you to sew a dress. You take the material and make a dress the way you think best. In impression the material, the design, and all other details are given to you as the most essential and goal-fitting for the plan of the moment.

Both techniques are ways of communication. One is like symbolic communication, the interpretation of which depends on your state of evolution and achievement. The other is direct communication which is not conditioned by your interpretation.

In a sense, you have more freedom of translation in inspiration than in impression. Inspiration is translated according to the degree of your response. Impression is projection by the higher centers, and it stays as it is.

We may say that the picture projected on the screen is an impression. The energy that hits certain crystals, which through reaction to the energy take special form, is like inspiration.

Inspiration is invocation. Impression is evocation.

Sometimes great Teachers inspire a person with great ideas and visions, and the person tries to work out the inspiration through certain ways and forms, breaking the voltage of the inspiration through his own effort of translation. But in the case of impression, the whole voltage is there and it must be transmitted almost without change.

Impressions are given for certain levels, and they can be used accurately on these levels. Inspiration can be used on any level. For example, one is on the Olympic swim team and he swims very well, but toward the end of the race he has one mile left and he feels very tired. His friend jumps into the water and swims with him to encourage him. He is receiving inspiration, but he must do the work.

It is possible to be impressed by your Soul, but be inspired by your Master. It is possible to be impressed by your Master, but be inspired by the Hierarchy. It is possible to be impressed by the Hierarchy and inspired by Shamballa and so on. Impression is more accurate and precise communication.

If impression is transferred prematurely, it creates illusion. Inspiration can be adapted to many occasions and conditions.

In the transmission of impression special communication lines are built through which the impression travels and reaches the receiving agent. But in inspiration the communication line is temporary and is sometimes built by your Soul or special devas and then removed.

Sometimes alcohol, drugs, or special rhythms of drums or other instruments stimulate the brain cells, the etheric centers, and the mental atoms and build a channel of inspiration given by low-level entities or black forces. Some contemporary music, dances, and paintings are inspired from such sources through alcohol, drugs, and certain rhythms.

Impression cannot come through such means. It comes when the Golden Bridge is built between the Monad and the personality.

One must always try to find the sources of his drives, stimulations, or inspirations. What or who is controlling you? Once you find the answer to this question, you have a great chance to control your actions, or at least make efforts to control them.

Inspiration is the method of higher forces to help the evolution of humanity without its conscious approval and cooperation. In impression the same forces act with the cooperation and approval of the human consciousness.

In inspiration you have almost no choice. In impression you have choice, but you follow the impression almost exactly anyway because you intuitively see the highest beauty and the purest goal-fittingness of the impression.

It is also interesting to notice that maya, which is an etheric congestion or accumulation of energy, is dispelled by inspiration. Inspiration has the power to wash out the congestion in any center and release it into proper activity.

Glamor, which is an emotional congestion and crystallization, is cleared away by the light of the love of the Soul, which creates clear thinking, discrimination, and analysis.

Illusion is a mental crystallization which is shattered and cleared away by the energy of illumination, thrown into the mind from the center of the Spiritual Triad.

The Dweller on the Threshold, which is the combination of these three accumulated around the axis of the human soul, is burned away by the power of the Monadic flame.

This whole cleaning process has one goal: to establish a direct communication line between the Monad and the personality so that the individualized Divinity, the human Spark, may manifest Its supreme beauty and fulfill Its duty.

27
The Art Of Lecturing

Let us begin with certain details in the art of lecturing. These are very important details because lecturing is a means of contact with people. A contact is a serious thing. It can hinder progress or open the way for new achievements.

Before you lecture, have a retreat and contact your Higher Self for at least ten minutes. Even if you are the best speaker, it does not matter. It is not the ability to speak that is important but the energy you transmit through your words. You may have defective grammar. You may not know how to make smooth phrases, and so on. But if you have made the inner contact, the energy passing through your words will inspire and uplift people. This energy from the Higher Self amplifies the essence of your words and visions and expresses itself through your actions and looks.

While you are in retreat for ten minutes before you lecture, speak to your Higher Self and say, as Saint Francis of Assisi did, "O Lord, make me an instrument of Thy peace. Where there is hatred, let me sow love. . . ." When the contact is made, you yourself will be surprised by the inspiration pouring out through your words and even composing the most beautiful sentence structures for you.

You will see that often at the time of your lecture you are inspired and uplifted by the energy passing through you because of the contact.

Lectures should not be

— For entertainment

— For showing off

— From a need for recognition

— To increase information

— To increase our followers

— To acquire money

— To satisfy our glamors

Our lectures should be like beams of directed energy of realization and transmutation to

- Cause changes in people
- Heal them
- Expand their consciousness
- Make them strive
- Inspire them with greater beauty

- Challenge them to greater achievement
- Simplify the goal

The best lecture is the lecture that remains in the mind of the audience and offers an opportunity for improvement. This means that it must have an architectural construction and be simple enough, but with roots toward deeper visions. It is possible to present highly charged pictures in allegories or parables which remain a long time in the minds of people and cause changes if interpreted in an advancing light.

The lecturer must have simplicity with profundity. Simplicity does not mean superficiality or absence of value and depth. On the contrary, simplicity cannot be achieved if the man does not know his subject. One must not only know well the subject of his lecture, but he must also have certain realizations and experiences on the line of his subject. Then he must consider the level of the audience, who may not know the higher technical terms very well but are very sensitive to deeper meanings, if they are presented in a way that they can understand.

The deepest doctrines are taught by Masters in very simple parables or stories. Read, for example, the Teachings of Buddha and Christ. They are so simple when not distorted by theologians or scholars. But with Their simplicity you touch the spirit of Buddha and Christ, or Infinity. . . .

It is more difficult to make things simple than to make them complicated. We are even told that the complex machinery which we are using in various departments of human labor will be simplified in the future by more advanced scientists who will better understand the laws of Nature.

Very often things are not understood because the giver is not sure what he is doing, or the theory and experience in him are in conflict.

In lecturing there are many subtle ways that you can hurt people, take revenge, or give them a hard lesson. But all these effects create hindrances between the personalities and human souls of your audience. For example, do not say:

> "I know, but if I explain it to you, you will not understand it."

> "I have my degrees and diplomas. . . ."

> "I have this or that connection with such and such people."

> "You need to grow to understand this Teaching."

> "You are still babies, you need to grow."

and other expressions which demonstrate vanity, pride, and superiority.

The best speaker speaks as if he were the audience. Every time an audience is humiliated, the radiations of their souls become fainter.

People advance and enjoy the wisdom or the instruction if the speaker affirms the Divinity in them, gives them joy and hope, gives them future, encourages them toward new heights, and tells them they can do great things. They have the possibility to grow when the speaker respects their innate Divinity, their innate possibility. Only thus can he communicate with their souls and impress their minds. If the speaker does not respect their visions and their ability, they reject him and he cannot reach them. The greatest leaders recognize your future greatness and present possibilities.

The speaker can go even further and say that what he is presenting now is just to create more interest and that he is sure their interest will carry them farther ahead than where he has reached, if they strive for it.

Stay on the line of your topic as much as possible. Some people do not even refer to the subject about which they are supposedly speaking!

Sometimes the introduction is so long that the time is over before the main topic is started. It is good to say a few words as an introduction, but then go immediately to your subject.

Before you speak, generate love and deep respect within your heart. Remember that people are spending time, energy, and money to listen to you and to be nourished, inspired, and encouraged by you; they are expecting certain help from you. After such a consideration, you will be more careful and feel greater responsibility toward them so that you guide them in the right direction.

Look at them and with your smile let them know that you love them, you respect them, you care for them. Unless you really do, you cannot transmit the power of light to them.

You can even think about your audience before the lecture with the following consideration: "I wonder how many confused persons are in the audience, how many hurt souls, or broken hearts, or wounded people; how many searchers, anxious to know more. . . . Lord, make me love them, and let Thy wisdom guide me to help them." Such thoughts give you more realistic and many-sided approaches to your subject and open new channels of communication between you and your inner source of inspiration.

When you really care for your audience and sincerely want to help them, greater inspirations pour down into your mind to such a degree that you even wonder where these new ideas came from into your mind. I have been surprised many times when I answered questions that I never thought I could answer the way I did.

The Inner Guide is waiting to radiate out, and the best opportunity for such radiation is the sphere of a loving heart who cares for his audience.

You know it is ugly to make people feel that you are superior. But it is also very ugly to make yourself inferior. People do not like inferior speakers or leaders. They also do not like you to make yourself superior to them. They should see your value without your advertising yourself or showing off. If they do not see it, all the efforts you make to impress them bring the reverse result.

Humility is not inferiority. Some speakers say, "This subject is so deep. I wonder if I will be able to understand it." This is the wrong way to start. After that, no matter what you say, the audience will think, "I wonder if he knows what he is talking about."

You must have the confidence of your audience, and you cannot buy it either by humiliating yourself or advertising yourself.

I have heard many times someone speaking about a subject and saying, "Some people think about this subject this or that way. Other people think thus. And I do not really know which of them is right or wrong." There is no need for such a comedy. Audiences must listen to the things that you really believe or you really reject. Confusion and uncertainty reflect on your reputation. If you know something, say that you know about it. If you believe something, say that you believe it. Do not create uncertainty in the minds of the audience.

You can say, for example, that beyond this point you are not sure, or it is under investigation, or it is the subject of greater research, etc. But the audience must have a foundation under its feet.

Speak with all your faith and knowledge, or never speak at all. It is a crime to make people believe something which you do not apply in your own life or which you have never understood. Many great concepts can be communicated only because the speaker wholeheartedly believes or knows whatever he is saying.

If you give a great lecture without your conviction and faith, it will be rejected subjectively and it will be a burden on the audience's minds.

Your speech must radiate your inner conviction. Contact is created only through conviction. When a man has faith in his knowledge of himself and in his actions, he is a source of enthusiasm, and it is enthusiasm that inflames the hearts. Real speakers have the fire of enthusiasm. It is this fire that creates conviction and faith, and then action.

Your speech must have the following elements:

- An introduction

- A development, unfoldment, or expansion of the subject, perhaps into many branches but without losing the trunk and keeping the sense of proportion with the trunk

- A conclusion with a vision of the future

Let us take these one by one.

1. The introduction may explain why the subject of the lecture is necessary at this time and how it meets the needs of the present moment. Make a short definition in the introduction; then pass to the body of the lecture.

2. Develop, unfold, or expand your lecture on a set but flexible plan. This work must be done like an engineer. The difference between many lectures is the difference in handling this second point.

Some lectures are just a heap of good things — not organized, systematized, or categorized — just ideas stacked upon one another without any foresight, plan, or order. Such a lecture creates chaos in the audience's minds. There must be construction, an architecture in the lecture.

Ideas must be developed and expanded in proportion to each other. Each idea must fill a need, and all together must exist only for the one building. Of course, you can emphasize certain points of the construction without losing the importance of the whole.

Sometimes I try to develop my subject like a flower, petal by petal. Sometimes I unfold it like a building. Whatever one does, it must be architectural if one wants his lecture or book to be impressive and constructive.

Your ideas must have the proper dress, color, music, and movement to fit the occasion. Once you find the secret of right construction, you will have great magnetism because the human soul is architectural, not chaotic.

If you have one big idea and you present it in a clear, harmonious way, you do greater good than taking ten ideas and creating chaos in the minds of the audience.

Some people try to build their lecture or writing from the roof or from the window, and they make it very difficult for people to understand. Start with the foundation; raise the walls; put the roof on; work on the windows and door openings; then put in other details as needed.

Start with the soil, the seed, the roots, the trunk, the branches, the leaves, the flowers, the fruit.... Or start from the spring, the fountainhead, the creek, the river, the fields, the canyons, the ocean. . . .

Thus the engineering design is very important, and also it helps you remember your speech and guide you in your talk.

3. The third point is the conclusion. We have the introduction, the unfoldment, and then the conclusion. Try to complete your building; make your tree bear fruit; let your creek or river reach the ocean, but do not put an end on your vision. Leave the door open for a new flowering, for new additions, for a new future. The conclusion must be complete, but the meaning must fly to the far-off worlds. People must depart with a spirit of aspiration and an expectation of something which has no name. They must hear music in their hearts as they depart.

The building process of a lecture is a continuity of successive steps that are taken logically to a conclusion. Your conclusion must be short, impressive, and clear but not dogmatic and limiting. It must be like a door which may open to a new and higher path.

Some speakers conclude with an appropriate saying of a Sage. This is good if care is taken that it does not sound like an authoritative command but rather as a synthesizing statement.

You can also use your visualization before you come to give a lecture. Visualize yourself talking, inspiring, answering questions in joy, in love, in freedom. Visualize an accepting attitude in your audience. Visualize your Master shielding you, inspiring you.

Many lectures are successful because the visualization before the lecture is successful. Our success starts from inside. All victories are first won within ourselves. Outside success is the reflection of the success achieved inside.

Voice control is another point. Test yourself with a tape recorder. Are you monotonous? Are you able to control and adjust your voice according to words, ideas, and meanings?

Your voice makes a great difference in impressing your words. You do not need to have a hypnotic, monotonous voice. One thing you must avoid is a voice that induces hypnotic conditions. You need your audience to be awake, alert, and responsive, not hypnotized. Great ideas are often lost because they are given as posthypnotic suggestions.

No idea can really bloom and turn into a mighty action until it is received by those minds which are awake, alert, and responsive.

You must have voice control; you must use the right pitch, the right note, and change it in a way that in its totality it is music, not a monotonous noise. Different notes create responses from different centers of the brain and keep a man awake.

You can practice voice control while you are talking to anyone. Observe and see how and on what note you are speaking. Experiment by changing your tonality, speed, shades of softness and loudness, and by approximating your voice to the content of your speech.

Mannerisms are very important in your lectures and conversations. The movements of your body, your hands, your fingers, your eyes, your facial muscles, and your mouth add to your lecture, or decrease the value of your lecture. All your movements must fit the general pattern of your speech and voice. Jerky, nervous movements will distract attention and even cause rejection.

Your dress must be appropriate for the occasion. Do not forget that beauty always increases if it is not artificial. Your body and your dress must be part of your lecture. Even the color of your dress must match the general tone of your subject.

A lecture is a living flow. All that accompanies it must be harmonious and arranged in a way that the true meaning of the lecture is amplified.

Some dresses or suits create responses that do not fit the subject. Some colors irritate people and create discord.

Subjects have their own special chord and color. One can experiment with such an idea.

Solemnity must prevail throughout the lecture. It should not be an artificial solemnity but a realization that you are standing there in the presence of so many respectful people and trying to bring them the message of the Great Ones. All idle remarks and ugly jokes and gestures must be avoided.

Humor must be present in solemnity. Humor helps people make a breakthrough. Solemnity does not mean to be stern, sad, or unexpressive. It means to be dignified and in harmony with the supreme goal toward which you are heading.

Facial expressions are also very important. Some facial expressions do not harmonize with the mood of the speech. Sometimes a speaker says beautiful things, but if you watch his face, he is almost crying.

Eye contact is another point. Your eye contact must harmonize with the general tone of the lecture. This must be so natural that it does not require your attention and deprive you of the energy which you need to use for your thinking and lecture.

Eyes can express almost all kinds of moods. It will be helpful if you speak in front of a mirror and experience certain expressions.

Voice control and energy go parallel. Some lecturers start loudly and energetically, but close to the end they seem exhausted. It should be the reverse. You should start very mildly and gently, with a controlled voice. As you go on, you must wind yourself up and become more energetic, ending the lecture with power.

The focus of the consciousness or attention of your audience weakens toward the end of your lecture. You must use extra energy to keep their attention and interest alert. If you have saved energy at the beginning, you can use it at the end. Your audience generally departs remembering your conclusions.

Some people do artificial things to draw attention. It may be necessary in public meetings, but is it not necessary in esoteric lectures. Your beauty, your power, your dignity, your ideas, your visions, and your radiance will be enough to create focus and attention. Mechanical means evoke personality attention.

If the person is an initiate, his aura will evoke the music in every heart.

Some people ask, "Should we memorize our lecture?" You must do anything necessary to make a good lecture. You can memorize but not recite it. Recitation sounds mechanical. Your lecture must be a living expression.

I write my lecture and read it many times until I see the plan or the architecture of it. Then I impress my brain with the keynotes or key ideas, and ten minutes before the lecture I forget all about it. Sometimes it happens that I do not say at all what I wrote, but the key ideas control me or guide me, and I follow the inspiration I receive through my heart and head centers.

I take into close consideration the level of the people. Sometimes for one worthy person I dwell on an idea to make him understand it; then again I pass to the general level of the audience.

My intention is to communicate with my audience on their level and inspire them with ideas and visions. Any time I go over their heads, I feel guilty. So, when you are preparing your lecture, you can remember the above possibilities and be ready for them.

I would not give any lecture without preparation. I even think about the questions the audience may ask and prepare myself, but I always open myself to new inspirations. In my experience, new inspirations come when you prepare yourself thoroughly. Preparation helps you give the right expressions to your inspirations and visions. Preparation also helps you not to be influenced by the thought currents of visible and invisible guests.

You may bring your paper with you and place it on the podium. You need not refer to it, if you can do without it. It may be just a safeguard for you in case anything goes wrong.

You may visualize yourself giving the lecture. This is giving a lecture on the mental plane, and you may attract many devas as your audience who will follow you to your lecture, helping you and reinforcing your ideas.

Try not to be satisfied with whatever you did. Leave it behind. Do not be flattered by the praise of the audience, and do not be depressed if some do not appreciate you. Everyone looks at you from his own level and interest. Your goal is to do your best, in whatever way you think is best. You may adjust many points in your lecture after due consideration of the remarks of the others but — this is important — not without your own agreement.

Good lecturers need good auras. This means that the lecturer must equip himself with a highly radioactive and magnetic aura. Such an aura can be built through meditation, sacrificial service, and silence. If you talk nonsense all day, or gossip, or make idle or harmful talk, your aura will not have the energy to support your esoteric lecture. Filthy, harmful conversations sap the energy of your aura.

Many great speeches are given after a day or a week of silence. Silence charges the aura, purifies your motives, and deepens your realizations.

A leader leads by his example, his beauty, and his creativity. A leader must try in all ways to improve himself so that he creates a great urge in others to improve.

The greatest damage is done when a speaker presents to his audience a large quantity of indigestible material and forces them to eat it. This is how one creates hatred toward the very objects he wants people to respect and love.

The speaker must always present the speech on a gradient scale. He will not leave any word or expression unclarified. He must explain his ideas through examples from daily life. By using concrete, real, and genuine examples, he slowly builds his speech upon a solid foundation.

A speaker must know what the foundation, the walls, the doors, and windows are. He must know what the roof is, and if it is necessary to build another story.

An "architectured" speech is a speech that becomes a source of inspiration and interest to the listeners.

It does not mean that one must be dry and cold. There must be beauty of expressions and manners. There must be joy, enthusiasm, and power.

Leaders especially, and group members generally, must develop a sense of good listening. A leader must listen exactly to whatever is told to him or asked of him. We may even say that he must not only listen carefully to what is said to him, but he must also be able to hear the motive behind the words. Careful listening is the first step toward a deeper insight.

When you talk or lecture or answer a question, stay on the subject. Do not drift here or there; do not fluctuate. Stay on the line and try to speak only on the subject.

People often take wrong roads in their speech. They announce that they are going to talk about California, but they end up with New York. When such an action is repeated, the leader loses those whom he was supposed to serve.

Changing the line of conversation or the object of conversation denotes lack of concentration, lack of willpower, and instability of mind.

Be impersonal in your answers or speech. Even if your answer hurts you, be honest.

Do not use your audience for your own self-gratification or propaganda. Do not use your lectures to secure your own interests. The best speaker is one who tries to meet the needs of others.

Do not try to force your glamors, illusions, prejudices, or vanities on others. If you are hurt, it is better to retreat. No one can speak from the spirit if he has hurt feelings.

Do not direct your attack toward any person or personality. A leader has nothing to do with personalities, groups, or organizations. His main target is *ideas*. He can discuss ideas but avoid personalities. He emphasizes principles, but he does not condemn those who violate principles.

The leader has no right to condemn because condemnation invites hatred and attack. He condemns those ideas which are not inclusive or evolutionary and not based on the spiritual and lasting interests of people.

When you speak, let it be organized in an engineered beauty. Chaotic speech evokes rejection and creates confusion and criticism.

At the time of your speech try to catch the attention of the whole audience. You can even throw a few words toward those who are not alert. There are many ways to do this. A question awakens them; a look awakens them. Or if you know their main interest, you can bridge your topic to their interest for a few moments until they are tied to the lecture.

What to do when questions have been asked:

1. Do not try to answer the whole question if it is composed of many interlocking questions. Divide them, enumerate them, and answer them clearly, one by one.

2. Do not give the impression that you gave the whole answer. Leave a part for the questioner to search for.

3. Do not answer on a level that will not be understood.

4. Do not answer to prove that you know. In some cases a question can best be answered by neglecting it and giving a chance for other questions.

5. Some questions are traps or attacks, and a wise leader must find a way not to debate or be trapped. In certain cases this can be handled by a question to the one who asks the question. Your question can subtlety imply an answer and impart a lesson.

Christ used this teaching method in great beauty.

Negative and harmful questions can be handled by presenting an experience or an event of a positive and constructive nature.

Do not immediately assume that there is an attack upon you when someone asks a hard question. Remember that if you stand as a spiritual fire, you will evoke the spirit from your audience.

Sometimes hard questions are tests for you to make you find where you stand. Remember that charged with psychic energy, you can dissolve almost any bad intention, divert attacks, and win those who were not sympathetic toward you.

Your life must go parallel with your speech and conversations. People learn from your life more than from your words.

Those who do not live what they preach create mechanical reactions. Then their followers develop a machine-like character which acts by the forces coming from outside. These are the people who can be used by any charlatan or demagogue.

Try to make people realize that they must follow the path by their own incentive, by their own choice, and by their own free will.

It is the duty of every Future oriented leader to make people less mechanical. Our lower bodies are very eager to be mechanical. They like to take over any activity and run it without the conscious participation of the subject. People are mostly personalities; they have their three bodies aligned and integrated, and because of this the whole personality is carried away and becomes mechanical. This phenomenon must be controlled within our own system and within our co-workers. Conscious activity must be our daily goal. Whatever we do, we must be conscious of it.

Mechanicalness uses the etheric body without charging it with psychic energy. Such a mechanical activity wears out the etheric body, and you feel exhausted. This is why in every conscious action you gain energy. Whenever you are "spaced out," you lose energy.

In your speech and your relationships be dynamic and do not concentrate on yourself or your interests; concentrate on the need, and find out in what way you can approach the need and on what level you can communicate with the one who is in need.

The speaker must speak for the group, not for himself. This is the key. He must not try to manipulate people because they will reject and hate him.

Our speech must come from Soul levels and be directed according to the needs of the group. If they cannot hold the energy, then do not give it. The greatest lecture reaches the public and meets their needs. Sometimes you must even give less than they need in order to create aspiration and effort in them.

Any time you paralyze the audience, you will create rejection. A good speaker evokes challenge from the audience.

Give your speech at their level. The introduction must be short. Then enter directly into the subject. It is very dangerous to let the audience believe that you do not know your subject.

Never say the subject is too big for the audience. It depresses their mental effort. Show the steps to the subject and level out at the end.

Be practical. Make the subject practical, useful. If it has no relationship to present life, then it is not useful. Interwoven with daily life, it has an immediate effect.

Make the audience struggle with you slowly on some thoughts. Admire some great quotations. Always give the impression of having much time. Do not make the audience hurry to understand you. Make the audience think; do not give everything quickly and easily. Sometimes struggle in finding deeper words or meaning. In this way the audience is struggling too, and they join the aura of the speaker.

Speak joyfully. Joy is insulation.

Speech shows inner realization and integrity. Right speech is the result of meditation and silence. In right speech man is shifting the emphasis from personality to

Soul consciousness. Man is touching something great within himself, and because of that contact and change, there is a tremendous pressure to share this with others.

The cause of effective speech is in building the Antahkarana. The Antahkarana unites all mental levels. It extends a cable line from the focus of consciousness to the Chalice, and all treasures stored in the Chalice then come into the mind. This creates an electrical polarization to the core of intention and Teaching, and the speech flows out.

Insulation is important when speaking so that the manners, auras, thoughts, words, and emotions of others do not reach and affect the speaker. The disruptive person distorts the aura of the audience as well as that of the speaker. When this happens, the magnetic aura of the audience with the speaker is broken. Then the audience cannot evoke energy from the speaker.

The Solar Angel of the speaker sometimes speaks through the speaker because of the need. Frequently, we find ourselves saying something that we did not know we knew but that really helps someone or the group.

When our co-workers are speaking, we must support them with our smiles. We must radiate our smiles toward them, so that they receive courage and energy. We must visualize them in the light of their Souls.

In speaking, the technique of definite programming and slow building must be used so that the audience knows where it is going to land. Structure is very important in order to keep the audience's attention always with the speech.

The speaker will measure himself not by praise received but by his vision. The speaker must find out how to improve continuously.

When we are standing for someone or for some cause, we have power. This power coming to us is not personal but the result of greater visions and ideals. We must stand for something to be effective.

Speech is the fire of thought released into sound. Speech is concrete power; it puts the builders into action and creates changes. In thinking a person realizes the idea and formulates it into workable, understandable terms, plotting out the correct sequence and timing. Speaking can only come after this; otherwise it only creates confusion. If a person's thoughts are scattered, he cannot direct any energy. Then when words are spoken they will be scattered and empty, having no energy.

"Energy follows thought." If a person's thought has penetrated clearly into the higher vibrations of Space, it will attract very high-voltage energy, hooking into the reservoir of all related ideas.

In meditation the mind is prepared to formulate the thought pattern, to send it into higher realms, and then to bring back unchanged to the concrete mind any ideas that are encountered. In silence a person is receptive to the incoming energy and ideas that the thought attracts. Silence also allows a person to see what is going on in the mind and what hindrances there are to accurate reception. In my own experience, when I have totally stopped my mental chattering I can then see needs or issues clearly and directly.

Why is there the tremendous pressure to share with others something great within oneself? It seems to me that when the Soul level is contacted, people realize the interrelation of all things — one person cannot operate effectively alone. All ideas, energies, realizations of problems, causes and effects must be circulated to be put into action. When the Soul is contacted, a tremendous power is released into the person, thus creating pressure. A fuse may blow in the person's circuit if it is not expressed outwardly, continuing the circulation.

Sometimes a speaker's thoughts are very clear in the reception of an idea, but when he speaks the words, they are not right for the audience. This is where meditation and silence help. The speaker must practice mentally giving talks to different groups in different ways on some idea contacted. Gradually the idea will become clearer in his brain. When the idea becomes so clear and simple that he can say it in many ways, then in speaking he can put more attention on the wavelength of the audience and react according to their need. The less attention a speaker puts on himself or on his ability to speak, the more radioactive he can be.

When we "stand for some idea," we hook into the energy currents and thoughts of that idea and of all those who are also working with that idea. A much greater understanding and force of energy comes in when we open our whole heart and mind to a person or idea. We become a pure channel radiating the energy and thoughts to others.

If someone is only speaking about a person or idea from an intellectual standpoint, it may be interesting, stimulating, or unusual but it will not evoke any effective response from the audience. It will not touch their hearts, opening them to the larger currents of energy and self-forgetfulness. A purely academic speech frequently keeps people in separation, emotionally and mentally, allowing distortions, arguments, and petty differing opinions. When a speaker is one with his idea in experience and radiates that power — particularly in joy — the people's higher unity is electrified and fused, regardless of personality differences.

Thus we must look ahead to the future, filled with success and radiance. We must receive our joy from within as it pours down when we stand for a great cause. We avoid the interference of our personality and its problems while we are in a state of transmission of the light of the Soul.

We must know that some people who were trapped in drugs, in various psychic phenomena, in smoking, etc. are not really bad people or agents of dark forces. Some of them are very valuable people, and that is why out of their curiosity and interest in the unknown they were trapped. The dark forces are interested in promising people and attack them and trap them to prevent their future usefulness for the Forces of Light.

When such people come to your meetings, do not occupy yourself with their weaknesses or vices. For six months watch them and try to emphasize pure living and the pure Teaching. Try to show them the beauty of a true spiritual life. Eventually when you see that they are stuck to the Teaching, then start to shape them. Before that, be careful and even make them feel that you are not interested in their shortcomings.

For example, you meet a man or woman and ask, "Are you doing Hatha Yoga?"

"Yes."

"Oh, that is not good; it hurts you."

This is not the way to win people. Start with something in him that you like. For example, if he is doing meditation, say, "Isn't that beautiful! You know, it is so important for your spiritual growth." Start by emphasizing the best points in him. When the best points of his nature increase, automatically they will clean the bad parts.

Suppose that people come with specific questions. Even here you must discriminate and not hurt them. The first thing you must do is to create love and confidence in yourself; even offer a smile or keep silent. They will read your intentions and live accordingly.

When you are forming your group, open your door and let many people in. Do not reject those who want to come, even if you know that they practice Hatha Yoga, smoke marijuana, use some drugs, or have various other hang-ups, because among them can be found some jewels, some future co-workers. After a while those who are not fit will leave you, and those who want to stay with you will be ready for your discipline, advice, and correction.

Sometimes the devil makes a man show his worst characteristics so that you reject him. Thus he comes with his ugliness, and his ugliness is blown out of proportion at the time he meets you, so that you reject him. Once you reject him, the devil rejoices because the devil feels he was successful in making you reject a man whom you could attract and lead to the path of liberation.

Sometimes we think that when a man asks big questions it signifies that he has a big understanding. This is not true. He can ask questions that are projected into his mind by dark forces to sidetrack the speaker or the group. They can be hypnotic questions, planted in his mind unconsciously, that are now coming out because of the law of association. Such questions can be the result of individual vanity and pride, or they can have the motive to hurt someone.

In all these cases you must be very careful about how you answer or not answer the question.

Sometimes the most stupid people ask the most tricky questions. Before you attempt to answer an odd question, immediately ask the person another question to measure his intelligence. In this way you can see if he is intelligent, informed, and ready or if he is a tool for confusion. Your question must be very clear, loving, personal, and related to the point of his own evolution and progress. If he cannot answer it properly, you must be careful in answering him.

Some speakers find an opportunity to demonstrate their own vanity in trying to answer big questions in complex ways. To be bribed in this way is to lose the line of the common good of the group.

Some speakers think, "If I do not face the challenge and answer the question of that lady, what will the audience think of me? I am the important one. It is better to show off than to follow the Teaching of simplicity and humility."

In answering some odd questions you are wasting the time of the audience and creating confusion in their minds. If the man who asks is a very important man and an intelligent person, you may invite him to see you privately after class to discuss the question.

All of this means that you must be very discriminating in answering questions. You must not become involved in critical, debating conversations or be trapped in your vanities.

Sometimes you even need to transfer the question onto another level and play with it in a way that you say what you want to, in spite of the question. You may even play the part of the fool and not answer directly, but say the thing he needs to know.

Leadership must play with such people; the leader must take care of his flock.

The most important thing in your lectures is to find the level of the people and start working on that level, then slowly lift them up to higher levels after the foundation is built. It is always better to start with the foundation.

People who cannot understand you reject you. People whom you do not understand are lost for you. Try to find an affinity with them, and slowly increase their beingness and knowingness; take them on your wings and fly.

We must be progressive in all our teaching techniques, learning from each other and continuously trying to improve ourselves and our techniques. If we proceed in vanity and by showing off, we lose some very valuable people and future co-workers.

Whoever is coming to your classes is drawn by you or sent by karma, by his Solar Angel, or even by a Master. Handle them very carefully, and try to see what you can do for them as very precious ones. Do not grasp them and pour upon them the wisdom that you do not have.

Go slowly. See their needs; find the doors and windows to their minds, if necessary. But if needed, take immediate action. Be like a surgeon. Wield the knife in the right place and save them from spiritual death.

Do not use anyone for your personal interests. If they want to help you, let them know that they are serving the Plan and not you. Let them not expect from you personal favors, but let them learn to serve without expectations.

Learn the science of fishing. Not all fish can be caught by the same hook and the same bait. You must use various methods, ways, and means for various people.

Study people to know what they are and what they need. A cat sometimes waits for three hours before catching the mouse. He knows that if he makes any motion at the wrong time, the mouse will be lost.

People sometimes reject you when you give them the things they want. So how can you play the game? You are not going to give what he wants but what he needs. He cannot reject the things that he needs, but he rejects the things that he wants. Most people want things that they do not really need.

When you have people in your group who are troublemakers, "smart" people, and they intentionally ask questions to cause trouble, do not answer them. Find another "smart" person and let him answer the question. Even appoint three other troublemakers to attack him, while you sit and watch them. When they are tired, bring the discussion to an end, or say a few more words and close the subject. This must be done in a way that others do not feel too bad or bored.

You may also not answer by saying that this is not the time to discuss the subject, but if you are interested in it, read the following books, etc.

If you do not know anything say, "I do not want to speak about it." And if it is a serious question and you really do not know, go and search for it and learn, making yourself ready for another time.

When new people come the leadership must entertain them with beauty, wisdom, and solemnity, but not with artificiality.

28
Book Review

A leader may find it necessary to give a review of a book that is important for his co-workers. Here is an effective way to give an oral book review.

1. Show the book and say a few words about the title.

2. Give the place of publication, number of printings, translations, and the recommended use for the book — general, specific, schools, etc.

3. Discuss the author — his background and specialization and other works or activities he has.

4. Summarize the subject matter of the book.

5. Give seven or nine main ideas presented in the book, reading excerpts, if possible, which clarify the main ideas.

6. Choose five or more questions which are answered in the book. You may ask the audience the answer to the first question. Whatever answer is given, say, "Let us see what the author says about this question." Then read an excerpt which answers the question and explain it. Follow the same procedure with the other questions. This technique creates an intense interest in the book itself.

7. Conclude with why this book is important and how it may be distributed.

You must believe whatever you say. Your duty is to let the book speak, not your individual ideas. Your intention should be *how to spread the book to more readers*.

The following are suggestions for giving a lecture based on a chapter from a book:

1. Introduce the book as a whole for three to four minutes, summarizing the chapters and the main idea of the book. Then come to the chapter under discussion.

2. Give the keynote of the chapter.

3. Enumerate the main ideas.

4. Choose excerpts (paragraphs or sentences) which illustrate these main ideas, and discuss these excerpts.

   — Start by analyzing words and sentences. Concentrate on technical words and explain them in a simple way. After the words are understood, explain each sentence until the paragraph is completed.

— Repeat this step with each paragraph.

— After analyzing the paragraphs chosen, repeat the main ideas enumerated in Step 3 and try to associate them with the main idea of the chapter.

— You may conclude with how the book helped you, how it may help the audience, and where it may be purchased.

29
Effective Lecturing

It is very important that those who lecture or speak to special audiences come together once every three months to discuss ways to improve their lectures or speeches and to share with each other the techniques they are using and the experiences they are having.

One of the steps that can be taken by speakers is not to use any notes for reference when they speak. Sometimes the existence of notes prevents direct thinking and the flow of the speech. One must cultivate self-confidence in order to increase the effect of his speech.

Self-confidence cannot be built if one always depends on his notes or paper. Of course, it is possible to give a great lecture, using some notes, and one must use notes if

1. He did not have enough time to assimilate his subject

2. He cannot remember, because of his busy schedule, important points in his speech

We are advised to take time in preparing our lectures and make them useful factors for the transformation of the lives of those who listen to us.

There is a great amount of energy flow when a speech is delivered without interruption. This also helps build a bridge between what the speaker thought or accumulated in his mind and his brain. Many people do not have completed communication lines between the mind and brain.

When people forget what to say or when things evaporate from their mind, this means that there is not yet a bridge between the mind and the brain. Later, one must also build the bridge between the brain, the mental body, and the consciousness. When the bridge is extended to the consciousness, the person turns into a fountain of continuously flowing ideas, wisdom, and energy.

Memory is the sign that there is a bridge between the brain and the mind. But sometimes this memory of what you prepared evaporates when you stand in front of an audience. Sometimes it totally evaporates; sometimes half is lost; sometimes it is all there.

In trying to speak without the aid of a paper, you begin to cultivate control over your memory and reject all those influences which make you forget your lecture. These influences can come from associations within your mind or push buttons in your emotional nature. These must be controlled by your effort to deliver your message without the help of any paper.

It is possible that you will fail a few times, but your goal is to be successful and attain mastery over your nature and influences. Besides associative ones, exterior influences which may disturb you are the feelings and thoughts that the audience projects on you. But you can conquer all exterior influences through continuous striving and efforts to speak without notes.

To be able to give a lecture without notes, you need first to write a paper and think deeply about your subject until you are sure of what to speak about and how to speak. Preparation gives you self-confidence, which in turn increases or creates your audience's faith in you. The faith of your audience eases your speech and inspires you to contact new ideas and not lose the chain of your lecture.

There is a better way to remember your lecture. First of all, you must know the subject of your talk. Second, you must draw the blueprint of it. Then you must divide the plan into parts. For example, you have the plan of a house. The parts are the rooms — kitchen, bathrooms, walls, doors, windows, roof, and perhaps a chimney.

These parts must be divided according to the time you have. Let us say you have forty-five minutes to speak. Introduce your plan or your subject on broad lines for a few minutes, and then speak for four minutes on each of your ten parts. It is very important to abide by your time-plan. Stay four minutes on each part, trying to give complete ideas or thoughts about each part. You must give four minutes only to each part of your plan and then reach a conclusion.

You can frame your talk on the symbolism of a house and easily remember each part related to your subject. For example, take the topic of fear. The plan is what is fear, what it does in general, and how one can handle it.

1. Foundation — the causes of fear

2. Walls — how fear grows and what barriers it may create

3. Doors — Through what agents or conditions fear creeps in

4. Windows — How a place full of fear can be ventilated

5. Roof — How one can protect himself from the attacks or precipitation of fear

6 Chimney — How one can burn uninvited fears in his system

When we say plan, we refer to a symbol, to a story, to a parable. All these can be used as a plan upon which we build our lecture. A plan or a symbol can serve the same purpose: to have an organized and balanced talk.

You can take the symbol of a tree and build your talk on that, with earth, roots, trunk, branches, leaves, flowers, fruits, birds. You may also take more advanced symbols, such as a parable, a dance, or a geometrical figure. You do not need to reveal to the audience the symbol you are using as your scaffolding. Just hold it in the background of your mind and proceed with your talk. The symbol is the structure upon which you build your lecture.

There is another step ahead in which you tell a story and use each part of the story to present an idea. This is called a two-dimensional talk. For example, taking a parable and interpreting it properly is a two-dimensional talk. You say, "Seeds grow in good earth and in right conditions." Then you can continue, "A child is a seed; he needs a good home, love, education, and security as a seed does. . . ."

You can visualize a blooming flower or a running river and make that symbol operate your talk. Such an effort brings a great amount of intuitional energy into your talk which in turn inspires your audience.

It is also possible to use ideas to build a symbolic form in the minds of people through your lecture. For example, virtues are the flowers of the tree; the psychic energy is the sap; striving forms the branches; the influence of our beauty is the fragrance of the flowers. When you build the symbol, you impress the minds of your audience with the symbol, and they relate the symbol to your ideas.

The difference between presenting the ideas before the symbol and presenting the symbol before the ideas is that in the first case you come from the abstract to the concrete and in the second case from the concrete to the abstract. If your audience is mystical, give the ideas first; then build a concrete image to ground them. If your audience is down-to-earth, give the symbol first; then lead them to the abstract levels of thinking. These two ways can be used to balance your audience, according to where they are.

An unorganized, unorchestrated talk causes confusion, rejection, and even headaches. But if your talk is organized and architectural, you impress people. No matter how good are the ideas and words you present to people, the audience will not like them if they are not sequential, systematized, and organized. A simple, organized talk is much more influential than an unorganized, long, and forceful lecture.

Your first duty is to create certainty and disperse confusion; then to present deeper ideas on a gradient scale. When you learn how to use symbols upon which to build your lecture, you slowly calm down and relax and let your soul speak. Once you have such an experience of speaking as a soul, you will be a source of new ideas not preconceived during the preparation of your lecture. After you speak as a soul, you will feel that you are standing in the light of your Inner Guide and you are surrounded with ideas and inspirations beyond your expectations.

There is another step forward. When you, as a human soul, step into the Spiritual Triad — occasionally, by accident, or permanently — you transmit the glory and beauty found on that level. This is rare, and only after the Fourth Initiation can one enjoy such experiences permanently.

Coming back to the idea of wholeness: Never transmit a distorted picture or a half-built picture, but always transmit a picture that is whole, complete. You do not necessarily need to present a picture of an airplane, but you may present a complete picture of a part in the engine of the plane. A complete picture creates certainty, confidence, and joy. Half-built pictures and mixed-up pictures create rejection and headaches. This is why the important words in your lecture must always be defined clearly, to make people know what you are saying.

If you have a complex subject to talk about, do not distort the minds of the audience by trying to fill their heads as if you are hurrying to fill their bags with all kinds of things. Take one part and finish it; then take the others, always keeping the line of relation with the parts clear.

There is another method that you can use. This is called the question and answer method. You ask questions and give the answer. Take "the five W's":

>   What

>   Where

>   Why

When

Who

Then add the "how." For example, take gratitude and try to answer:

- *What* is gratitude?

- *Where* can you use gratitude? Where can you find gratitude?

- *Why* is gratitude important?

- *When* can gratitude be used or cultivated?

- *Who* can express gratitude?

- *How*: What are the techniques and discipline involved in gratitude?

You do not need to ask questions to the audience. Ask them to yourself and talk to the audience about the answers. Sometimes the best lectures are answers to intelligently prepared questions.

Have fifteen to twenty questions in a lecture, and prepare your lecture as an answer to these questions. When you lecture, you need only to remember the questions. The answers will come easily when you remember the questions. In this way, you may solve many questions in the minds of the audience and plant new questions in them.

Planting questions in the minds of the audience is one of the ways to focus their minds and create interest. Many speakers are like tape recordings. You wind them, and they talk and talk, but without any transformable effect. When you talk mechanically without being in your talk, you create rejection of your subject and yourself.

This is why you must master your subject, then come to the lecture as if you did not do any preparation, in order to give your Higher Self a chance to take over.

There is a network in our mind which is called the network of interplay. This network connects everything in your mind like a computer, and you can use any topic or button to make the network associate ideas connected to your topic. This mechanism works only within the boundary of your mental body. But if your Antahkarana is built, this network can be a transmitter for the sources of ideas outside of you, in Space or anywhere on Earth. Inspired speakers like Buddha, Christ, Apollonius, Pythagorus, and Akbar had such a mechanism. Because of it, they were eternal sources of wisdom and beauty which could move multitudes.

All parts of your talk must be given equal time to be heard. If one part is emphasized more than the others, it creates imbalance in the audience's consciousness. If there is a part that is really important, it can be taken as the subject and the other parts as parts equally divided.

If you take a face and emphasize the nose for forty minutes and speak only a few seconds about the other parts, it creates an unbalanced reaction in the audience. It is possible to emphasize one or two parts in the lecture, but this must be done in the prelude. Then for each part, equal time must be given.

Sometimes talks are very badly delivered, as if the speaker has a truckload of goodies and he wants to dump them into the mental bags of the audience. Or the speaker goes through an "ego-trip," trying to make everybody feel that he knows things that no one knows. Showing off is very ugly in speech, and it creates personality reactions.

You may also use a spiral plan in your talk. Take your points or parts and first define them; then speak about them with more explanation; then in the third round, you can go more deeply into each part. This is a great technique which prepares the consciousness of the audience to climb gradually and feel joy.

People have no idea that a one-hour speech creates a formation in Space, with colors and geometrical forms. The challenge is how to deliver a lecture that has beautiful colors (ideas that are factual) and balanced forms (time and sound).

People may not notice the unbalanced form you are creating in Space, but they feel that there is something wrong. This feeling creates a barrier in their minds toward your talk and your ideas.

In regard to your language: Do not use words that people will not understand. Simplicity and clarity are very important. Also, your sentences must not be too long or filled with too many clauses. Such sentences create suspension. People become "spaced." If they do not understand five words or a few sentences, their minds wander and they do not listen.

It is important to breathe well and easily when you speak. To be short of breath during your speech makes people very uncomfortable. Calmness and smoothness are very attractive in speech. When things are clear in your mind, take it easy; you will do very well. Some teachers advise taking fifteen or twenty deep breaths before you start your lecture.

Your voice must be audible and your words must be pronounced well. Every time your audience misses words or does not hear you, a gap is created in the consciousness of the audience. If these gaps increase, the audience will not listen any more. It is very important that as a speaker you keep the attention of the audience continuous.

You can also use the technique of intervals of pauses, as in music. Say something important; then stop for a few seconds. Thus you give the audience an opportunity to take in your idea and ponder on it. In the pause, you also charge yourself with new energy.

Sometimes you must think that the mind of the audience is like a garden. If you intend to plant a few seeds, you need to prepare the garden, weed it, fertilize it, and then properly plant the seeds. This is a science which must be learned.

Your words are important, but more important is the meaning you put into your speech. Without meaning and energy, your words are empty decorations. People come to restaurants to eat. Similarly, they come to a lecture to get satisfaction about a topic. If you do not feed them, they do not come again. You must make your lecture tasty, beautifully presented, so that they feel hungry for more after a few days.

It is not your words that carry the whole voltage of the ideas, but it is mostly your voice. Your voice presents the level on which your consciousness is.[1]

Some lectures sound very monotonous, although there are great ideas in them. A monotonous voice stops the mental striving of the audience and makes them passive and in a hypnotic state. Speech is actually slow singing. You must speak as if you were singing, with variation, emotion, vision, and energy.

Another very important item is to make your preface or prelude very attractive, shocking, or concentrated, in order to pull the attention of the audience and focus it on your subject. Then after you are successful, you will have their full attention. You may then take it easy and relax their tension without letting the attention be dif-

---

1. See also *The Ageless Wisdom*, Ch. 19, "The Voice."

fused. Actually, the whole lecture should be a detailed analysis or explanation of the prelude.

If you start heavy and feel that your audience is not ready for it, you can bring your talk slowly to their level, to help them expand their consciousness.

It is important that you speak directly on your subject, instead of going around and around it. You must not talk about any ideas that are not related to the chosen subject.

Sometimes people talk about subjects they do not believe in or about which they have doubt. An honest speaker must believe what he says. If he does not believe what he is saying and he tries to make other people believe it, he creates a condition in the consciousness of the audience which is called in the old country, "broken gears." People lose their faith in a subject which is delivered to them by a person who has no faith in it. This is why hypocrites were called the destroyers of faith and they were considered worse than the enemies of faith.

You must show enthusiasm and faith in which you talk. Enthusiasm is electricity through which your message reaches the hearts of people.

It is good to talk about your experiences, without emphasizing yourself, but analyzing the experiences.

The best lecture is not the talk you give about all that you know. The best lecture is the talk that meets the needs and expectations of your audience. The best lecture gives them hope and future, expands their consciousness, takes confusion away, clears their minds, and creates the spirit of striving in them. The best lecture is the one that brings improvement in the life of the audience.

Lecturing is a service. You must hold this idea in your mind while you are talking. You must know what the audience needs and try to meet that need.

There are some basic needs:

1. Knowledge
2. Expansion of consciousness
3. Destruction of fanaticism and crystallization
4. Increasing of viewpoints
5. Clarification of certain issues
6. Building a broader understanding
7. Eliminating habits
8. Breaking certain vanities
9. Abolishing ego
10. Opening new horizons
11. Leading people to their Real Self.

When you try to meet such fundamental needs, you render a great service for the spiritual progress of your audience. This is why before you lecture you must have a time to ask yourself: What is the need and how can I serve it through my words? If you do not meet the need, your lecture becomes only a show-off or a waste of time.

Besides meeting the need of the audience, you must try to make your speech

— Full of light. It must have solid and real knowledge. You must know the subject well and pass real knowledge to the audience.

— Magnetic. Your speech must be full of love and understanding. It must be charming and beautiful.

— Powerful. Your speech must have power, conviction, and directness.

If you think that you have no experience about the subject you are talking about, try to

- Do some research.

- Think if you know people who have some experience about your subject.

- See if you have experiences that are related to your subject.

The human being has many experiences, but he either forgets them or does not pay attention to them. If you develop the power of observation, you will find yourself surrounded by jewels.

Suppose you are talking about enlightenment. You may think, "I don't know anything about real enlightenment. I am not enlightened like Buddha or Christ, so how can I give a lecture about it?" But if you think deeply on the word, you can find many experiences of enlightenment on your level. For example:

1. You found something that was lost.

2. You remembered something.

3. Something made sense to you.

4. You understood the real meaning of an event.

5. You solved a problem.

6. You had a deeper understanding about a friend or about yourself.

7. Suddenly you realized your mistakes or saw your ego.

8. You suddenly knew what your goal is.

9. You suddenly saw how people were cheating you.

10. You suddenly understood the meaning of a book.

11. You suddenly realized that your emotions are controlling your life.

12. You suddenly saw that you are building a fanatic within yourself.

If you talk on this level of simplicity, you can render a great service to people and make them observe the precious moments in their lives. You might also suggest how a nation or the world could be enlightened if they were to see the above twelve points in their lives.

The level that you are on is very important, and you must serve on that level. People need to walk and run on runways before they are able to fly.

Once a lecturer explained enlightenment as follows: "All the day I was fighting with my wife and children and then suddenly I saw why I was doing it. This was an experience of enlightenment which cleared my mind, and I changed my behavior." People in the audience told him that they loved his concrete examples about enlightenment.

This does not mean that you cannot speak about higher experiences you may have had. But you must stay on the level of the audience and be honest with yourself. Your experiences must be presented as objects of analysis and not as means to present yourself or praise or condemn yourself.

Your lecture must have a personal, national, and global vision. For example, if you are talking about the integration of the personality, expand it and think what it means on a national level; what it could mean on a global level; what could be the fruits of integration for humanity. And always end your lecture with a future vision, with hope and trust, or at least with optimism.

30
Lecturing with Feeling

We are told that thinking has two main layers, external and internal. External thinking is expressed through words, but internal, deeper thinking is expressed through feeling. There are feelings that cannot be expressed in words. Such thinking has a great influence on people.

Sometimes feeling is expressed through a gesture, movement, voice, or exclamation, which tells more than the words do. The speaker can utilize deeper layers of thinking, using his feelings as the expression of his thinking.

Thoughts expressed through feeling can move people and lead them into striving, but dry words do not touch their hearts. When thinking is expressed through feeling, it immediately affects the etheric centers, charging them and inspiring them into activity.

Lectures are not given to make people into storage rooms but to make them create movements within their souls and within their environment.

Knowledge and information take a direction only when they are associated with a feeling. The feeling indicates that the knowledge and information are going to be used by a deeper thought. Man seldom turns into a hero through knowledge, but he turns into a hero through feelings.

When words are charged with feelings, they evoke deeper thoughts from the audience.

Knowledge and information can easily be reflected on the mirror of the mind without penetrating into the being of man. But when thought is assimilated in the heart, it turns into feelings. This is why the Ancients used to say, "Speak through the heart."

When speakers turn into tape recorders, they fall into a grave danger; they close the pathway that leads to the heart.

When we speak about feelings, we are not referring to emotionalism or the various dramas or comedies that emotions can create. We are referring to the blooming of inner, harmonious thoughts. When thoughts turn into words, they stay in Space as crystals; but when they turn into feelings, they form a flame, a river which touches the hearts and circulates around the globe, carrying a mighty current of uplifting light.

Real art is not the product of surface thinking but the result of a deeper thinking expressed in feeling. Mechanical creativity lacks feeling, although it can be built by the engineering of thoughts. Creativity that is produced by feeling carries high-voltage thoughts and penetrates into the essence of people.

Feeling is composed of three elements — light, love, and Intuition. Light is knowledge and thought. Love is heart and life. Intuition is affirmation and psychic energy. In feeling, there are also the combined fires of prana, matter, and mind.

Speakers must go through a period of self-training during which they must try to be aware of thoughts that are expressed in feeling. Remember, speakers must turn into transmitters of a fire that creates.

Books are there to give you inspiration and confidence. They are not there to be memorized and repeated as if they were your creation. You must have all possible information but use the spirit of the information and adapt it to the needs of daily life without making your talk commonplace.

A lecture should have at most three ideas explained in terms of daily experiences. Do not fill the mind of the audience with many ideas and subjects. Take at most three, and dwell on them from various viewpoints. For example, here are three *ideas* on which to build a lecture:

- Purity of body
- Heart quality
- Clarity of mind

Give fifteen minutes to each idea, and you will have forty-five minutes. Do not go beyond this. Keep your talk always on your subject. For example, on the idea of purity of body, you may take the following viewpoints:

— Washing the body

— Drinking pure water

— Eating uncontaminated food

— Changing your clothes and shoes

Then you may discuss *why* purity is important

- Because it is healthy
- Because it is beautiful
- Because it does not attract germs
- Because people feel it and it causes good relations
- Because it makes the cells happy and they breathe better

Then you may go to what purity does to the mind, then to the heart. You have one idea, but you are looking at it from various viewpoints. Thus you build a form in the consciousness of the audience, which can be used for their practical life. Do not give any lecture that cannot be applied to practical life, or else your lecture will have no value as far as we are concerned.

In your lecture, you may refer to other books, saying, "If you want more technical information about this subject, refer to (book title), page (number)." One of your aims in lecturing is to help people to

a. go deeper into the Teaching

b. become better friends of your group and help support it

c. grow in their spiritual evolution

Lecturing is an art, not a science. This is why you must speak through your heart and not turn on the tape recorder in your mind and think you are giving a lecture. During your lecture, you must create reactions or responses. They must love your lecture or feel very uncomfortable, but they must not think that you are an intellectual nut.

Before you go deep into your lecture, define the words of your title. Then choose not more than three ideas and plan the viewpoints you are going to take, five viewpoints for each idea. You can also use the following viewpoints for your ideas:

>The form
>
>The quality
>
>The purpose
>
>The cause
>
>>or

1. Personality viewpoint
2. Viewpoint of the soul
3. Viewpoint of the Inner Watch
4. Hierarchical viewpoint

>or

1. Present viewpoint
2. Past viewpoint
3. Future viewpoint
4. Infinity viewpoint

>or

1. Personal viewpoint
2. Group viewpoint

3. National viewpoint

4. International viewpoint

Choose your *ideas* and *viewpoints* carefully. It is very important to be able to discriminate between ideas and viewpoints.

People think that lectures must carry intellectual reasoning, logic, and information. This is only one part of the story. The second part is that the lectures must carry fiery *heart feelings* such as joy, indignation, admiration, wonderment, serenity, striving, suffering, divine anxiety, expectation, and so on.

Lecturing also has another subtle point which manifests when one is on the path of actualization. This is the part that causes transmutation in the essence of the audience. We call it *radiation*. This radiation starts when, during the lecture, the human soul contacts the layers of Beauty, Goodness, Righteousness, Joy, and Freedom and his consciousness penetrates into higher spheres.

It is this radiation that causes you to feel uplifted and free, that makes you meet your Self, make decisions, change directions, raise the focus of your consciousness, see your responsibilities, and purify your heart.

Choosing *ideas* and *viewpoints* carefully, having *heart feeling*, and having *radiation* or *actualization* are the first three aspects of lecturing that must be experienced by all those who feel responsibility to impart to the public a greater light, beauty, and joy. Actually, lecturing is an experience of transmitting energies to the audience after achieving mental, emotional, and spiritual integrity.

There is a fourth aspect in lecturing which comes naturally when the first three aspects mentioned above are done in the right way. This fourth aspect may be called *dramatization* of the three.

Dramatization is an effort to make the essence of your lecture visible and audible to the audience through subtle changes in your voice and through making your voice a true expression of your ideas, visions, and feelings. Dramatization is an effort to make the essence of your lecture visible through your eyes and facial expressions, through the movements of your hands and body. But if the first three factors are not conquered and actualized, your dramatization turns into a burden and sometimes even a comedy.

Most lecturers are crystallized in their vanity, and they feel hurt if you try to shock them and expand their awareness. Such lecturers must go through training before they can again deliver lectures to an audience because they transmit their vanity through their well-formulated and well-packaged lectures.

The fifth factor in lecturing is *magnanimity*. The meaning of this word is easier to feel than to understand, but let us try to define it. Magnanimity is the natural radiation of your spiritual achievement. It evokes respect, admiration, and deep love from the souls of the audience. They see a vision in you, a "path through which they may achieve."

Magnanimity touches their souls and releases the energies of their souls into the field of their personalities. Magnanimity is a continuous flow of joy and solemnity which starts to operate immediately when your soul fuses with your Inner Lord or when your soul tunes to the sphere of the Hierarchy. Magnanimity radiates through your posture and your voice.

We may conclude by asking a question: How can one turn into a good lecturer or a servant of light, love, and beauty? The answer is only by trying to expand your consciousness and reaching a higher degree of self-actualization or beingness.

31
Lecturing as an Art

Public lecturing is a delicate art. One of the complications in this art is that the consciousness of the public is on various levels. The speaker must not only find a common denominator but must also touch the highest and lowest levels of consciousness without making the highest bored or the lowest confused. The first step in mastering this art is to express ideas that are deep in essence and simple in form.

Let us consider this first step. You must give the definitions of the most important words you use. This builds bridges in the mind of the audience through which to offer your ideas. If you make a statement without building steps to take the consciousness of people toward the statement, you create confusion and you fail.

Statements are syntheses of ideas. People cannot grasp ideas if the proper steps are not taken to lead the consciousness gradually toward the statement. For example, you state, "Symbols are embodiments of ideas." This is good, but you did not define "idea" and "symbol" and prepare the consciousness of the audience to accept the statement. They will be in confusion. When you make additional statements without building ladders to them, you suspend the consciousness of the people. They begin either to dream, sleep, be confused, or fight internally with you. People reject you if you forget the *Law of Graduality*. For example, you say, "Every symbol is related to other symbols," but you do not lead them to understand such a relationship. Things have separate existences for them, and they were not made ready to connect them.

A good lecturer is a builder of ladders, bridges, and relationships between ideas, their meanings, and statements. The most successful lecture is one which, like concentric circles, expands in the consciousness of people. This can be done through simplicity.

The best way to express ideas that are deep in essence but simple in form is to use parables which contain condensed Teaching but in appearance are just stories. A few of such parables will give enough food and pleasure to those who are beginners and enough challenge for advanced ones to penetrate to the depth of the meaning presented by the symbolism of the parables.

Second, the art of lecturing requires that a successful lecturer be a responsible lecturer. Do not waste the time of people or confuse them. Start building the foundation so that people have certainty in their minds. Some people try to build the foundation for forty-five minutes, and then they speak about their topic for five to ten minutes. This also creates rejection. A good lecture must be like a basket of flowers of various kinds, tied together with their essence.

Third, it is very important that speakers have a reserve of energy. To influence people with your speech, your ideas, and your voice, you must have energy. This energy must be accumulated by resting, by meditating, by eating the right foods, and by saving energy. When you stand up for your lecture, you must radiate energy. When you have finished your lecture, people must feel that you are not exhausted. When you are tired or exhausted, your words will sound like empty shells, and they will create repulsion, pity, or criticism. People do not like to buy chestnuts whose insides are empty or rotten. It is the energy behind your words that creates interest, conviction, and joy in the audience. If energy is lacking, people pity you and are sorry that they wasted their time listening to you. Your spiritual visions, ideas, and thoughts need energy in order to impress people.

Some speakers exhaust themselves within ten minutes after starting their talk, but they continue talking, spending their reserve. Then at the end they collapse. When you begin to speak, you must have enough energy to carry your speech to the end with increasing dynamism. It is this increasing dynamism that captures and enthuses people. Even if your speech is weak in grammar or vocabulary, you impress people because of the energy.

Things told with energy create acceptance, admiration, and joy. Things told without energy create indifference, even if they make sense. This is the reason why you must not lecture, sing, dance, or counsel people if you feel tired.

It is an ancient tradition that those priests who are going to serve Holy Mass or deliver the sermon on Sunday must stay at the church on Saturday and sleep there in a special room. All day Saturday the priest contemplates on his sermon and rests in the garden or in his room, away from family or social problems. Thus he charges himself, focuses his mind, and makes himself ready for Sunday's duties. I have seen such priests in the old country. When they sing, read, or preach, they radiate a great amount of energy throughout the service. After the service, the people do not feel that the priest is exhausted. On the contrary, they see he is charged even more. It is the energy that creates magnetism and meets the psychological needs of people. When we are tired, we strain our voices and we make artificial movements to cover our exhaustion. People feel this immediately.

For every audience, the speaker is like a wrestler: They want their man to win in his fight for Beauty, Goodness, Righteousness, Joy, Freedom — radiating the Teaching. The audience feels very bad when their hero shows signs of weakness or exhaustion. The audience even feels a deep anxiety.

Once in our orchestra, the pianist showed exhaustion. The conductor was very angry. When the performance was finished, he scolded the pianist in front of the orchestra, calling him an empty bag who lacked the sense of responsibility and respect for the audience. Then he added, "An exhausted musician is like a flat tire in the orchestra."

The Teaching must be delivered with dynamism. If you have a small amount of energy, speak only for fifteen minutes. Sing one song or play one piece but never force yourself to perform longer if you cannot charge your expression, manners, and voice with dynamism.

Physical energy is gained by

— Rest and relaxation

— Eating right

— Conserving your sexual energy

— Sleeping well

— Controlling your imagination

— Keeping away from worry and anxieties

Psychic energy is gained through

- Meditation
- Contemplation
- Tuning in with the Guardian Angel or Teacher
- Raising your mind toward the future and Infinity
- Dedicating yourself to the service of humanity

Real energy does not need forcefulness. It is a steady radiation of preciseness, joy, humor, depth, and control of the voice, manners, and ideas.

The enemies of the Teaching wait for the moment to see the servants of the Teaching exhausted. This is the moment that their victory begins. They mercilessly attack the speaker and disqualify him, either in front of the audience or behind his back. My mother used to say that an exhausted speaker or artist is like a mouse in the paws of a cat.

The speaker, singer, or dancer must have not only physical energy but also psychic energy in order to radiate the beauty of the Teaching. A Great One says, "The most difficult thing for people is to coordinate the utmost rapture of spirit with inexhaustible action."[1] "Inexhaustible action" is fed by the fuel of physical energy. "The utmost rapture of spirit" is attained through psychic energy. Both must be present if one does not want to turn into a "windmill."

---

1. Agni Yoga Society, *Heart*, para. 35.

To improve our talks and to bring greater help to the audience, we must also improve in the following areas as much as possible.

1. *Organization*. Organize the ideas sequentially, on a gradient scale, so that the whole talk has a beginning, development, and conclusion. You must give ample time for each of the three sections so that you do not create cleavages or congestion in the consciousness of the audience. Metaphorically speaking, you must give time for the seed to sprout, to grow, and to bring fruit. If you present the fruit before the seed sprouts or grows, you create confusion. Confusion is the absence of integration.

2. *Tonality*. You must listen to a recorded tape of your talk with objectivity. Besides the ideas, you must also check your voice. It should not be monotonous, running on one or two notes with the same pitch. To improve your voice, talk for a few minutes and tape it; then listen to it. See if you can make your speech as if you were talking to your friends. See if you can make it more pleasant by changing your tonality and pitch.

Some people's voices drill into your brain or create a hypnotic atmosphere. Some people's voices block your receptivity or irritate you. A good speaker keeps the audience alert, even aggressive. He makes the audience run with him, discover with him, accept him, or reject him. At the end of the talk, the audience is more alert than before. A speaker's voice must not block his ideas from evoking interest in the audience.

3. *Pauses*. Some people talk like a machine gun. The words run after each other as if they were racing. This creates a very uncomfortable state of consciousness in the audience. If the ideas are mediocre, they cause rejec-

tion. If the ideas are of high-quality, they cause headaches.

When you give a speech, you must have pauses between your sentences, paragraphs, and even certain words. Pauses allow time for assimilation, concentration, and reconsideration. Pauses must be irregular and meaningful, giving people a chance to ponder upon what you said. Pauses also help the ideas to sink in and be assimilated.

4. *Speed.* The speed of your talk must be considered. Too much speed is mechanical. Too slow a speed creates lethargy. You must talk at the right speed when you deliver your talk. Generally, you must consider the level of consciousness of the people and the level of your ideas. If their response mechanism needs a slower speed, be slow. Do not throw the balls in the game at such a speed that the other person cannot catch them.

Sometimes a speedy talk is a result of a damaged tape recorder. Sometimes it is like a well-blown tube which has no valve to regulate the outflow of air. Some speakers are like a man with a bucket in his hand who tries to empty it as soon as possible and run away. When you are talking, realize that you are watering a plant in a small container. It needs time to absorb only a little water at a time, not the whole bucket at once.

5. *Emotions.* This is a very important point. Put emotions in certain words or certain expressions. It can be any kind of emotion: love, anger, command, grace, power. Sometimes even repeat the same words with different emotions. Create wonderment, admiration, ecstasy — even surprise.

6. *Ending.* Your talk must not end like an emergency brake but with a conclusive, synthesizing expres-

sion to emphasize the basic idea and its purpose in a pleasant and effective manner.

7. *Dramatics.* Some speakers are like mannequins: There is no life in them. Speech must be dramatic, using your voice, gestures, and movements of your hands, head, face, and body. Dramatization tells the audience things that your verbalized thoughts leave untold. Of course, we are not referring to clownish kinds of dramatizations. Amplification of ideas and thoughts needs polarity, which dramatization provides, to make your talk more impressive and complete.

8. *Emphasis.* For some lecturers, every word in a sentence has equal value. They use the same tonality and the same speed with every word as if they were all potatoes or tomatoes. The reality is that speech is not only the utterance of words but also the emphasis laid upon certain words, to broadcast the meaning and make it impressive in the minds of the audience. Have you ever noticed that it is not your sentences that convey the exact ideas you have, but the emphasis you lay upon certain words? Sometimes you cannot even convey your idea correctly if you put your emphasis on the wrong word, or if you utter your sentences like a machine.

You must practice emphasizing certain words in your speech until you learn the art of right emphasis. When you emphasize certain words, using a different voice, speed, or tonality, you not only give a clearer picture of your thoughts, but you also keep your audience awake. Mastery over words is accomplished by right pronunciation and emphasis. When your words drop from your mouth without being emphasized, people will eventually stop listening to you. Emphasis, right pronunciation, and amplification of certain words create magnetism and intelligent responses.

32
Leadership and Speech

Leadership is a very heavy responsibility, and one of the fundamentals is a sense of responsibility in our speech and in our letters. Our speech and written words must be guarded in such a way that we do not betray, in the slightest degree, our leadership position.

The average man can escape the consequences of his speech, paying a considerably smaller karmic penalty than a leader. Because of his position, the leader produces greater damage with his wrong speech than the average man.

The purpose of the leader is to inspire people to transcend themselves, to surpass their former level of beingness, and to live and be conscious on higher levels. The leader affects people by the way he walks, talks, thinks, and feels. He is under a great obligation to improve himself on all paths and to inspire those who are with him as his co-workers.

The leader must have faith in himself if he wants to inspire people to heroic action. How can this faith in oneself be developed?

First of all, you must create a reason to have faith and trust in yourself. You must work hard, strive, dare, accomplish certain things, and build faith in yourself.

In different conditions and crises you must try to hold your fundamental principles high and prove that you can pass various tests without losing your spiritual principles and visions. These are the elements that increase your faith in yourself. This faith does not come as a gift but as a result of long-lasting labor on the path of striving and achievement.

One of the things that really weakens your faith in yourself is your failure to observe your principles at the time of conversation or speech. Such a failure can have dreadful consequences on your service and your creative leadership. You are going to create reasons to convince yourself, your inner watchman, that you are really beautiful even in tempting conditions. You will be careful of talking about things that belittle yourself in your own eyes.

There are five rules to guard your speech, and no great work can be done without these five points. If you think that you can do great service for your fellow beings, if you think that you can be a worker for the Great Ones, if you think that you can achieve a higher level of transformation, then you should observe these five rules in your daily life. Your knowledge and talents are not enough to make you a leader of souls. You need more than this. If you do not observe these five very essential points, you are constructing a building which will eventually fall on your head.

Leadership is measured by the degree of mastery that the leader has upon his tongue.

1. You must keep silent about your own personal affairs and personal relationships. When you are dealing with your co-workers as a leader or as a co-worker, words about personal affairs and personal relationships bring the entire spiritual work down to lower levels and make it impotent, unmagnetic, and harmful.

Once you bring down your image to the level of your personal affairs, complaints, and relationships, you eventually build a low-level image of yourself and you lose your trust or faith in yourself. This image is a thoughtform which hangs around you and discourages you in all your attempts of daring and striving. It weakens your faith. You no longer respect yourself, and people slowly lose their respect for you. When you lose your respect for yourself, you want to take revenge on yourself. You take yourself away from the Path and from the Teaching so that you do not have any reason to be uncomfortable with your image.

If one wants to be somebody, something, in the progressive efforts of the world, he must not lose his trust and respect for himself.

In higher levels of human achievement, the personality must not be carried with you, nor should it bring embarrassment in your work. Wrong speech and speech about your personality problems, affairs, and relationships with others is a great obstacle on your Path and a danger for others. If you have problems you can talk with specialists, with your Teachers, even with your elders, but only to receive help and not for the sake of cheap talk.

Not only must you stop unnecessary talk, but you must also avoid those people who have no control over their speech and do not discriminate in their words.

Beware of those co-workers who have loose and wild mouths. They are dangerous and can ruin your work.

If a member of a spiritual group is keeping people busy with his personality problems and failures, he is preventing the progress of the group. He must be isolated until he learns the lesson of right speech.

2. Exercise severe discrimination in your speech — how to talk, why to talk, what to talk about.

Check your thoughts before you speak. If you do not know exactly what to talk about, do not talk at all.

If you know what you are talking about but do not know how to talk, wait until you learn how to talk. If you do not know why you are talking, keep silent until you find a noble reason to talk.

We make most of our mistakes through our speech. When wrong speech is released, you build karma. When your karma increases, your trust in yourself decreases. You lose your respect for yourself. No matter how wrongly you act, there is still someone watching you.

It is also very important to know when to speak. Words that are uttered at the wrong time are either powerless or harmful. In both cases, energy is wasted.

Economy in speech expands the dimension of your aura.

We are advised very strongly to think before we speak. This is not easy advice, but the reward is very great once we practice it.

3. Exercise control of speech in moments of excitement, success, failure, fear, or anger. These are moments when you can lose control of your mechanism and your physical body, your astral elemental, or your urges and drives and your subconscious tapes may control your speech. In these moments you will be extremely careful to guard your words through your thoughts. It is in these

moments that you may hurt people, insult them, reveal things entrusted to you, or fill yourself with vanity, pride, and hatred.

Once your astral elemental takes over your mouth, it leads you from one trouble to another until your whole image is lowered and spoiled. It is at these moments that crimes are committed, and hatred and jealousy are evoked with various kinds of attacks. A leader must try to watch such moments in serenity, in self-control, and with a smile.

Anything that makes us lose control of our mechanism must be avoided.

A leader should not involve himself in unnecessary problems, taking sides, or separate interests. He must stand above all of these things. He must keep his neutrality and balance and if necessary protect the interests of both parties. For the leader, there is not one side to things but always two sides. A leader falls into the hands of one party when, at the time of excitement, success, failure, fear, or anger, he does not control his mouth and takes sides. Those who are involved in separate interests lose the power to lead.

Once my Teacher in the monastery called a boy who was ready to be promoted into a leadership position. He took him under a tree and told him some "grave secrets" about the monastery. Two days later, the Teacher made the boy really angry and made him go to the garden and carry on his work.

Three other people were designated to watch him. Two hours later the boy went to another and complained about the Teacher. Then he told one of the "secrets" to his friend. Before he went to bed, he told all the "secrets" of the Teacher to at least five people. The next day everybody knew about the "secrets."

The boy was called to the leadership class. The Teacher, with great humor and sadness, revealed the test and invited the boy to explain why he had acted that way. He was not allowed to advance with that class any more; he had failed.

You can be very beautiful in your written reports, but the reports do not mean too much to real leaders. They look for your true being, your character. This is why a Sage stresses that people not be promoted in haste but slowly and gradually as one senses the beauty of their character.

4. Develop the ability to watch the dosage of information or insight passed to your co-workers or friends through your words. How much must you say? How much must you reveal? How much light must you shed on a problem? The wise leader knows the quantity of information or insight he should pass to others. A slightly greater dosage can flood their mind and paralyze them. A slightly greater dosage can make them lose their control or enter into total confusion. A little less information may lead them into errors or dangers.

How much must you give so that you help others grow and unfold, increase their striving, and inspire their spirit? The dosage is so important.

Do not open your mouth wide and say everything that you know or you think you know. You must take into consideration not only people's ability to understand, to discriminate, and to use safely the given information, but also you must consider their environment, their associates, their past.

If you are careful about these points, you will become a successful leader and help people grow without endangering their life.

Have the right dosage when you are scolding someone or disciplining him, when you are giving instructions, when you are informing about certain critical events. The right dosage is found only by wise leaders.

A leader must also be careful not to reveal the whole procedure, difficulties, trials, and dangers of the path of discipleship and initiation. Too much light blinds people; too much information discourages them. The mother eagle does not take her babies to the precipice until they grow wings. A leader does not show the depth of the abyss before the students develop daring. Also, when the jar is cracked, do not fill it with precious fluids.

Thus, when you speak of things that do not have the approval of your Inner Self or of your principles, you lower your image of yourself and lose your respect for yourself. Any person who loses respect for himself can no longer continue to be a leader.

When you act according to your spiritual principles and virtues, you will respect yourself more and more. Your faith and trust in yourself will increase, and you will become a true leader.

5. Develop the ability to answer the motive of the question rather than the question itself. The leader must use the eyes of his Intuition to penetrate beyond appearances and not be trapped in words and arguments. Christ was a perfect example of such an attitude. He answered the motives, not necessarily the questions. For example:

"Master, do you think one must pay taxes?"
"Give me a coin. Whose image is on it?"
"Caesar."
"Things that belong to Caesar give to Caesar; things that belong to God offer to God."

When you are able to answer motives, you knock down the evil in your adversaries or you enlighten them about the true issues of the question.

Some questions are intended to trap you or to create suspicion about you through your answers. You must be very careful to stand on the foundation of truth but not give a reason to the questioning one to hurt you. Remember also that there are many errors in excessive words. Shortcut answers can save you time and energy. Initiates are those people who speak only the most essential.

6. Develop the ability to resist your nosiness in the personal affairs of others or from their private lives. People may come and talk to you about their private life for advice. As soon as you understand the problem, you do not need to know the details. Speak to them about principles and how to abide in principles. If hatred is involved, you do not need to hear all the forms or expressions of hatred. Speak about the necessity of love, respect, compassion, and understanding.

People may come to you to justify their attitudes or position. Do not justify them or condemn them; speak about principles and let them try to appropriate their lives to these principles.

If they are ugly, emphasize beauty. If they are full of ill will, emphasize goodwill. If they are full of lies, emphasize the necessity of truth without taking any side because you cannot be one-sided. A leader is an all-sided man.

You must never put your nose in the personal lives of others and in their private affairs. If you suspect that someone is really dangerous, you can report to the authorities. Beyond this, you must respect the freedom of others.

Nosiness leads you to totalitarianism, involves you in the problems of others, and awakens in you the spirit of using others for your selfish interests.

A spiritual leader must impress the minds of people around him with the idea that he is interested in their soul and not their personality life. This does not mean that people must have a double nature — a soul nature and a personality nature apart from each other. It means that the spiritual leader is not interested in the sexual problems, financial problems, housing and eating problems, or social problems of his people; but he is interested in how to raise the consciousness of his people to the higher levels of values and principles and make them able to live according to the contacted values and principles.

I remember once during wartime in 1942, ten young people were given a chance to work in the army of a certain country. We were waiting by the door when the commander himself opened the door and said, "Come in." He sat on his chair by a huge table. Then suddenly he got up and said, "I will be back in a few minutes."

We waited more than five minutes and began to talk and walk around. We saw that there were letters on the table marked "Top Secret." Some of us immediately kept away from the table. Others hung over them and began to read. When they heard he was coming, they stepped away. He came in and asked a few questions to each of us. Then he told seven boys to leave the office. Then he questioned the three of us who were left and recommended that we start our job immediately.

When we were leaving his office he said, "By the way I appreciated your keeping yourself away from my desk. One must mind his business if he wants to work in the army."

Outside we were happy, and we concluded that all the time during his absence he was watching us.

7. Develop the ability to strike a viper with not more than five words.

If you see anybody in your group, church, or organization who is corrupt or degenerate, do not wait long. Open the door and lead him out. A leader is fearless but cautious. In the moment of necessity, he is fast and his decision is final.

You need to have strength to do this, and your strength first of all comes from your own image. If you have faith in yourself, in your integrity, beauty, and sincerity, you have strength. People feel that strength emanating from you and indirectly destroying in them the walls of darkness and evil.

8. Be forgiving and resolve problems correctly. One of my Teachers used to say that forgiveness is noble when you are sure that your forgiveness will not encourage the criminal to continue his actions.

One of the easiest things to do in the world is to blame others whenever you have failed in anything. This is a common sickness, and it is widespread. There is also the reverse of the above. Whenever you are involved in any trouble or problem you heavily blame yourself. This is another kind of sickness.

The healthy attitude is to cool down and find out the real cause of the failure without blaming yourself or others. In this case you and others are not important; the important thing is to find the cause of the failure, annihilate it, and introduce new causes which will result in success. Such a procedure needs cool observation, without involving your emotions, without blaming others, and without blaming yourself.

It may be possible that you made some miscalculations and others took advantage of them; or others made miscalculations and you were not alert enough to catch them.

It is impossible to solve a problem by blaming others. The way to solve a problem is to find the real cause and try to change it.

Many friendships are broken and many future possibilities evaporate because of blaming each other. In blaming ourselves harshly, we develop an inferiority complex and kill the spirit of striving and effort within ourselves. Then we eventually turn into weak creatures, dependent on others.

It is known that people blame others in order to cover their own guilt and past mistakes. People blame themselves when they are identified with the guilt of others. All such complications can be healed only by developing cool-headed observation and honesty. Another way to overcome psychological weaknesses is to strive toward beauty, harmlessness, and kindness.

9. Beware of those who gossip. They are distributors of germs which are very hard to annihilate. Dark forces work through gossipers to create disturbances in the hearts and minds of people, and they agitate groups dedicated to the service of unity, harmony, and cooperation.

Do not encourage gossipers by listening to them. They will talk the same way about you to others.

Gossipers are sick people. Their heart center is covered in a gray mist, and their consciousness is in the process of degeneration.

There is a service you can do for those who gossip:

a. Ask if they are perfect.

b. Ask if they have things in their nature which are vulnerable.

c. Ask if they really know who they are.

d. Ask if they have the same character as their victims.

e. Ask the reason why they want to gossip.

f. Ask them to go and talk to their victims.

With these six questions you will unveil their true face.

Never repeat the words of gossipers to anyone, for any reason. To repeat gossip means to spread it. As far as you can, kill the gossip immediately and never talk about it.

In the meantime send a blessing to the victim and pray for him.

In cases of danger or treason, let only the victim know about the traitor.

It may happen that someone gossips and damages your reputation although you have done nothing to him. The reason is that the gossiper is hating in his heart a certain man who did wrong to him in the past, and you remind him of that man. Actually, you are an image and a victim of a hatred with which you had nothing to do. This is called esoterically "the confusion of images and time."[1]

It also happens that the man you hate is the image of a former man whom you hated and whose position you damaged. You tried to ask his forgiveness, and either he did not forgive you or you did not have the chance to receive his forgiveness. This is a complicated situation. You hate an image and make that image suffer from your hatred, while that image has nothing to do with you.

Such a hatred often creates reactions from the "image," and your problem becomes even more complicated because the image changes into exactly the person you hated.

---

1. See also *The Subconscious Mind and the Chalice*, especially Ch. 19, "Observation."

33
How to Organize the Work

Any successful enterprise is the result of planning and organizing the work. Planning requires a great amount of co-measurement. One must take many factors into consideration besides the present need if he wants his plan to work.

It is very helpful if the entire work is divided into five levels. Each level can have as many personnel as is needed. In the beginning one can start with five people.

The *First Level* is called the *Leadership Level*. The Leadership has a goal and a purpose.

The *Second Level* is the level of *Operators*. They analyze the purpose and do the planning. The plan states the ways and means to fulfill the purpose.

The *Third Level* is the level of *Communicators*. They receive the plan and organize the performers with discrimination according to each performer's quality, ability, and fitness.

The *Fourth Level* is the *Performers' Level*. Performers work out the plan in objective manifestation. Performers present their program to the Operators, and the Operators present it to the Leadership before it is put into action.

The *Fifth Level* is the level of *Distributors*. Distributors are those people who take the product and work for its best distribution.

The Leadership is divided into five sections:

1. There is the President — the Leader of Leaders.

2. There is a Leader who observes the Operators and works with them as their Chairman and as the reporter in the Leadership group.

3. There is the Leader who observes the Communicators as their Chairman and as their reporter in the Leadership group.

4. There is a Leader who observes the Performers as their Chairman and acts as the reporter for them in the Leadership group.

5. There is the Leader who works with the Distributors as their Chairman and as their reporter in the Leadership group.

In the *Leadership* meeting the Leaders are kept aware of all that is going on within the four departments of work. They are the Leader-Chairmen.

The Leadership's "orders" must be very clear. The orders must be written, and copies must be kept in the folders of each Chairman. Date, duration, and place can be indicated very clearly. One of the most important qualities of leadership is clarity, which means simplicity and directness. As much as possible, confusion and the possibility of misunderstanding must be avoided by all means.

Operators must refer to the Leadership group, via their Chairman, if any doubt emerges in their minds between the purpose and the plan.

The duty of Operators is to understand the purpose presented to them by the Leadership. The Chairman can help to clear any confusion if it exists. They must formulate the plan as clearly as possible. The plan is the ways and means of how to actualize the purpose. Their duty is to explain the plan to the Communicators and be sure that there is no doubt in the minds of the Communicators. Operators must also know how much information will be safe to impart to the Communicators.

The Communicators' Chairman must keep very close watch on the Communicators to make sure they are efficient and accurate in their job.

Communicators translate the plan, analyze it, divide it into parts, and select those people who fit each part and are able to carry the plan into construction. Communicators will discriminate between those who please them and those who are able and qualified to carry on the work of construction faithfully.

Communicators never work by favoritism. They do not have favored or unfavored ones. Only the work is important to them. Working with the Leader of the Performers, they have the hard job of choosing people who can fit into the right position. They alternate the Performers if necessary. They emphasize punctuality, accuracy, and persistence. Communicators must not only know the mental abilities of the Performers, but they must know about their emotional qualities and energy limits.

Communicators never force the Performers beyond the limits of their capacity to work. Forced work leads to failure.

Once the Performers are selected, the Communicators never belittle them in any way, either by word or gesture. Any time a deficiency is observed, the Communicators arrange training programs to make them more efficient, or transfer them to another part of the plan where they can be more efficient.

Performers must try to understand their duties accurately and keep harmony and understanding between each other through direct communication. They must try to work together in spite of many differences of character and personality. They must try to work with each other without being limited by any personality reactions which may surface because of past or present affiliations. The more detachment they have from the personality, the more successful will be the work of the Performers.

Performers, or any group below the Leadership, must not take orders from each other. It is the Chairman's duty to translate the order of the Leader or give sub-orders if necessary.

Distributors must be experts in organizing, advertising, and communicating with people. They must care how they dress, how they talk, how they approach people, and how they hand over the perfected project. They must have all their techniques ready to face various conditions and different needs.

Distributors are leaders on the distribution level.

In the activities of all the levels, tension must be eliminated as much as possible. Overloading the workers leads to failure of various kinds. The workers must have their days of rest, vacation, and entertainment.

Joy must be preserved in all relationships.

To keep the work alive, up-to-date, and under continuous observation, the Leaders must have a meeting at the end of every month. In these meetings the Chairmen-Leaders must report on their own departmental problems, plans, etc.

Every three months, all members of all levels must meet with the Leadership to present their viewpoints and suggestions for improvement, which all must be recorded and filed properly for future use.

Anyone who wants to be promoted must start from the lowest level and work his way up. The best of each level must be promoted to higher levels after three years' work on their own level.

The President-Leader must work in each different level as an assistant worker for a day each month. This will help renew his information on each level and give him firsthand knowledge about possibilities and problems. The Leader must leave open the communication line between himself and the workers on all levels, allowing them to have direct contact with him by a simple appointment.

The principles which must control the activities of all departments are Beauty, Goodness, Righteousness, Joy, and Freedom through self-forgetfulness, harmlessness, and right speech. Each Chairman must be extremely careful that these principles are observed by all related to the work.

Let us apply this procedure to book manufacturing. The *Leaders* will decide the book to be published, and for various reasons they may choose various books. They will read the book chosen for publication and make the needed corrections or alterations. They will also decide the amount of copies to be published.

The *Operators* will take the book and decide the following:

— paper

— typeface

— cover design

— printer

— diagrams, etc.

The *Communicators* will take the manuscript and choose all those who will be able to meet the requirements of publishing such a book. They will have the artists draw the diagrams, cover design, etc. They are the people who understand the problems of publication and are familiar with the printing business.

Performers will find the right printers, will proofread, make needed corrections, and handle various problems.

The *Distributors* will receive the copies of the published books and will do the following:

1. Check the pages, covers, paper quality, etc.

2. Store them in the proper place

3. Advertise the book

4. Sell the book

5. Keep clear accounts

6. Research for a new edition

7. Return the manuscript and proofs to the Leaders

It is the Leadership group who reviews the work done by each group and gives the results to them in written form.

34
Leadership and the Ability to Organize

Leadership will not be successful if the spirit of organization is lacking. To organize means to arrange those ways, means, personnel, places, etc. in such a way that a desired goal is achieved with the least resistance, within a proper duration, and with the least expenditure of time, energy, and matter.

In an organizational effort there are important factors to be considered, for example:

1. Timing
2. Personnel
3. Place
4. Clarity of Goal

5. Awareness of obstacles and weaknesses

6. Sources that may sustain the organization and make it grow

7. Future possibilities of various changes

8. Focus of intention and willpower

9. The needs of the present and the future

10. The field of service

11. Contribution to other affiliated organizations

12. Meditation

If these twelve main points are considered by the leadership, it can really organize and bring greater success for people.

1. *Timing* is very important. Many, many organizational efforts have failed because of wrong timing. Astrological timing is very beneficial, but there are other factors to be considered when one wants to organize, for example:

   a. The political, social, and economic situations

   b. The personnel who are going to be part of the activity

   c. The maturity of the plan

   d. The psychological atmosphere of the persons involved or of society

Of course, many organizations were started and continued with great success under adverse conditions.

The duty of the leader is to find those moments which help him to be successful under the most adverse conditions in history.

Timing, in its esoteric sense, is the ability to synthesize all conditions and to find the best moment to release the arrow so that it reaches its destiny more easily through the rings of obstacles rather than in open air.

The leader must use and exercise his sense of timing with daily things, in his daily relationships. Throughout the day he must try to find the right moment to speak, to ask, to give an order; a right moment to keep silent, to act, to start a labor, to rest, to plan. Through such exercises he can learn the operation of many esoteric laws which man does not usually profit from because of his ignorance.

A letter written at the right moment is more effective. A call made at the right moment brings great results. There is a right time to do everything.

In the light of the above suggestions one can investigate the moments when he did something which ended in failure. Such research will teach him many lessons.

2. *Personnel.* Organizational work cannot be carried on if the personnel are not chosen in the right way. The "right way" does not mean to choose the best people but the right people. The right people are those people who:

    a. Are creative and catalytic

    b. Know the plan and have the skills

    c. Are diligent and energetic

    d. Are cooperative

    e. See beyond their personal interests

f. Have less interference from their personality problems

g. Are in good health

a. There are some people who are difficult to get along with — but they are accurate; they are perfectionists; they have clear observation; and they can act as catalysts. Pleasant and easily agreeing people are sometimes trouble-producing people, and one cannot advance further with them.

b. The personnel you choose must have the skill or be eager to learn the skill. They must know why they are in your company and something about what your developing plan is. The plan makes them adjust their lives and skills accordingly.
There are, of course, instances when the plan must not be fully revealed to the co-workers, but proper goals must be set.

c. Organization work cannot progress if the personnel are in apathy or inertia. Psychic energy makes the whole machinery work. Inertia is a very contagious disease, and it retards the centers of other co-workers and slows the work.
Diligent people are integrated people, and they are good conductors of energy.

d. Cooperative people must be chosen for organizational purposes. An organization or organism is the manifestation of the spirit of cooperation. Cooperation multiplies the energy and lets it flow through all parts of the organization.

In cooperation people work for the project, for the plan and purpose, and stand above their personal problems.

Uncooperative people push their personal glamors into the labor and create divisions.

e. Those who enter any organizational work with self-interest eventually create an atmosphere of refusal around them, which can be quite a painful experience for them and for the personnel of the organization.

Personality interests are the source of exploitation, and one cannot exploit people and situations without creating contradictory directions in the organization.

f. One must be as little influenced by his own personality problems as possible to be really useful to the purpose of the organization. When personality problems, hatred, fear, jealousy, greed, anger, and family situations are constantly carried into our daily duties and responsibilities, we cannot function at full capacity. We eventually become a problem in the organization in which we work and prevent its growth and development.

Those who are involved in their personality problems cannot understand the dimensions and the sanctity of the spiritual work. They must be trained and purified before they are invited to work in a spiritual organization.

g. Good health is very important. The spiritual work puts increasing pressure upon the physical, emotional, and mental natures and thus exposes their weaknesses and brings out defects which otherwise would remain dormant.

Also, unhealthy people bring into the organization not only their problems, pains, and sufferings but also their irritation and karma.

The leader must see that those who are going to handle heavy duties and responsibilities are healthy people.

3. *Place.* The most important factor in organizational work is to choose the right place. Many failures in organizational work are due to the fact that the leader chose a wrong place to start his work. A place is the climate, the location, the psychological, religious, economic, and political atmosphere where the organizational work will be carried on.

If the atmosphere proves to be unfriendly, then the work must not start there. Of course, through heroic efforts one can conquer adverse situations, but why waste time, energy, and money if there is a place which is more favorable for the work?

The new plants must be protected until they reach a state where the winds or animals cannot push them. Gardeners know where to plant their seeds, where to plant their trees. The Teaching is like the seeds and trees. The Teacher must know where to spread them to bring the most abundant result.

The right place also means the karmic purity of the place. Great spiritual development cannot take place in those areas where crimes are committed and dark and destructive activities are carried on constantly.

4. *Clarity of goal.* From the beginning of any plan the goal must be clear: what do you want to do?

The goal can be progressively revealed. For example, this year the goal is to master the physical body or build the walls of the temple. Next year's goal is to master the emotional body, or to finish the water system in the temple. The next year's goal is to master the mental body or to install the electricity in the temple, and so on. You can see clearly that goals are successive steps leading you to your *purpose.*

In the above case your purpose may be to produce a master man or to have a beautiful temple for meditation.

When the goal is clear, you have a better opportunity to be successful and you do not waste time, energy, and money in uncertainty, in confusion, or in a frequent change of goals.

A goal clearly defined and geometrically planned prevents confusion in the minds of co-workers. An undefined goal creates doubt, confusion, and lack of efficiency.

The purpose is a mosaic; goals are pieces in the mosaic.

5. *Awareness of obstacles and weaknesses.* No leader must proceed in his organizational work without being aware of the obstacles on the path and the weaknesses of the people working with him. When the leader knows about the obstacles, he can prepare himself or the work in such a way that the obstacles turn into assets and the weaknesses of some workers increase the strength of the others.

Before the organizational work begins, the leader must thoroughly research possible obstacles in individuals, groups, and the society such as:

Physical — weather, climate, etc.

Emotional — traditional, religious

Mental — philosophic, political

He must try to see where weaknesses exist and on what line. For example, are there weaknesses in concentration, in dedication, in silence, in solemnity? Knowing the weaknesses, he can either fortify the weak points or eliminate or replace the objects of weakness.

It is possible to make impotent certain weaknesses of people by placing such people in appropriate positions where their weaknesses cannot bring harm.

When the obstacles are known, the leader decides if he can surmount them; if it is worthwhile enough to battle against them; if it is necessary to ignore them or to wait for a better time or better condition. A little research done on obstacles and weaknesses will save much time, energy, and headaches.

6. *Sources that may sustain the organization and make it grow.* The true leader must realistically find those sources which will give his organization moral support, financial support, and spiritual support. This is the total expected income of the organization. It is not only money or material help but also moral and spiritual help that can assist an organization to grow and serve.

One can list those whom he thinks will support him morally with their attitudes, words, and contacts. He must also know those who will support him financially by making pledges and regularly helping the organization. These people can be approached in the right ways, by the right people, inspiring them with the beauty of the purpose and by the description of the service to be rendered. Proper literature, documentation, and recommendations can be presented to them, and personal visits can be arranged with them to make them really interested in the various projects.

Real success needs time and preparation, but once all is ready, the growth can be accomplished easily and swiftly.

7. *Future possibilities of various changes.* Every organization must be ready to grow cyclically and submit itself to new changes. Time after time the leadership

must try to adapt the organization to the needs of the time.

Many organizations grow, then petrify and die. A really healthy organization must be like an organism which grows and shoots new branches, new roots, and new trees. It must be a living entity, sensitive to the changes in the environment, to the needs of people, to the visions of advancing students and co-workers.

Periodically the course of the organization must be checked to see if it is in harmony with the time and with the original vision on which it was established. One must be ready to introduce changes in programs, in leadership, in the politics of the organization without hurting the principles and the vision of the organization.

The leader must train the future leaders in such a way that they will be able to introduce changes as they see the need and not follow him blindly. New conditions demand new ways of approach, and the future leaders must be inspired by the spirit of freedom to take new actions without any guilt feelings.

The curriculum can be adapted and elevated into deeper levels of study. The ceremonies can be enriched and made more clear and powerful. The decorations, rooms, and gardens can be changed. The system of correlation between the departments can be improved. New advances can be added. But all this must be done after detailed study and without the spirit of vanity or self-interest.

After the original leader leaves, the future leadership must be very careful and cautious for a long time before introducing changes. Time is necessary to make the new leadership see the real issues and the reasons for the previous procedures.

Before introducing new changes and meeting new challenges, a leader must test the group to see if it is spiritually and physically ready to step up to a higher dimension. The group must be ready for change, or else the new proposals will cause confusion and hurt.

To make the group ready, one must present new and higher disciplines and longer hours of service so that the group is able to see the next step of its evolution and constantly strive for it.

If the group is not able to actualize the lessons already given to it, it is not wise to present new lessons. New lessons may lead the group into vanity, refusal, or confusion.

The group must be progressive, but the progress will be designed and introduced slowly and with the acceptance of the group.

Thus the leadership can change the programming and the placing, but the changes must prove that the group can actualize the initial purpose in a better way and with less friction.

The leadership must be very cautious of those people who promise great success in a short time if certain changes are made. Often changes are introduced with wrong motives or at the wrong time. Such changes can be disastrous for the group for a long time.

It is also wise to test changes before adapting them as permanent procedures. A testing period reveals the weaknesses of the changes and the short-sightedness of the introducer of the changes.

The leadership must be careful in choosing leaders. We are told that personnel from other groups must not be brought in and given responsibilities. This is a very risky action or effort. It is better to promote the young ones from the group, after careful observation of their lives.

Various interests can damage a group, if the group is continuously exposed to them.

8. *Focus of intention and willpower* are necessary to keep the group steady on the path of its service and development. The organizing leader must see that the co-workers have willpower and that their intention has focus.

Flickering lights, weakhearted ones, must not be invited to daring labor. Motives and intentions must be observed very carefully, as well as their duration and strength.

It is possible that people have right motives and right intentions for a short time and during periods when their higher nature is stimulated by the presence of the leader. But sometimes this stimulation does not last when new interests and new obstacles force their presence.

One must watch the applicants not only during their successes but also during their failures and moments of difficulties for a period of at least three years. The promotion must be slow and gradual.

Small and big responsibilities and sometimes complicated, tiresome labor must be given to the applicants to make them expose themselves and to see if they are stable in their efforts, labor, and intentions.

9. *The needs of the present and the future.* A healthy organization must be an answer to a need. This need must be a present need and a future need. Unless the organization answers a present and a future need, it cannot survive.

The leadership must find the need that can be met by an organized group. It must be a real need. For example, one organizes a group to bridge gaps between people. This can be done on political, educational, philosophical, artistic, and scientific fields, as well as in religious or economic fields. This is the immediate need. The leadership must decide how to meet this need, on what level, in what field, and through what kind of approach.

Then the future need must be considered. Where will this bridging process lead us? Are we looking for political, economic, or religious unity only, or are we also looking for a psychological unity, a spiritual unity, a unity between centers in man, between nations and planets, a unity within the solar system, a unity in the galaxy, and so on?

When one has a future vision his efforts and labor steadily harmonize themselves with the vision, and the future need strengthens and encourages the efforts to fulfill the present day's need. It is between these two points that adjustment and changes must be introduced. There is the starting point. There is the goal. And every change must prove that the present labor is in closer harmony with the future labor and a better preparation to render a better labor for the future.

10. *The field of service.* It is very important to be clear about the field in which the service will be rendered. The organization must fit the field. There are seven main fields of service, and each of them has many branches:

>Politics
>
>Education
>
>Philosophy or Communication
>
>Arts
>
>Science
>
>Religion
>
>Economy

A field must be entered after specialization, after equipping your organization with knowledge and experience.

No organization can survive by changing its field of service frequently. It is possible that as an organization grows new fields can be introduced, but not without preparation and new personnel.

Every organization can eventually develop seven fields of service within its own borders. For example, an educational organization will have its leadership which formulates the politics of the organization. It can have a committee for communications, arts, science, religion, and economy; but all serve the educational plan.

If certain members of the group develop different interests, it is better for them and better for the mother organization if they go and form a new organization with new goals and new methods. There is no reason that the new organization should be in conflict with the parent organization, if the parent organization gives freedom to its members to follow their hearts.

11. *Contribution to other affiliated organizations.* Any healthy organization must contribute to those other organizations which carry out constructive work for humanity. It is through strengthening each other's efforts that the greatest changes can be brought about within the life of humanity.

Each organization must have a yearly convention dedicated solely to review the ways and means to help other organizations in any possible way. A selfish organization cannot grow, and if it grows it becomes a danger to humanity.

Those organizations which help the growth and wellbeing of other organizations grow in a healthy way and serve humanity.

An organization must help others without self-interest and without selfish motives. For example, an organization can help a needy organization by raising funds for them, by giving them furniture or machines they are not using, by presenting musical and theatrical performances for them, by sponsoring lectures, and by giving moral and spiritual help. The more an organization helps others, the longer will be the duration of its own life.

An organization grows not through what it receives but through what it gives to people and to organizations that are engaged in the welfare of humanity.

It is very important that from the beginning the leadership makes it clear that it is absolutely forbidden to criticize any organization dedicated to the human welfare. Each has its own work to do, and each labor is a field of test and examination for its leadership. Outer interference must not be exercised by a noble leadership of any group, though warnings can be given if any affiliated organization is in danger.

12. *Meditation.* The leadership of the group must set a special time every day for meditation or thinking to observe the function of the organization, to rededicate it with greater enthusiasm, and to fit itself to the new challenges. If this is done, the organization becomes an organism which always renews itself, recharges itself, and blooms.

An organization is a multiform mechanism which tries to fulfill the duty programmed by the leadership. An organism is an integrated, living entity, sensitive, telepathic, spontaneous, and simultaneous in its responses and reactions.

The goal of an organization is to form an organism in which all parts are aligned and harmonized to a high degree to meet the challenge of the time and to prepare for a greater service.

35
Festivals, Parties, and Entertainment

A leader needs energy in order to work, and this energy is of two kinds. The first energy is that which is released within him through his contact with his Inner Dweller, his Master, his Ashram, etc. The second type of energy is the energy field which is produced by his contact with his followers and co-workers.

When a leader is charged with Soul or Ashramic energy, his contact with other people creates a release of energy in them. This released energy must be coordinated, harmonized, and oriented through various duties, responsibilities, and sacrifices which the leader presents to them.

As his followers and co-workers respond to his call, the field of energy expands, strengthens, and becomes very magnetic which then attracts new energies. This magnetic field, or the energy field of his followers and co-workers, is of various kinds. There is an etheric energy field, an emotional energy field, a mental energy field, and a spiritual energy field. Also, there is a field in which *all* the above fields are present in a very harmonized and beautiful way.

The energy field of etheric radiation is mostly created by enthusiasm directed toward great goals. The emotional energy field is created by devotion, worship, and dedication. The mental energy field is created by building a mental group interest in a project or a plan, or through synchronous meditation. The spiritual energy field is created by focusing the attention of the co-workers and followers on a great sacrificial service inspired by an intuitive understanding of the purpose of life.

All these energies are created and harmonized in great beauty and with great influence in cyclic festivities; for example, full moon festivals, Easter festivals, Christmas celebrations, in parties celebrating birthdays or wedding anniversaries, or the anniversaries of group formations, etc. In all these and other festivities, the leader or the leadership readies the group-created energy field for later use in greater service for humanity.

In these festivities we have physical, emotional, mental, and spiritual integration, alignment, coordination, and communion — all superimposed by a vision which the leader presents through his person, his works, or his sacrificial life. In the great opportunity presented by the festivity, this vision slowly penetrates, and the energy field then forms on a higher dimension and creates links, relationships, and responses within the parts and the whole.

In future incarnations this energy field becomes stronger and pulls toward itself all those who participated in forming the field. Thus the leader will have under his direction an ever-increasing field of energy and co-workers who will provide the facilities for the expression of the Plan and Purpose on Earth.

It is in this way that the armies of the Great Ones are created. Imagine the followers of Christ, three, twelve, seventy-five, five hundred, the Hierarchy, the New Group of World Servers, and all those who in some degree answer His call. Now we can see why the Great Ones created festivals — festivals celebrating Their birthdays, celebrating the remembrances of Their great works and Initiations, festivals celebrating Their sacrifices and "death."

Through all these festivities, They accumulated and brought together various Sparks on various levels and inspired them with a great vision of achievement and service.

These festivities are not only used to create the energy field which will be used as a distribution center for ideas and activities of the Future, but the festivities are also cycles of testing the leader's followers and co-workers.

The leader's co-workers and followers are tested in the following points:

1. In their sincerity

2. In their emotional responses

3. In their ability to use their minds and to organize

4. In the sacrifices they make

5. In the opportunity to express their love and dedication

6. In their selflessness

7. In their recognition of the value of the leader and their reverence for that value

Birthday Parties

Let us say that an initiate or a disciple or a leader is having a birthday party. This occasion is an opportunity for him to see his followers and co-workers in a different light and to test their personality and Soul responses so that in the future he uses them in the right place, at the right time, in the right proportion, or he leaves them to one side for a future use.

Let us examine the tests:

1. Was your *sincerity* tested toward the leader? Did you have conflict within you? What was the conflict? How did you resolve it?

2. In your *emotional responses*, were you jealous or envious? Did you act funny because a hidden jealousy or other emotion made you talk, act, or appear in abnormal ways?

3. Did you *organize* the festivity in the best possible way you could? Did you see your failures and defects in handling and fulfilling your duty?

4. Did you *sacrifice*? What was it? The leader does not actually need your gifts, but he needs to create a sacrificial nature in you. You will never reach greatness until you learn how to sacrifice for someone, for a Teacher, for a leader, for a cause, for a plan; and all this starts with practicing the spirit of sacrifice.

What did you really offer to the leader? The best? Or was it just mediocre? This will measure the position you have on the path of your evolution.

It is a very shallow and false excuse when you say, "I give my whole life to the cause he presents, so I do not have to sacrifice anything valuable for him." This is self-deception. This is why Christ said, "If you do not love a brother whom you see, how can you love God Whom you cannot see."

Your Master's contact with you is only through the disciple who watches you and your whole attitude toward your Master. Thus the disciple protects the Master by revealing your nature to Him and by preventing an unready one from reaching Him.

5. In what ways did you *express your love and dedication*? Every time we lose an opportunity to express our love and dedication, we lose an opportunity to unfold and radiate and to expand our consciousness on a higher plane of light and activity.

On what level do you really express your love for him, your dedication to him? With a kiss? With a gift? With a great decision to serve the cause to which he is dedicated? With a lofty decision to perform certain creative activities which will make it easier for him to render his responsibility on the Path? Will you erase some emotional or mental blocks which are preventing your full cooperation?

Do you express your love and dedication by maintaining a greater personality *detachment* and giving him greater freedom to work in the light of his Soul, or by withdrawing your physical, emotional and mental demands, attachments, and criticisms of him?

In what way do you express your love and dedication? Remember that your Teacher or leader is the door toward your spiritual realization. He is an individual in his own right but also a symbol of greater Beauty.

6. The next test is that of *selflessness*. Was your selfishness tested? What did you find out about yourself? Did you act selfishly or unselfishly? Do acts of greatness on the part of your leader hurt you and make you jealous and envious of him?

Did you act in a way that showed you wanted recognition and praise from people? Did you act in any way to get them to give recognition and praise to you?

7. The last test is that of *recognition of the value of the person and reverence for that value*. Never forget that when you love someone, when you respect someone, you send a ray of Soul or spiritual energy to him which thus strengthens his heart for greater responsibilities and labors. Leaders know this, and they need that support because without it certain daring labors cannot be performed.

A leader is an architect and a builder. He must use all that is offered to him to create those conditions in which conscious blooming will be possible. In this way the path of glory and the path of achievement will be built.

By observing his followers and co-workers on different occasions and in different relationships, the leader is able to promote them in their duties and responsibilities and gradually, but very wisely, lead them from lower attachments toward higher identifications and unifications.

You are leaders or disciples in your own right and in the proper places where karma has put you. Therefore *respect yourself* and make people respect you — not because you are a certain somebody but because you present the flame of the Almighty Life. Repeat to yourself:

Om Mani Padme Hum

Repeat this mantram inwardly toward all whom you meet. Repeat this mantram especially toward your Teachers, Leaders, and Elder Brothers.

Organize birthday parties and other festivities to love and be loved. Organize the festivities with the purpose to serve a cause and try, try very hard to become lost in that cause. Be a little wheel in a greater wheel.

As you start trying to do these things, you will begin to see the nature of your friends. You will also see something very important that you cannot often see: the effect your life has on others. What kind of people do you attract to yourself? What changes are created in them because of the attraction? To what level of understanding do you lift them? What new steps will you take to create a greater field of energy to further the Plan?

Did you stand in your spiritual purity and bliss when they were respecting, honoring, and praising you, and did you, in turn, dedicate all the praise and recognition to your own Teacher and Master and humanity? While all this was going on were you seeing the *jewel* in each of those who were praising and recognizing you, the jewel which must be honored and respected as a flame from the one fire?

Always remember, you are as you are because of your Teacher, and your Teacher is as he is because of his Teacher, and so on. All of us are Teachers and centers of energy, and also we are petals forming greater energy centers.

Let us remember the words of one of our Teachers:

> *Precisely by love should one teach how to deal wisely with the sacred concept of the Teacher. There are no thirty shekels for which one may hire various teachers. As wisely must one select disciples. The same silver thread binds each Teacher with each*

> *disciple. Once the pledge is pronounced it becomes the foundation of karma.*[1]

One of the greatest dangers for a leader is the possibility of falling into vanity and selfish interests and using his energy field for the satisfaction of his ambitions and desires. This danger can easily be overcome if the leader is in constant contact with his Soul or Master through his meditation, self-examination, and retreats. A true disciple never falls into such a danger, but if at any time he does fall into it, he must recollect himself and stand up in the light of his Soul with even greater selflessness and sacrifice.

A question may be asked here: If a co-worker or follower of the leader notices any slight possibility of failure on the part of his leader, what should be the co-worker's attitude toward the leader?

The answer will be surprising for the average man but very logical for the co-workers. They must stand by him always and in all conditions, focusing their attention on his Innermost Spark and expressing greater trust, greater love, and deeper expectations of his greatness and beauty. Only in such a way can the leader be helped and any mistake in judgment discarded, thus averting any resulting negative action.

Criticism is the tool of Satan which is used to destroy the works of the leader in the field of the Hierarchical Plan. Thus, patience must be learned, wisdom gained, and discrimination cultivated.

The extreme action that a member of a group can take is resignation from the group with all respect and gratitude.

---

1. Agni Yoga Society, *Hierarchy*, para. 300.

Festivals and Entertainment

A group or an organization must have days of entertainment for the average public. On such days of entertainment:

— The talents of the members must be revealed. These include singing, dancing, reciting, etc.

— The dignity and the prestige of the group must be demonstrated by the members in their relations and performances.

— The presentations must lead to a goal. They must be joyful, but meaningful, and in line with the goal of the group.

Such occasions are opportunities for contact with those people who are related to the group in some way but are not followers of the Teaching for various reasons. Entertainment days are opportunities to impress upon them the beauty of the group, the beauty of its goals, and the beauty of its members. People evaluate others not when they are in meditation or giving lectures but at the time when they are free in the spirit of entertainment.

Many disciples are drawn to serious work after meeting qualified people in the group at such events.

On these occasions members can exercise their organizational talents or learn how to organize a goal-fitting party or an entertainment night. Those who have the ability to organize must teach others how to organize. But to organize is not enough if the goal of the group is not yet known or realized.

Some people think that in parties and entertainment evenings the Teaching must be left behind and the presentation must be on a common level. This is a wrong idea. Whatever the group as a whole and members as individuals do will reflect on the value and the prestige of the group. People will know others by what they are and by what they give.

A disciple or an aspirant must not be two-faced — sometimes solemn, beautiful, and dignified and other times vulgar, cheap, and common. Those who are not familiar with your Teaching will have the impression that your Teaching is exactly what you are, and they will stay away from you if you are two-faced, even if you invite them to hear you give a great lecture.

The time, money, and energy of a disciple are very valuable. He cannot waste them without purpose because his time, money, and energy do not belong to him. They belong to the Hierarchy, and he cannot waste them in entertaining physical or emotional bodies.

If the group's intent is to present common entertainment, why not let people go to common places to find it? People come to a spiritual group because they are lonely, they need consolation, they need their sorrows and troubles taken away, or they want to know what the group is.

The entertainment can be joyful and full of laughter, but it must also be uplifting, expanding, and instructive. It is sometimes easier to melt crystallized attitudes through laughter.

The program of entertainment, as a whole, must be a complete cycle. There should be a beginning, a development, and a conclusion. Each part of the program must lead to the next.

If at any time the plan calls for the public to join in the program, a group of trained students must first demonstrate the program; then the public should be invited. For example, if a dance is scheduled, first the trained dancers must demonstrate the dance; then the public should be invited to dance. In this way an artistic performance and a vision are offered, and at the same time the public is given a chance to join in the program.

Public performances, parties, and festivals must always have guests of honor who should be presented and honored in special ways, for example:

1. They must be seated in a special corner with other special people such as the current or past officers of the group.

2. They must be introduced to the gathering, and the person making the introduction must speak about their relation to the group.

3. They must be given special service, and those who speak with them will give them a clear idea about the activities of the group, its future visions, plans, and — very tactfully — its needs.

4. When they leave, a group officer must accompany them to their cars.

Officers, current and past, must always meet the new people at any party and sit and talk with them, answering their questions intelligently and broadmindedly, always striving to present an attractive impression of the group. In such conversations no other groups must be criticized or condemned, and no public figure must be belittled. In the case of direct questions, it is better to hand the question back to the person and expect his full opinion about the one he is asking. The best thing to do is to keep him busy with his own questions.

Farewell Parties

For esoteric students a farewell party is an occasion to remind of responsibilities and duties, a time of gratitude, confession, and forgiveness, and of making a pledge to continue the path. Such a party must be attended by the high officials of the organization and by a selected membership. The committee of the party must organize major speeches.

Usually the chairman will open the party with the Great Invocation, announcing the occasion and speaking about the goals of the group and its future plans. He must relate these ideas to the person who is leaving the group (for various good reasons such as moving to another state or country, or being sent to form other service activities) and encourage him to meet his responsibilities and spread the light of the Teaching.

A proper song should follow.

Then the secretary will speak about how the person is qualified to meet the challenge, or what other outer requirement he needs to be able to spread the light. His speech must be clear, up-to-date, and organized.

Then another song or some music should follow.

Next the chairman will invite the departing person to deliver his speech. He must start with, "The President, the chairman, the secretary, board members, and dear fellow members...." He must express his gratitude, being factual and real, first to the President, then to the board of trustees, then to the fellow members.

Then he must speak about mistakes he made and his failures in relation to the leader and the group and promise not to repeat his mistakes. Then he must speak about his plans and goals for the Teaching. He must express loyalty to the group ideals.

Then the president speaks. He may say, "We have been building our spiritual family here, and the karmic ties built by the call of the Hierarchy will last a long time. Such spiritual ties receive strength and power as we, individually and as a group, work with the same plan under the banner of the Hierarchy.

"The procedure of the service is as follows: First there is a nucleus, then a group which receives inspiration and gives inspiration, then the field of service. The group continues for a while, and when a degree of maturity is reached, the co-workers are naturally spread abroad, each to form his own field of service.

"It is in this private service field that the group members pass the test of *leadership*. The test of leadership is based upon the sense of responsibility, the sense of righteousness, and the sense of freedom.

"We are approaching such a cycle in which many of you will create your own field of service and use that field as a test, examination, or challenge."

The president's duty is to advise the departing member about the work, warn him about various dangers to which he should be alert and sensitive, reveal a few weak points which he must work upon, encourage him, and bless him.

The closing ceremony is as follows:

The president lights a candle, from which the chairman and secretary light their candles. They in turn light the departing member's candle together, saying, "This is the light of the Hierarchy. Carry it in your heart and let your light shine out."

Usually something must be presented as a remembrance. The goal and the future of the work must be emphasized in a symbolic or direct way. The gift can be presented by the youngest member of the group who says, "I am presenting this in the name of the whole group."

The leader will conclude by emphasizing the importance of developing divine carelessness. Divine carelessness is an unexplainable feeling. It contains joy, peace, confidence, and laughter.

Those who are serving the Lord must develop *divine carelessness* toward all actions and plans of darkness. The protecting Hand will be there, and karma will watch very closely. The worker knows these two inevitable forces work together for the success of the leader and the worker on the eternal Path.

36
Psychic Energy and Willpower

We are told that willpower is refined and sharpened psychic energy. This energy is everywhere in Space, and a person can charge himself with that energy through

— Expanding and raising his consciousness

— Living a life in harmony with higher principles and virtues

— Living for the good of all that exists

The charge or flow of psychic energy will then be transmuted and sharpened by heavy, creative labor, with focused concentration, and turned into willpower.

There are seven rules or factors which must be observed to organize labor

1. Discipline
2. Challenge
3. Unexpectedness
4. Demandingness
5. Concentration
6. Joy
7. Accuracy

1. One cannot perform a continuous labor without keeping his personality and his time under *discipline*. Discipline of thoughts, emotional reactions, speech, and actions are very important. Discipline of time, punctuality, and speed in labor are necessary for success.

2. Labor must be *challenging* to your physical, emotional, mental, and spiritual resources. It must not be easy. Every phase of labor must challenge not only your knowledge but also your virtues, your health, and your insight and foresight.

3. Your labor must have the element of *unexpectedness*. It must be conceived and organized in such a way that you do not fall into routine or habit and easily see your next step. On the contrary, your labor must keep you alert every moment with a shock of unexpectedness.

Metaphorically speaking, you will face a door and you will find it is a wall. You will see a stream, and you will find it is frozen lava. You will depend on someone and find out that he was a traitor. Or you will touch a rock and find it is a jewel. You will sit in darkness, and it will turn into light.

A leader must develop the ability to be calm and patient as he confronts every moment as an unexpected event.

4. Labor must be *demanding* of your time, your resources, your undivided attention, and your devotion and dedication. It must demand the dissipation of your ego, vanity, glamors, and illusions. And it must always demand greater light, greater love, greater wisdom, and greater sacrifice.

Demandingness is a superior technique to evoke from your Self resourcefulness, abundance, and the release of precious energies from hidden reservoirs of your deeper being.

5. Labor must be done with the highest *concentration*, which means with all your heart, mind, soul, and spirit. Unless labor is met with integrity and wholeness, there can be no transmutation of psychic energy into willpower.

6. Without *joy*, labor is slavery carried on under the pressure of self-interested people. It is joy that changes the character of labor and causes transmutation into psychic energy. Joy makes labor a source of happiness and pleasure. It is in joy that labor turns into a voluntary discipline.

Joy takes away the pressure caused by efforts and striving and makes you feel that it is an exercise of self-unfoldment. Joy makes you labor, not under the demands of others or under the demands of time, money, and recognition but under the direction of your Higher Self. Once joy enters your labor, you no longer count your time; you no longer work because of money or recognition; you work only for the joy of creativity, service, and unfoldment.

7. It is important to learn to be efficient and *accurate* in your labor. Without accuracy, the labor turns into a source of problems and complications. Every part of the labor must be performed with accuracy and with maximum effort to reach perfection. Accuracy in thinking, feeling, and expression, as well as accuracy in action, are extremely important in each labor.

Through these seven factors, the stone of the alchemist is created, or the psychic power is changed into willpower, or the Niagara Falls of psychic energy is transformed into electricity.

It is necessary that we organize our labor in the light of these seven rules and eventually develop the will.

— The will offers to humanity and the planet the greatest help.

— The will paves the way to Higher Worlds.

— The will gives us power over energies and forces in Nature and use them for the betterment of life.

Willpower is the source and foundation of all virtues, all creative processes, all achievements and attainments. It is through willpower that psychic energy is put into conscious and goal-fitting use.

There are several reasons why willpower is a source of help in the world:

1. Willpower carries the direction of the Great Life. In every act of willpower, the charge of the ultimate direction is present. Any action in harmony with the ultimate direction is an action that is the least resisting path toward success.

2. As willpower manifests, it brings all hidden treasures into expression from our being.

3. Willpower expands our consciousness and makes us exercise inclusive thinking.

4. Willpower reveals to us the most essential in our thinking, actions, and speech. It sharpens the power of our discrimination to such a degree that we occupy ourselves only with the most essential. This saves time, energy, matter, pain, and suffering.

5. Willpower connects us to the Higher Worlds. Actually, continuity of consciousness is built on the foundation of willpower. All obstacles on the path of continuity of consciousness are removed by willpower. All attacks during a flight to Higher Worlds are annihilated by willpower. Right direction in Space is maintained by willpower.

6. Willpower is a destructive factor for all kinds of limitations, hindrances, and obstacles. It gives freedom to those who possess it. It gives freedom to those who work and live in the field of a person who has willpower.

7. Willpower helps a person fuse himself with the expanding reality of the Cosmic Self. Greater blessings in life are given to us by people who have developed willpower.

Glossary

Ageless Wisdom: The distilled human experience on any level of life. The sum total of the Teachings given by great Spiritual Teachers throughout time. Also referred to as the Ancient Wisdom, the Teaching, the Ancient Teaching.

Antahkarana: The path, or bridge, between the higher and lower mind, serving as a medium of communication between the two. It is built by the aspirant himself. It is threefold: the consciousness thread, anchored in the brain; the life thread, anchored in the heart; and the creative thread anchored in the throat. More commonly called the Rainbow Bridge [or Golden Bridge].

Aquarian Age: The esoteric name given for the next cycle that we are about to enter, which is exemplified by universality and the expanded consciousness of man. Also known as the New Era.

Ashram: Sanskrit word. Refers to the gathering of disciples and aspirants which the Master collects for instruction. There are seven major Ashrams, each corresponding to one of the Rays, each forming groups or foci of energy.

Astral Plane: The plane in which the emotional processes are carried on. Sometimes called the astral or emotional world. Also known as the Subtle World or the Astral Realm or the Emotional Plane. See also Cosmic Physical Plane.

Aura: The sum-total of all emanations from all the vehicles of any living thing.

Bailey, A. A.: (1880-1949) A teacher and author of numerous books including *Esoteric Healing*, *Esoteric Psychology*, and others; founder of the Arcane School.

Blavatsky, H. P. : (1831-1891) Founder of the Theosophical Movement, author of many books including *The Secret Doctrine* and *Isis Unveiled*.

Center: Any energy vortex found in a human, planetary, or solar body. Also known as Chakra. Man has seven major centers known as: base of spine, sacral, solar plexus, heart, throat, ajna, head.

Central Sun: The Central Spiritual Sun; the Core of the solar system. The Sun is triple: the visible Sun, the Heart of the Sun, and the Central Spiritual Sun.

Chalice: Also known as the Lotus. Found in the second and third levels of the mental plane (from the top). Formed by twelve different petals of energy: three knowledge petals, three love petals, three sacrifice petals, three innermost petals. The Chalice contains the essence of all of a person's achievements, true knowledge, and service. It is the dwelling place of the Solar Angel.

Consciousness thread: One of three threads composing the Antahkarana. See Antahkarana.

Continuity of Consciousness: The ability to be conscious and function on the subtle planes as well as the physical plane simultaneously.

Cosmic Physical Plane: Refers to the totality of the seven subplanes of manifestation, from highest to lowest: Divine, Monadic, Atmic, Intuitive or Buddhic, Mental, Emotional or Astral, and Physical; each with seven subdivisions, totaling forty-nine planes of manifestation.

Cosmic Magnet: The invisible center of the Universe.

Cosmic Planes: The seven planes of cosmic manifestation: Cosmic Physical, Cosmic Astral, Cosmic Mental, Cosmic Intuitional, Cosmic Atmic, Cosmic Monadic, and Cosmic Divine.

Dark forces: Conscious agents of evil or materialism operating through the elements of disunity, hate, and separativeness.

Dweller on the Threshold: The lower self, the totality of the personality hindrances. The totality of the maya, glamors, and illusions. The main obstacle to overcome for further expansion of the consciousness.

Esoteric: Refers to hidden, deeper, or concealed meaning and significance. The wholistic understanding and explanation of the world events.

Great Ones: Those Who have the ability to control their physical, emotional, and mental bodies and are able to function in higher worlds.

Guardian Angel: Also known as the Solar Angel, Inner Guardian, Higher Self, or Transpersonal Self.

Hierarchy: Composed of Masters of Wisdom, or Great Ones whose members have triumphed over matter and have complete control over the personality, or lower self. It is the Hierarchy that formulates the Plan of action for our planet. The dynamic center of Love-Wisdom of the planetary Soul.

Karma, Law of: The Law of Cause and Effect or attraction and repulsion. "As you sow, so shall you reap."

Logos, Planetary: The Soul of the planet. The planet is His dense physical body to provide nourishment for all living forms. Planetary intelligence and Love-Wisdom.

Masters: Individuals Who mastered Their physical, emotional, mental, and Intuitional bodies.

One Self: The universal consciousness pervading all existence.

Other Worlds: Those planes of existence that are beyond the dense physical plane.

Path: The route that an individual takes to fulfill his purpose in life.

Plan, The: The formulation of the Purpose into a workable program by the Planetary Hierarchy for all kingdoms of Nature for this planet.

Purpose: Refers to the Divine Intent.

Roerich, Helena: (1879-1955) Responsible for the numerous books in the Agni Yoga Series and on Buddhism. Wife of Nicholas Roerich.

Roerich, Nicholas: (1874-1947) Artist, writer, explorer, founder of the Agni Yoga Society and Peace Through Culture movement. Reputed to have painted over 7,000 paintings depicting his travels in Asia, Europe, and the United States.

Self: The capital "S" Self is another term used to refer to the Core of the human being. The True Self is the developing, unfolding human soul who is trying to liberate himself, go back to his Father, and become his True Self. Also known as the Real Self, the True Self, Divine Self.

Seven Fields of Human Endeavor: Politics, Education, Philosophy, the Arts, Science, Religion, Economics and Finance.

Seven Rays: The seven energies which manifest as the seven fields of human endeavor.

Shamballa: Known as the dwelling place of the Lord of the World, the Father, where the Divine Purpose is formulated and where "the Will of God is known." Dynamic center of the Will of the planetary Soul.

Solar Angels: Very advanced beings who act as the teachers and guardians of human beings. Also known as the Soul, Guardian Angles, Inner Guides.

Soul: The Solar Angel when written with capital "S".

soul: The small "s" soul is the human psyche, the Spark, traveling on the path of evolution. Also know as the evolving human soul.

Spiritual Triad: The field of awareness of the human soul in the Higher Mind, the Intuitional Plane, and the Atmic Plane. This field comes into existence when the human soul is able to function on the Intuitional Plane and higher.

Subtle World: Refers to the Astral or Emotional Plane.

Teaching, The: The Ageless Wisdom.

Transfiguration: The stage of complete purification of the physical, emotional, and mental bodies.

Transpersonal Self: The Solar Angel. The inner Teacher or the Inner Guide.

Index

A

Abundance
 and economy, 210
Achievement
 individual and group, 115
Adaptation
 and human development, 281
Adaptation, science of
 and cooperation, 199
Advancement
 and lecturing, 336
Alarm
 and stage of co-worker, 156
Ambition and vanity
 tendencies of, 142
Antahkarana, 351, 370
 and effective speech, 351
Applicants
 and how to test, 140
Aquarian Age, 250-251
Armies of Great Ones
 how created, 431
Art
 and mystery in man, 175
Art, real
 and feeling, 380

Ashram(s), 21, 24, 44, 75, 91, 106, 113-114, 116, 120, 143-147, 185-187, 276, 429
Ashramic contact
 prerequisite for, 116
Ashrams
 how formed, 143
Ashrams, externalization of, 106
Assistants
 how chosen, 215
 See also Co-workers
Attacks
 and verses to repel, 188
Attacks on others
 used as cover up, 264
Attacks to groups
 how protected against, 187
Attraction, energies of
 and group, 132
Aura
 and how built, 123
Aura, expansion of
 and speech, 398
Aura, group
 and cooperation, 154
Authority vs. Leadership, 15

B

Babylon, tower of, 116
Bailey, A.A
 letter to secretaries, 119
Barriers, removal of
 and group work, 115
Beatitude, sense of, 194

Beauty, 31, 40, 65, 77-78, 85-86, 89, 92, 94, 108, 135, 154-155, 161, 165, 180, 183, 193, 195-196, 233, 239, 242, 246, 253, 263, 266-267, 281, 304, 318, 384, 390, 411, 433
and leadership, 19
as evocative, 252
Beauty & challenge
and Leadership, 14
Beauty, life of
and impressing children, 283
Beauty, sense of
beauty developed, 193-194
Beauty, striving to
and weaknesses, 405
Beingness, 16, 63, 82, 90, 154, 183, 222, 250, 267, 280-282, 356, 386, 395
and childhood, 280
and value, 222
how formed, 281
Betrayal
sources of, 227
Blaming others, 404
Blavatsky, H.P.
as a lion, 161
Bliss
and beauty, 194
Book printing
as example of organization, 411
Book review
how to, 359
Breathing
and lecture, 371
Bullheaded people
defined, 144

C

Center, heart, 103, 405
Center, ruling within
kinds of, 238
Center, sacral, 102
Center, solar plexus, 103
Center, vibration of
and training, 271
Centers, various
use of for leader, 272
Ceremony, closing
for departing member, 441
Changes in group
how to handle, 422
Chasm
and co-worker, 163, 165
Children
and vision through literature, 33
how to teach, 280
Christ, 21, 36-37, 53, 89, 103, 129, 158, 161, 175, 177-178, 189, 211-212, 221, 246-248, 250, 263, 282, 306, 318, 335, 348, 370, 375, 401, 431, 433
and born again, 89, 176
as spirit of unity, 282
Claim making
and leadership, 67
Cleavages
and cooperation, 203

and criminal behavior, 307
Clothes, color & style
 and lecturing, 342
Co-measurement
 defined, 183-184
Co-worker
 as creative person, 167
 four qualities of, 162
 requirements for, 155
 stages of, 156
Co-worker, nature of
 and fusion of, 200
Co-workers
 and personal problems, 221
 and protection, 185
 and responsibilities, 228
 and testing of, 432
 how built, 54
 qualities to look for, 139
Commands, internal and external, 275
Common Good, 14, 155, 181, 205-206, 210, 265, 283
 and cooperation, 210
Commune living, 189
Compassion, 125, 152, 195, 263, 267, 402
Complainer
 and how to handle, 133
Complaining
 and co-worker, 166
Condemnation, self
 and leader, 295
Conflict, inner
 and failed promises, 288

Conflicts, inner
 and how to solve, 304
Confusion
 and dangers of in group, 187
 and decision making, 243
Confusion & disturbances
 and promises, 286
Conscious actions, 349
Consciousness, continuity of, 75, 96, 127, 135, 447
Consciousness, expansion of, 56, 151, 241
 and cost of, 83
 and values, 63
 and vision, 29
Consciousness, path of, 12, 20
Consciousness, shifting of
 and values, 240
Consciousness, small
 defined, 182-183
Contemplation
 defined, 23
Conversation skills
 and leader, 347
Converting people
 and internal conflict, 279, 282
 as crime, 282
 problems with, 279
Cooperation
 and co-workers, 153
 and surfacing of vices, 210
 and use of adapters, 211
 as agreement, 277
 defined, 197

inner process of, 199
true meaning of, 178
Cooperation with others
and internal cooperation, 203
Cooperation, kinds of
and three parts of man, 205
Cooperation, spirit of
and personnel, 179, 200, 416
Core in leadership, 257
Core-centered life, 261
Cosmic Magnet, 9, 125, 192, 196
Cowardice
causes of, 162
Creative energies
and response mechanism, 125
Creative forces
and speech & thought, 289
Creative forces, planetary
and cooperation, 204
Creative principles
how contacted, 162
Creativity
and decisiveness, 244
and energy of vision, 32
defined, 175
how increased, 90
Creativity and leadership
defined, 48
Creativity, suppression of
and leadership, 77
Crime prevention
and vision, 35
Criminals

and "integrity", 302
and cleavages, 305, 307
Crises
and leader's role, 177
and role of summits, 174
Criticism
and leader, 294
causes for, 248
Criticism and gossip
effects of, 140
Crucifixion, 315

D

Dancers
and co-workers, 155
Danger
living in, 308
Dangers and problems
and help to leaders, 320
Dark forces, 25, 98, 140-141, 185, 187-188, 227-228, 244, 277, 325, 354-355
and victory, 98
Dark forces, techniques of
and group disunity, 185
Deception, self
path of, 152
Decision making
and principles of the Teaching, 134
Decision-making
centers of, 238
Decisions
and secrecy, 290

explained, 290
Decisions, right
　safeguards of, 239
Decisiveness
　and time, 96
　defined, 237
Defeat
　and causes for, 305
　inability to, 301
Defeat, self
　causes of, 302
Democracy
　and leadership, 250
Depression
　and broken promises, 286
　and vision, 34, 99, 217, 225-226, 233, 240, 286, 296
Depression, healing of
　and vision, 34
Disciple
　and false self-image, 68
Desert
　symbolic of, 160
Dictatorship
　and leadership, 61
　how formed, 10
Dignity, 61, 70, 265, 344, 437
Direction, wrong
　and signs of, 141
Disciple
　and dependency, 223
　defined, 113
Disciple, guiding
　and role in group, 120
Disciple, pseudo
　vs. real disciple, 68
Disciple, real, 69
Disciple, sign of
　and labor, 81

Disciples
　kinds of, 20
Disciples, of New Era
　& needs of, 18, 108
Discipline
　and group members, 114
　and labor, 444
Discrimination
　and group life, 147
Discrimination, sense of, 194
Divine beingness
　and expression of, 246
Divinity
　and how revealed, 89
　as creativity, 92
Divinity, expression of
　and creativity, 175
Domination
　and result in leadership, 57
Doubt
　and disintegration, 280
　and group life, 187
Duality
　and improvement, 94
Dweller on the Threshold, 74, 330
Dweller on Threshold
　how cleared, 330

E

Economy
　and cooperation, 210
Economy, discipline of
　and increasing energy, 130
Education

and change, 63
and lack of vision, 33
Ego
   and leadership, 265
   how formed, 74
Ego in leadership, 257
Egos
   and group work, 133
Elders, committee of, 312
Emotional energy
   field of, 430
Energy
   and lecturing, 389
Energy accumulation of
   and economy of discipline, 130
Energy circulation
   and focus, 35-36
Energy fields
   and kinds of, 430
Energy, physical
   how gained, 390
Engineer, invisible
   and repairs in groups, 131
Enjoyment
   and group labor, 178
Enlightenment
   defined, 29, 194-195
   examples for lecturing, 375
Enthusiasm, v, 41, 110, 164, 166, 219, 225, 339, 346, 373, 426, 430
   and lecturing, 166, 339
Entities
   and Teacher, 233
Essence, man's
   how grown, 124
Essential, most
   and developing sense of, 130
Etheric body
   and mechanical actions, 349
Etheric energy
   field of, 430
Evolution
   and cooperation, 201
   and inspiration, 330
Evolution, direction of, 276
Evolution, path of, 15
Evolution, superhuman, 40
Expansion, human
   and cooperation, 208
Expectations
   and promises, 289
   why minimize, 291
Experience
   and inquiry, 158
   and lecturing, 374
Externalization
   how done, 129

F

Failure
   and cause of, 404
   and faith, 320
   and i.d. with lower self, 310
   and leadership, 57
   defined, 32
   kinds of, 311
Failure of business
   and self-interest, 207
Failure thoughtforms, 295
Failure, feeling of, 24

Failure, in group
  and how handled, 134
Failure, moments of
  as catalysts, 97
Failure, reasons for
  how to deal with, 86
Fairy tales
  and vision, 32
Faith
  and leader, 317
  how obtained, 320
Faith in oneself
  and leader, 396-397
Fear
  effects of, 302
Fearlessness, vi, 33, 159, 161-162, 165, 215-216, 268
Feeling
  and internal thinking, 379
Festivities
  and use for, 430
Fiction
  kinds of, 242
Fiction reading
  and dangers of, 240
Flattery
  dangers of, 217
Flickering lights, 139
Focus
  and creation, 35
Forced work
  and failure, 410
Formulation
  defined, 23
Freedom, 65, 85-86, 89, 94, 108, 135, 154-155, 161, 180, 183, 194-196, 233, 242, 246, 253, 261, 263, 266, 281, 304, 318, 384, 390, 411
  and leadership, 16
  and basic principles, 64
  and cooperation, 200
  and servility, 265
Full moons
  and group vision, 41
Full moons, three major
  and kinds of vision, 42
Future, v, 63, 65-66, 96, 116, 121, 128, 154, 173, 179, 318, 349, 383, 414, 420, 431
  and vision, 31
Future disciple of, 128
Future, groups of
  how formed, 121, 173

G

Gears, system of
  and cooperation, 210
Glamor
  defined, 50
  how cleared, 330
Glamors and illusions
  and impersonality, 246
Goal, clarity of, 418
Goal-fitness, 130
Goals
  and cooperation, 206
  and speed, 226
Goals of body
  and integration, 204
Goals, professional
  and selfless service, 34
Goals, true
  qualities of, 205

Goodness, 31, 40, 65, 77-78, 85-86, 89, 94, 108, 135, 154-155, 161, 180, 183, 195-196, 233, 239, 242, 246, 253, 263, 266, 281, 304, 318, 384, 390, 411
Gossip, 405
Graduation, real
  and beingness, 82
Greatness
  how recognized, 248
Greatness, presence of
  and reaction to, 248
Group and Plan
  and relations to Hierarchy, Shamballa, humanity, 110
Group balance
  and attraction and repulsion energies, 132
Group conscious
  and advancement, 116
Group Consciousness, 101-105, 113-114, 116, 120-121, 126, 179, 189
  and real group, 113
  and unfolding synthesis, 126
  defined, 120
  how formed and created, 115
  kinds of, 101
  signs of, 104
  signs of lack, 102
Group consciousness, human
  three levels of, 102
Group entertainment
  and parties, 438
Group expansion
  how to, 220
Group formation
  and cooperation, 202
  and kinds of people, 354
  and labor, 178
  and Plan, 185
  obstacles of, 37, 106, 241, 419, 447
Group goals
  and cooperation, 205
Group labor
  and fields of service, 425
  and future vision, 424
  and role of leader, 185
  See also organization
Group leadership
  and meditation, 426
Group life
  and isolation of members, 61
Group Lotus, 115
Group meetings
  and arguments, 174
Group member
  and correcting weaknesses, 131
  expectations of, 110
Group members
  and advanced leader, signs of, 117
  and attitude toward dropped members, 120
  and dealing with delinquency, 113
  and group incarnation, 126
  and motive for joining, 185

and progress of, 120
and reasons for departure, 127
and spiritual striving, 111
and subjective unification, 112
Group membership
and obligations of, 107
Group readiness
and new changes, 422
Group self
and Hierarchy, 129
Group shortcomings
how dissipated, 129
Group unity, true, 250
Group work
and field of service, 424
resources of, 128
Group, discipleship
qualities of, 135
Group, esoteric
and how built, 109-110, 131
and likened to sentence, 109-110, 131
goal of, 112
Group, free formation of, 173
Group, Hierarchical
as center of transformation, 62
Group, power of, 128
Group, spiritual
and role of vision and service, 113
Group, subjective
and duty of inner core toward reactions, 125
externalized and qualities of, 121

Group, subjective and objective
and workings of, 126
Group, success of
and focus, 84
Group/family members
and contamination of, 107
Groupings
types and how formed, 103
Groups
and entertainment, 437
and magnetic field, 130
kinds of, 123
objective and subjective, 121
Groups, Ashramic
defined, 186
Groups, discipleship
and essential elements of, 133
Groups, esoteric
and expressing dissatisfaction, 132
and true function of, 131
goal of, 129
purpose of, 128
Groups, personality level
and growth pattern, 122, 125
Groups, subjective
and formation on three levels and response, 125
and lifespan of, 122
Groups, unrelated
and subjective cooperation, 127

Guardian Angel, 250, 391
Guide, subjective
 and group consciousness, 105
Guilt feelings
 and relation to attacks, 264

H

Harmlessness, 96, 102, 120, 128, 181, 250, 295, 405, 411
Harmony, world
 how created, 31
Hatred
 how manifested, 265
Health, 44, 83, 124, 131, 153, 165, 197, 201, 203-204, 207, 227, 234, 241, 244, 265, 282, 286, 290, 304, 417, 444
 and cooperation, 153, 202
 and personnel, 417
 and promises, 286
Hearkening
 defined, 158
Heart
 and group consciousness, 116
 and labor, 85
Heart center, 405
Heart, retarded
 effects of, 140
Hero
 and feeling, 380
Hierarchical work
 and group consciousness, 106
Hierarchy, 9, 14, 20, 24, 28, 30, 41, 44, 49, 52, 60, 85, 91, 104, 106, 110, 113, 117, 119-121, 127-129, 131, 140, 154-155, 162-163, 167-168, 173, 175, 181, 185, 187, 192, 196, 251, 297, 318, 328-329, 385, 431, 436, 438, 440-441
 and group inspiration, 117
 defined, 14, 128, 168
 path to, 140
Hierarchy, chain of
 and meaning, 251
Hierarchy, externalization of
 and group contact, 106, 129
Higher Authority, 267
Higher forces
 and distorted facts, 241
Human soul
 and factor in cooperation, 205
Humiliated audience
 and lecturing, 336
Humiliation, 271
Humility, 145
 and lecturing, 338
 how developed, 297
Humility, false, 246
Humor
 and solemnity, 343
Hurt feelings
 and leader, 347
Hypnotism

vs. impulse, 278
Hypocrisy
  and lectures, 373

I

Ignorance
  and results of, 178
Illumination
  and freedom, 282
Illusion
  and leadership, 68
  how cleared, 330
  how created, 329
Illusion, creation of
  and decisions, 240
Image, low-level
  and leadership, 397
Image-self
  and Future, 31
  and right speech, 401
  real and false, 60
Imposition
  and reaction to, 64
  kinds and defined, 251
Impressions, higher
  how received, 91, 255
Improvements
  how handled, 133
Impulse
  how activated, 277
Incarnation
  as a group, 126
Incarnations, past
  and effect of reliving, 56
Inclusiveness, vii, 29, 33, 35, 57, 103, 176, 194-195
  and cooperation, 208

Indecisiveness
  defined and causes, 243
Independence, growth of, 261
Inertia, 416
Inferiority complex
  and expression of, 248
Initiate, 94, 113, 117, 196, 244, 250, 402
  and role as leader, 113, 117
  and stability, 244
  defined, 113, 402
Initiation
  true meaning of, 89
Initiation, Fifth, 90
Initiation, process of
  and Self-manifested, 89
Initiation, stages of
  and signs of, 90
Inner Guidance, 272-273
Inner Guide, 28, 103, 157, 162, 205, 244, 276, 324-325, 338, 368
  how contacted, 157
Inner Lord, 157-158, 385
Inquiry
  and stages of co-workers, 156
Inspiration
  and dark forces, 22, 329
  and energy, 36, 198, 346
Inspiration, premature
  and results of, 327
Insulation
  and speech, 351
Integration of groups
  and results of, 129

Intention
  and leader, 310
Interests, personal
  and group interests, 140
Intuition
  and decisiveness, 96
Irritation
  effects of the leader, 140

J

Joy, 22, 44, 61, 69-70, 74, 78, 81-83, 85-86, 89, 94, 104-105, 108, 122, 124, 131, 135, 154-155, 160-161, 168, 178, 180, 183, 193, 195-196, 204, 207, 210, 225, 233, 242, 246, 253, 260, 263, 266, 270-271, 281, 287, 304, 318, 336, 341, 346, 350, 353, 368, 371, 384-385, 389-391, 410-411, 441, 445-446

K

Karma, 9, 169, 267, 321
  and group, 105
  and labor, 86
Karma, increase of
  and speech, 398
Karmic debts, 86, 302, 319
  and failures, 319

Karmic law, 307
Kingdom of Heaven
  why to seek, 99
Knocking
  and co-workers, 157
Knowingness, 281
Knowledge, accumulation of
  and maturity, 64

L

Labor
  and complaining against, 97
  and internal change, 86
  and motive, 86
  and psychic powers, 81
  defined, 94
  rules to organize, 443
  size of, 85
Labor, definition of
  and three stages of, 93
Labor, opposition to
  and response, 85
Labor, spiritual
  and Call the Spirit, 98
Language
  and lecturing, 371
Law of Group Progress, 108
Law of Hierarchy, 9
  law of successive experience, 9
Law of Karma, 9
Law of Synthesis
  and centers, 102
Leader, 232

and answering questions, 401
and attitude toward small workers, 173
and aura, 233
and being conscious, 246, 312
and class discussions, 174
and cooperation, 198
and dangers of vanity, 436
and deterioration of organization, 74
and development of direction, 56, 257, 277
and expectations from co-workers, 196
and failure, 294
and forgiveness, 404
and growth of organization, 421
and how to give Teaching, 226
and Leading self, 24
and need for energy, 429
and personal issues, 221
and personality life, 402
and personality relations, 221
and place of organization, 418
and Plan, 176
and process of progress, 226
and promises, 240
and psychics, 277
and sense of timing, 415
and separate interests, 399
and source of strength, 404
and sources of support, 420
and subjective groups, 121
and tolerance for others, 323
and use of power, 159
and vanity, 217
and vipers, 403
and youth of spirit, 165
as a servant, 11
as a Teacher, 235
as an architect, 434
as an engineer, 23
as creator, 162
as guru, 222
as Higher Self, 310
as lamp of desert, 156, 160-161
as magnet, 24
as transformer, 173
as transmitter, 158
as trustee of Plan, 227
as warrior, 180
Core-centered, 255-257
ego-centered, 255-257, 260
how destroyed, 74
how he conquers, 176
how to become, 14
reasons for being, 18
See also Warrior
Leader and co-workers
how to work with, 191
Leader of group
and correction of problems, 132

Leader tasks of, 133
Leader's Core
    and balance, 264
Leader's defeat
    how to overcome, 294
Leader's failures
    and response of co-
        workers, 436
Leader's followers
    and mechanical na-
        ture of, 349
Leader's path
    and obstacles, 37, 106,
        241, 419, 447
Leader's success
    and adverse condi-
        tions, 415
Leader, advanced
    and dealing with bad
        motives, 122
    and how promoted by
        Master, 119
    signs of, 117
Leader, advancement of
    and successors, 135
Leader, assistants to
    and negative qualities
        in, 218
Leader, crises of
    and co-workers, 227
Leader, departure of
    and new leadership,
        118
Leader, duties of
    and being judg-
        mental, 152
Leader, failure
    and co-workers of, 227
Leader, false
    defined, 253
Leader, followers of
    and detachments, 174
Leader, group of
    and why formed, 185
Leader, Hierarchical
    qualities of, 77
Leader, higher contacts
    of
    and meditation, 277
Leader, level of
    how conditioned, 76
Leader, life of
    and his association,
        178
Leader, of discipleship
    group
    and duties of, 135
Leader, office of
    defined, 13
Leader, progress of
    as a cross, 13
Leader, purpose of, 395
Leader, qualities of
    and sternness, 176
Leader, real
    and followers at-
        tracted, 88
    and leading others,
        250
Leader, Solar Angel, 135
Leader, speech and writ-
    ing of
    and use of centers, 272
Leader, true
    and labor, 85
    defined, 252
    goal of, 57
Leader, true sense of
    defined, 171
Leader, vision of
    and personality, 294
Leaders
    and lectures, 21-22
    and discouragement
        of, 295

and response to success, 297
how created, 18
why attacked, 76
Leaders in New Age
qualities of, 250
Leaders of related groups
and multi-group leadership, 128
Leaders of the Future
and virtues, 63, 66
Leaders, false
characteristics of, 87
Leaders, future
how trained, 58, 256, 258, 421
Leaders, true
defined, 47, 255
Leaders, unripe, 144
Leaders, young
and being sidetracked, 22
Leadership
and Esoteric field, 16
and favoritism, 18
and fields of endeavor, 14
and making plans, 22
and motives of followers, 17
and temptations, 16
and viewpoints, 13
and achievement, 53
and aim of, 58
and anarchy, 249
and assistants, 215-216
and awakening and energizing others, 222
and beauty in speech, 347
and choosing students, 229
and clarity, 235, 409
and co-measurement, 59
and compassion, 263
and dealing with failure, 309
and direction, 174
and ego, 265
and energy, 293
and failure, 57
and falsity, 259
and flexibility, 54
and focuses, 414, 423
and group unity, 250
and guidance, 275
and having energy, 222
and how protection is given, 184
and inner achievement, 155, 318
and labor, 81
and making claims, 67
and motive power, 77
and nosiness, 402
and past memories, 56
and personal interests, 357
and pressure by assistants, 220
and principles, 61, 254
and projection of false image, 61
and science of fishing, 357
and self-respect, 397
and small workers, 171
and trust in, 309
and vision, 225

and worthiness of followers, 76
as an example to others, 49
as creativity, 174
as guide, 251
as obedience, 262
as watchfulness, 55
causes for, 249, 253
defined, 9, 77
denial of, 9
exploitation, 10
how advances, 52
how refused, 11
power vs. domination, 56
principle of, 9-10, 12
two kinds of, 73
Leadership abilities
seven ways of, 19
Leadership and failure, 86
Leadership and whom to lead, 263
Leadership assistants
and dependency, 219
Leadership candidate
how trained, 268-269
Leadership changes
and leaving of original leader, 421
Leadership division
and organizing the work, 408
Leadership failure, 117
Leadership forces
and direction of, 173
Leadership group
how formed, 48, 128, 133-135, 173, 176
Leadership guidance
and criminal behavior, 150

Leadership neophyte
and reactions to leader, 258
Leadership organization
and twelve points of, 414
Leadership position
how selected, 135
Leadership preparation
qualities to watch for, 134
Leadership qualities
four kinds of, 50
Leadership success
and organization, 413
Leadership training
and quality of applicants, 263
and risks, 263
subtle forms of, 271
Leadership vs. authority, 15
Leadership, concept of
why spoken against, 249
Leadership, false, 250
Leadership, formation of
and service, 24
Leadership, four stages of, 116
Leadership, marks of, 221
Leadership, path of, 12, 258
Leadership, personality
defined, 74-75
Leadership, principle of, 9-10, 12
Leadership, Rays of
and response to failure, 296
Leadership, serious problems with

and how to solve, 76
Leadership, Soul, 74
Leadership, spiritual
  how established, 75
Leadership, true
  and imposition, 324
  and vision, 46
Lecture
  as a balanced form, 371
  based on a book, 360
  how to remember, 365
Lecture plan
  and T.S. method, 344
Lecture, the best
  qualities of, 373
Lecturer
  and need for energy, 391
  as a builder, 388
Lecturer, good
  qualities of, 385
Lecturers
  and auras, 345
Lectures
  and group need, 350
  as questions, 369
  ideas & viewpoints, 383
Lectures, true
  qualities of, 21
Lecturing
  and audience, 337
  and dramatics, 394
  and emotions, 393
  and emphasis, 394
  and external qualities of person, 341
  and five aspects of lecturing, 384
  and how to end, 393
  and hurting others, 336
  and level of audience, 356
  and meeting needs, 374
  and meeting to improve, 363
  and need to express, 352
  and pauses, 393
  and preparation, 345
  and purity as example, 381
  and satisfaction, 345
  and speed, 393
  and three main ideas, 381
  and use of symbols, 366
  and vision, 377
  as a service, 373
  as a soul, 367
  as an art, 382
  divisions of, 365
  ways to improve, 392
  why important, 333
  without notes, 363
Lecturing as art
  steps to, 387
Levels of organization, 407
Life
  how best changed, 64
Life, our
  and response/reaction, 124
Lion of desert
  functions of, 161
Listening skills
  and leader, 346
Lotus, group, 115
Love, of oneself
  and dangers of, 95

M

Magnetic field
 and vision, 27
Magnetism
 and leadership, 318
 how achieved, 24
 how increased, 21
Mannerisms
 and lectures, 342
Mantram of Disciple, 49
Master
 and notes of group, 112
Master, heart of
 and group, 106
Mastery, achievement of
 and disciple, 223
Maturity
 and cooperation, 199
Maya
 how dispelled, 330
Meditation, 19, 23, 35, 41, 69, 106-107, 112, 118, 128-131, 174, 176, 183, 187, 203, 271, 277, 305, 320, 345, 350, 352-354, 391, 414, 419, 426, 430, 436-437
 and groups, 107, 112
 and Leader, 23
 and lectures, 352
 and vision, 35
Meditation, full moon
 and visions, 41
Meditation, unanimous, 129, 131
Memory
 and building bridge, 364

Memory, weakened
 and promises, 287
Mental energy
 field of, 430
Mental plane, higher
 and group consciousness, 102, 121, 125
Mental states
 and assistants, 218-219
Misfortune
 reasons for, 83
Mobility
 defined, 164
Monadic intent
 and harmony of bodies, 324
Motivation
 and will and purpose, 78
 sources of, 264
Motive
 and labor, 86
Motives, real
 how revealed, 133
Motto, of server, 191

N

Nature, human
 transformation of, 83
Network
 in mind, 370
Neutrality
 defined, 244
New Era, v, 18, 108, 121
 disciples of, 108

O

Obedience, 259
  as a goal, 270
  qualities needed for, 267
Obedience to leader, 258, 268
Obedience training
  how done, 268
Obedience, real, 265-266
Obedience, science of
  and Inner Guidance, 273
Obedience, spirit of
  defined, 192, 196
Observation
  and failure, 87
Obsession and Possession
  signs of, 55
Obstacles in group formation, 106
Organization's health
  and answer to need, 421, 423, 425
Organization, goal of, 426
Organization, growth of
  See also Group

P

Parable
  and use in lectures, 366
Parables
  and lecturing, 388
Party, farewell
  how organized, 439
Past lives
  and disciple, 158
Path
  how entered, 156
Path, finding of
  and student searches, 137
Path, right
  and crises, 174
Peace within
  how achieved, 305
People, value of
  and dealing with weaknesses, 354
Perfection, path of, 31, 74, 96, 137, 235
Perfection, striving for, 90
Personal affairs
  and right speech, 397
Personality interests
  and workers, 417
Personality relationships, 121
Personality, transformation of, 81, 364
Personality-oriented leadership, 73, 75
Personnel
  how chosen, 415
Pity
  and danger to leader, 221
  and delinquent members, 114
Plan, 14, 24, 28-31, 36, 41-44, 48, 54, 73, 75, 85, 98, 109-110, 112-113, 116-117, 121-122, 126, 129-130, 132-135, 147, 162, 173, 175-178, 184-

185, 192-193, 196, 217, 227-228, 231, 233, 256, 276, 309-310, 317-318, 357, 431, 436
defined, 42
Plan, definition of
and our part in it, 30
Plan, Hierarchical, 28, 112, 129, 132, 135, 176, 195, 436
Planetary Logos, 28, 160
Polarity
and creativity, 35
how created, 99
Pole star
and leadership, 77, 79
Power
qualities of, 161-162
Power of leader
how used, 160
Praise
how to give, 299
Prejudice
and co-workers, 163
President's speech
to departing member, 440
Previous lives
and problems of, 323
Pride
as cause for failure, 297
Priests
and preparation to lecture, 389
Principle, central
and leadership, 184
Principles
and leadership, 61
defined and enumerated, 179

of human soul and leadership, 65
Principles of departments
and labor, 411
Principles, universal
how best used, 280
Progress
how achieved, 177
Progress, path of
and hindrances to, 76
Promise, dissolution of
and resulting pain, 287
Promise, to oneself
levels & ramifications, 288
Promises, 285
Promises, unfulfilled, 144
Promotion
and warrior, 181
guidelines to, 143
how done, 232
Promotion in a group, 422
Prosperity, 75, 83, 124, 131, 179, 201-202, 207, 210, 267
Psychic energy, 14, 84, 129, 159, 166, 244, 290, 349, 367, 380, 391, 416, 443, 445-446
how gained, 391
Psychic Powers
development of and labor, 81
Puissant, 156, 159
Punishment
guidelines to, 152
Purpose, 9, 14, 28, 36, 41-44, 110, 121-122, 125,

132, 160, 162, 193, 206, 209, 255, 258, 302, 431
and cooperation, 206
Purpose of life, finding of
and cooperation, 204

Q

Questions
and how to answer, 348
Questions, tricky
and how to deal with, 355
Quote:
Agni Yoga on co-workers, 167
on making claims, 70

R

Rays
and leaders, 296
Reactions
and group formation, 123
Reading process
as process to store, 271
Refusal of leader
and pride, 297
Rehearsal of lectures, 22
Religion
results of being forced, 283
seven levels of, 284
Religion, real goal of, 209
Religions, various

and beauty of, 282
Religious conversion
problems with, 282
Religious freedom
defined, 283
Religious harmony
how achieved, 284
Repulsion, energies of
and group, 132
Response
and growth of essence, 125
Responses
and group formation, 123
Responses, speeds of, 97
Responsibility
and leadership, 264
how increased, 90
Responsibility, denial of
and labor, 84
Responsibility, sense of, 43, 87, 91-92, 103, 146, 181, 218, 390, 395, 441
Rhythm
and group integration, 128
Rhythm, new
and group work, 130
Right speech, 96, 102, 128, 250, 350, 398, 411
Righteousness, 35, 45, 85-86, 89, 94, 108, 135, 154-155, 161, 180, 183, 195-196, 233, 239, 242, 246, 253, 263, 266, 281, 304, 318, 384, 390, 411, 441
Roerich, Nicholas, 54, 161, 165, 227

S

Sacrificial service, vii, 15, 19, 48, 71, 106, 108-111, 157-158, 180, 240, 306-307, 345, 430
Salvation, world
  and seven fields, 190
Sanity
  and cooperation, 203
Santa Claus, 241
Scientific thinking, 241
Secretarial work
  and cross-training, 219
Self, 9, 11, 20-21, 24-25, 28, 31, 36, 48, 52, 57, 60, 81, 83, 89, 91-92, 94, 96, 129, 152, 175, 177, 179, 198, 222, 240, 245-247, 254, 265, 288, 294, 301, 304-305, 310, 312, 319-320, 333-334, 370, 374, 384, 401, 445, 447
Self, denial of, 83
Self, Divine, 21, 81, 84, 222, 304
Self, expression of, 91
Self, finding
  and losing oneself, 177
Self, Higher, 20, 36, 152, 240, 254, 288, 310, 333-334, 370, 445
  and promises, 288
Self, Inner, 11, 92, 401
Self, lower
  and programming, 310
Self, Omnipresent, 83
Self, Real, 9, 28, 52, 60, 246, 374
Self, True, 48, 57, 89, 94, 179, 265, 294, 301, 320
Self-confidence
  how built, 364
Self-discovery, 82
Self-exertion, 52
Self-forgetfulness, 95-96, 102, 128, 208, 250, 252, 353, 411
Self-interest
  results of, 206
Self-respect
  and leadership, 52
Separativeness, 147
Service
  and discipleship, 81, 85, 311
  and vision, 29
  as a fragrance, 84
  group and individual, 115
Service, essential
  and non-essential, 112
Service, quality of
  how derived, 113
Servility
  and ego, 265
Shamballa, 28, 41, 91, 110, 162-163, 256, 318, 328-329
Shoppers in group
  effects of, 146
Show-off, 145
Showing off
  and false image, 60
Simplicity

and lecturing, 335
Sleeping Beauty
  and leadership, 92
Solar Angel, 135, 205, 351, 357
  and speaker, 351
Solemnity, 24, 46, 52, 70, 91, 105, 172, 176, 181, 196, 343, 358, 385, 419
  defined, 52
Soul, 17-21, 24, 27, 30, 32, 54, 73-75, 104, 107, 110, 112-113, 116, 118, 127, 132, 136, 155-156, 192, 204-205, 231, 238, 256, 260, 266, 276, 291, 294, 296-298, 303, 329-330, 350-352, 354, 429, 432-434, 436
  and plan, 27
  as group conscious, 116
Soul, human, 15, 27, 65, 78, 125, 156, 202, 205, 241, 257, 275-276, 278, 325-326, 330, 336, 340, 368, 384
  and purpose of, 78
  how gained, 83
Soul, of group
  and leader, 104, 132
Soul, selling of
  and labor, 83
Soul-oriented Leadership, 73
Space
  and time, 96
Speech
  academic approach, 353
  and audience, 347
  and Leader, 395
  and measure of, 351
  and role of co-workers, 351
  as fire, 352
  discipline of, 157
  elements of, 339
Speech, control of, 172, 234, 398
Speech, control over
  and excitement, 398
Speech, guarding of
  five rules for, 396
Speech, right
  and dosage of information, 400
  result of, 350
Speed
  becoming Space, 96
Speed, why to increase
  and labor, 94
Spiritual beggary, 82
Spiritual energy
  field of, 430
Spiritual forces
  and help and labor, 86
Spiritual impulses
  defined, 275-276
Spiritual Path, 83
Spiritual progress
  and labor, 94
Spiritual prostitution
  defined, 195
Spiritual tension, 324
Spiritual Triad, 28-29, 125, 238, 255-256, 294, 330, 368
Spiritual values, 74-76, 317-318

Story:
  destruction of authority / need for leadership, 251
  monastery / vices as traps, 38
  of boy & secrets / right speech, 399
  of co-worker game / separating followers, 315
  of depressed girls / vision, 34
  of divorced man / cooperation, 213
  of electrical wire / obedience, 262
  of girl & fire / true leadership, 11
  of girl and sexual needs / seeking self validation, 149
  of hard working Teacher / service, 307
  of man and many jobs / and losing independence, 220
  of man and pictures / false self-image, 60
  of man and wife / balance and cooperation, 203
  of man and wife / seeking self validation, 150
  of painter / vanity, 313
  of pianist/need for energy, 390
  of picnic / using own measures, 69
  of prison officer / lack of cooperation, 203
  of rooster / feeding the need, 59
  of smoking boy / cooperation, 211
  of swimming the river / breaking hindrances, 259
  of Teacher and lecture/inflated advertising, 69
  of Teacher tripping / ideals of leader, 313
  of teenagers / future vision, 33
  of two boys / obedience to Teacher, 261
  of wartime / nosiness, 403
  of water bowl / defeat, 314
  of young man looking for Path / insincere search, 137
  T.S. as principal / spirit of helpfulness, 166
  Tests of obedience, 261
Striving
  and decision, 324
Striving and discipline
  and role in unsatisfactory conditions, 133
Struggle of audience
  and speech, 350
Student
  offerings of, 234
Student, cycles of
  and self-decision, 260
Students
  best kinds, 17
  how chosen, 229
Students, kind of

and shoppers, 135
Students, new
   and qualities to avoid, 136
   See also Co-workers
Success, 44, 54, 57-58, 64-65, 74, 83-84, 124, 148, 153, 167-168, 187, 197-199, 201-202, 205, 209, 212, 227, 244, 247, 253, 267, 296-297, 308, 310-311, 319, 341, 353, 398-399, 404, 414, 420, 422, 442, 444, 447
   and basis of cooperation, 209
   and cooperation, 153, 199
   and formula of, 212
   and leadership, 58
   and response of leader, 297
   how guaranteed, 205
Success, inner, 341
Summits
   and crises, 174
Superstitions, 280
Sword
   symbols of, 159
Symbols
   and use in lectures, 367
Synthesis, age of, 126

T

Teacher
   and emphasis on principles, 180
   and gaining trust of, 260
   and your beingness, 435
Teachers, response to
   and wisdom, 15
Teaching
   and parties, 437
   and reason for lack of understanding, 136
   how damaged, 69
   understanding of, 108
Teaching, enemies of
   and exhausted speaker, 391
Teaching, goal of, 189
Teaching, living the
   & leadership, 20
Teaching, pure
   and spiritual impulses, 276
Teaching, true
   and qualities of co-workers, 140
   signs of, 194
Telepathy, 326
Tension
   and work, 410
Tests & festivities, 432
Thinking
   and two layers of, 379
Thinking, clear
   and promises, 287
Thoughtforms
   and promises, 286
Thoughts, petty
   effects of, 97
Time, conquering
   and Subtle Worlds, 94-95
Timing
   and success, 414
Tonality & pitch

and lectures, 392
Tower of the Future, 116
Traditions
 how & why returned to, 279
Transfiguration, 108, 119
Transformation, 105, 151
 how done, 227
Transmitting
 and co-worker, 158
Trinity
 and cooperation, 212
Trinity within, 202
Troublemakers
 handling of, 357
Truth, 31, 40, 77-78

U

United Nations, 103, 207

V

Value, human
 and Plan, 30
Value, sense of, 185
Values
 and levels of decisions, 240
 and source of creation, 252
 and students, 184
Values, greater
 and result of initiation, 90
Values, subjective
 and consciousness, 63

Values, transient and real ones, 50
Vanity
 and leader, 217
 and leadership, 68
 defined, 49, 51
Victory
 and leader's response, 298
 how gained, 98
Virtues
 and leadership, 222
Vision
 and creation of the new, 46
 and groups, 113
 and healing, 34
 defined, 27
 how manifested, 41
 how to give, 225
 why needed, 79
Vision and plan
 defined, 185
Vision of future
 and group labor, 424
Vision, energy pattern of
 and your creativity, 32
Vision, first contact with
 and resulting changes, 43
Vision, higher
 and demand of, 29
Vision, individual, 32
Vision, signs of having, 45
Vision, signs of losing, 44
Visions
 and readiness, 29
Visions and Plans
 and polarity, 99
Visions, kinds of
 and sources of, 28

Voice
 and lecturing, 372
Voice control, 342
Vows
 explained, 289

W

Warrior
 defined, 180
Warriors, great
 and technique for victory, 98
Weakness
 causes of, 162
Will, Divine
 how defined, 267
Willpower, 243
 and leadership, 74
 as source of help, 446
 defined, 443
Witness stand, 83
Workers, small, 171

Bibliographic References

Agni Yoga Society. New York: Agni Yoga Society.
    Agni Yoga, 1980.
    Community, 1951.
    Fiery World, Vol. I, 1969.
    Fiery World, Vol. III, 1948.
    Heart, 1982.
    Hierarchy, 1977.
    Letters of Helena Roerich, Vol. I, 1979.
    Letters of Helena Roerich, Vol. II, 1981.

Bailey, Alice A. New York: Lucis Publishing Co.
    Discipleship in the New Age, Vol. I & II, 1972.
    Esoteric Psychology, Vol. I, 1979.
    Esoteric Psychology, Vol. II, 1966.

Saraydarian, Torkom. Sedona, AZ: Aquarian Educational Group.
    Challenge for Discipleship, 1986.
    Five Great Mantrams for the New Age, 1975.
    The Psyche and Psychism, 2 vols., 1981.
    The Science of Meditation, 1981.

Saraydarian, Torkom. Cave Creek, AZ: T.S.G. Publishing Foundation, Inc.
    The Ageless Wisdom, 1990.
    Breakthrough to Higher Psychism, 1990.
    Other Worlds, 1991.
    The Psychology of Cooperation and Group Consciousness, 1989.
    The Purpose of Life, 1991.
    The Subconscious Mind and the Chalice, 1993.

About the Author

This is Torkom Saraydarian's latest published book. Many more will be released very soon. His vocal and instrumental compositions number in the hundreds and are being released.

The author's books have been used all over the world as sources of guidance and inspiration for true New Age living based on the teachings of the Ageless Wisdom. Some of the books have been translated into other languages, including German, Dutch, Danish, Portuguese, French, Spanish, Italian, Greek, Yugoslavian, and Swedish. He holds lectures and seminars in the United States as well as in other parts of the world.

Torkom Saraydarian's entire life has been a zealous effort to help people live healthy, joyous, and successful lives. He has spread this message of love and true vision tirelessly throughout his life.

From early boyhood the author learned first-hand from teachers of the Ageless Wisdom. He has studied widely in world religions and philosophies. He is in addition an accomplished pianist, violinist, and cellist and plays many other instruments as well. His books, lectures, seminars, and music are inspiring and offer a true insight into the beauty of the Ageless Wisdom.

Other Books by Torkom Saraydarian

The Ageless Wisdom
The Bhagavad Gita
Breakthrough to Higher Psychism
Buddha Sutra — A Dialogue with the Glorious One
Challenge For Discipleship
Christ, The Avatar of Sacrificial Love
A Commentary on Psychic Energy
Cosmic Shocks
Cosmos in Man
Dialogue with Christ
Dynamics of Success
Flame of Beauty, Culture, Love, Joy
The Flame of the Heart
Hiawatha and the Great Peace
The Hidden Glory of the Inner Man
I Was
Joy and Healing
Legend of Shamballa
New Dimensions in Healing
Olympus World Report...The Year 3000
Other Worlds
The Psyche and Psychism
The Psychology of Cooperation and Group
    Consciousness
The Purpose of Life
The Science of Becoming Oneself
The Science of Meditation
The Sense of Responsibility in Society
Sex, Family, and the Woman in Society
The Solar Angel
Spiritual Regeneration
The Subconscious Mind and the Chalice
Symphony of the Zodiac
Talks on Agni

Triangles of Fire
Unusual Court
Woman, Torch of the Future
The Year 2000 & After

Booklets

A Daily Discipline of Worship
Building Family Unity
Earthquakes and Disasters — What the Ageless
 Wisdom Tells Us
Fiery Carriage and Drugs
Five Great Mantrams of the New Age
Hierarchy and the Plan
Irritation — The Destructive Fire
Nachiketas
The Psychology of Cooperation
Questioning Traveler and Karma
Responsibility
The Responsibility of Fathers
The Responsibility of Mothers
Spring of Prosperity
Success
Synthesis
Torchbearers
What to Look for in the Heart of Your Partner

Video

The Seven Rays Interpreted

Next Book Release: **Leadership Volume II**

T.S.G. Publishing Foundation, Inc. is a non-profit, tax-exempt organization.

Our purpose is to strive to be a pathway for the transformation of humanity. We provide effective tools, by means of the applied Teaching, so that individuals may have the opportunity to transform themselves.

These fine books have been published by the generous donations of the students of the Ageless Wisdom.

Your tax deductible contributions will help us continue publishing and growing.

Our gratitude to all.

Ordering Information

Write to the publisher for additional information regarding:

— Free catalog of author's books and music tapes

— Lecture tapes and videos

— Placement on mailing list

— New releases

Additional copies of *Leadership Volume I*

U.S. $25.00 (Softcover)
U.S. $30.00 (Hardcover)
Postage within U.S.A. $5.00
Plus applicable state sales tax

T.S.G. Publishing Foundation, Inc.
P.O. Box 7068
Cave Creek, AZ 85331
United States of America

TEL: (602) 502-1909
FAX: (602) 502-0713